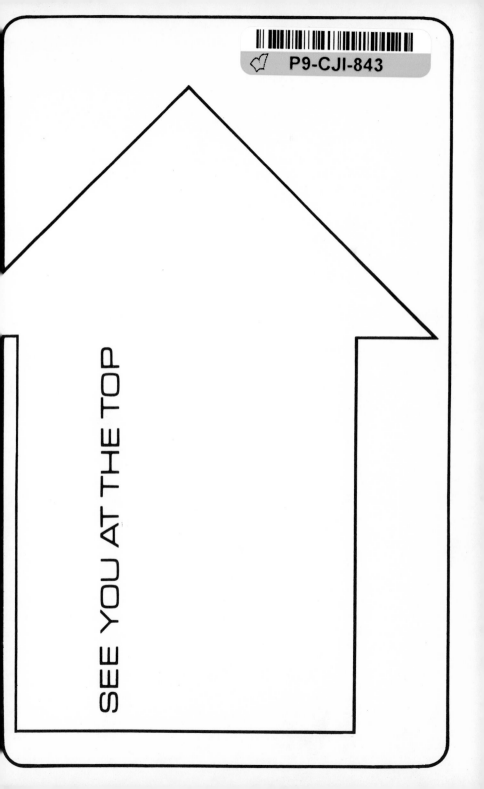

SEE YOU AT THE TOP

SEE YOU AT THE TOP

I BELIEVE

You can get everything in life
you want if you help enough
other people get what they want.

SEE YOU AT THE TOP

Formerly entitled
BISCUITS, FLEAS AND PUMP HANDLES

By ZIG ZIGLAR

Illustrated by Al Mayton

PELICAN PUBLISHING COMPANY
GRETNA 1979

First printing, July 1974
Second printing, April 1975
Third printing, May 1976
Fourth printing, August 1976
Fifth printing, October 1976
Six lt printing, February 1977
Seventh printing, June 1977
French edition, June 1977
Eighth printing, July 1977
Ninth printing, August 1977
Tenth printing, December 1977
Eleventh printing, March 1978
Twelfth printing, April 1978
Thirteenth printing, June 1978
Fourteenth printing, August 1978
Fifteenth printing, October 1978
Sixteenth printing, December 1978
Spanish edition, in publication

Ziglar, Zig.
   See you at the top = formerly entitled Biscuits,
fleas, and pump handles.

   1. Conduct of life.   I. Title.
[BJ1581.2Z53 1977]   131'.3   77-670008
ISBN 0-88289-126-X

THE ZIG ZIGLAR CORPORATION

12011 Coit Road, Suite 114
Dallas, Texas 75251
(214) 233-9191

Manufactured in the United States of America

Published by Pelican Publishing Company, Inc.
630 Burmaster Street, Gretna, Louisiana 70053

To Sugar Baby

The redhead who has been my wife and my life for thirty-one wonderful years — and the best is yet to come.

I BELIEVE

Man was designed for accomplishment, engineered for success, and endowed with the seeds of greatness.

ACKNOWLEDGMENTS

It would be impossible to more than scratch the surface in the form of acknowledgments to the many individuals who have helped me through the years. However, some have contributed so much that their names literally jump off the pages of my life and demand recognition. Heading the list is my "Sugar Baby" who gives my life meaning while making it fun and worthwhile. Her love has been the steadying and motivating factor that is and always has been present regardless of circumstances.

My mother, through her living examples of faith, courage, common sense, and love gave me the foundation for life and much material for this book.

Mr. and Mrs. John R. Anderson played a prominent role in my life. Mr. Anderson served as a "substitute father" and treated me like a son as he blended genuine interest with love and/or discipline as the situation demanded.

Mr. Walton Haining taught me a lot about "horse sense" and selling myself to the public. Ditto for Bill Cranford, my first sales manager, whose patience and personal interest transcended the normal sales manager-salesman relationship.

For sheer drama the short time I spent with P. C. Merrell is unmatched. He "turned me on, turned me around, and boosted me up" with the gift of believing in myself.

Hal Krause gave me national and international exposure through his company and made the road I traveled as a speaker and author considerably easier. My colleagues on the platform — Cavett Robert, Bob Richards, Bill Gove, Dick Gardner, Ken McFarland, and the late Charlie Cullen — all played an important part in the areas of encouragement, instruction, and inspiration.

Bernie Lofchick, "Brother Bern," whose advice, help, encouragement, and belief in me and the "Zigmanship" philosophy was vitally important in furthering my career and my personal life as well.

My friend, former associate, and fellow speaker, Dan Bellus, whose experience was invaluable in the publication of the original edition. Carroll Phillips, whose attentiveness to detail and specifics of instruction contributed greatly to the clarity and effectiveness of this edition.

Patti Bond, who typed page after page for both editions at an incredible speed and Jorita Symington, my secretary, who "held things together" through it all. Both rate reams of praise and a heartfelt thank you for their contributions.

Ann Anderson of Nashville, Tennessee gets a "special" bit of gratitude for helping to reopen my eyes to the joy of living a fuller, richer life on earth while making certain that I spend eternity with Jesus Christ.

I would be remiss and even ungrateful if I did not acknowledge the help given me by my brothers and sisters. There has always been a deep love and strong sense of encouragement among us. I hope this effort on my part will be meaningful to each of them.

Finally, there are my children. Each one is unique, different, and deeply loved in a special way. Suzan, my first born, provides me with much stimulating conversation and encouragement. Cindy, the middle child, quietly comes and goes as she makes her presence felt everywhere. Julie, the little one, is everywhere doing everything. Tom, the son whose belated but welcome appearance keeps me young and hopping. Each has given me much pleasure and occasionally a little pain. Each has contributed immeasurably to family enjoyment and solidarity. Each was a gift from God for which I thank Him every day.

To all of you whom I have named, please accept my deepest thanks. To you whom I have not named, please know that even though you are unnamed in this work, you are not unknown to me and you are appreciated more than you know.

To all of you, good luck, God bless you, have a good forever, and I'll see you at the top.

Zig Ziglar

IT'S TRUE

What lies behind us and what lies before us are tiny matters compared to what lies within us. *Ralph Waldo Emerson*

— AND —

You are the only one who can use your ability. It is an awesome responsibility.

FOREWORD

The word "different" will probably come into your mind every time you open the pages of *See You At The Top*. The dust jacket is different, and to start with "The End" is certainly different. The book is different in "feel," "subject matter," and "technique." For example, I will often "shift gears" on you and insert an analogy, example, one-liner, or power phrase to force you to pause and hopefully lead you to re-read the material to make certain you got the message. I will also emphasize a "different" theme in today's market place as I stress that you can get everything in life you want *only* if you help enough other people get what they want.

As the author, I believe that the entire book is different and effective, but my objective was not to write a book that was "different." The difference evolved because I wrote the book as I speak. [I'm like the crosseyed discus thrower. I don't set any records, but I do keep the crowd alert.] During the past 19 years, I have given the speech, "Biscuits, Fleas and Pump Handles," the original title of this book, over 3,000 times. Initially, the material only covered a forty-five minute presentation. Through the years that forty-five-minute talk has expanded into this full length book and the "I CAN" course which is being taught in schools and churches, and the Richer Life Course which is being taught in businesses all over America.

I cover a lot of subjects in *See You At The Top*, but my major objective is to communicate my feelings on faith, love, optimism, and enthusiasm. This is important because in today's world many people are confused about what real love and real faith is and are too "sophisticated" to show their true feelings and display real enthusiasm for anything.

On love — I plead guilty to loving the Lord, my wife, my family, my fellowman, and America.

On faith — I don't know what tomorrow holds but I know Who holds tomorrow so I approach it with confidence and thanksgiving. My Bible assures me that my past is forgiven *and* forgotten. That takes care of my past. Jesus Christ said, "I have come that you might have life and have it more abundantly." That takes care of the present. John 3:16 assures me I will have everlasting life. That takes care of my future. With my past forgiven, my present secure, and my future irrevocably guaranteed, why shouldn't I be enthusiastically optimistic?

See You At The Top is a philosophy, but there is little theory involved. The ideas, procedures, and techniques come from a lifetime of living. It incorporates thirty years of sales and people-development experience, as well as personal involvement with many of the world's top professionals from virtually every field of endeavor. The utilization of the ideas and techniques in this book will mean that you're learning from other people's experiences — not other people's theories. This is the only practical way to grow because it's too frustrating, too time consuming, and far too expensive to learn everything from personal experience.

I say with candor and complete conviction that had this particular book been available when I started competing in the game of life, my progress would have been faster and my results better. Obviously, I believe you'll be richer in many ways if you utilize this philosophy which I spent over 2,000 hours refining and committing to paper.

Within the body of *See You At The Top*, I use over 800 analogies, examples, "one liners," power phrases, human interest stories, and humorous incidents. The purpose is to hold your interest and keep you involved in the total message. Hopefully you will be like many readers of the first nine printings who enthusiastically stress that this is a book you never finish. That you can pick it up — open it to any page for a mental snack, read a chapter for a full mental meal, or read it from cover to cover as a way of life. Then you start over. God bless you and if you utilize the ideas in this book, I will "see you at the top."

Zig Ziglar

TABLE OF CONTENTS

Illustrations

SEGMENT ONE

STAIRWAY TO THE TOP

PURPOSE: I. TO OPEN YOUR MIND, STIR YOUR IMAGINA-
TION AND MAKE YOU THINK. TO AROUSE
YOUR CURIOSITY AND CREATE A HEALTHY
DISSATISFACTION WITH YOUR STATUS QUO.

        II. TO IDENTIFY THE THINGS YOU WANT IN
LIFE AND CHART A COURSE OF ACTION TO
GET THEM.

      III. TO AROUSE THE SLEEPING GIANT INSIDE
YOU.

      IV. TO ASSIST YOU IN RECOGNIZING AND OVER-
COMING YOUR LOSER'S LIMPS.

ADDITIONAL READING MATERIAL

William Glasser— *SCHOOLS WITHOUT FAILURE*

William Glasser— *REALITY THERAPY*

David A. Ray — *DISCOVERIES FOR PEACEFUL LIVING*

Solomon   — *OLD TESTAMENT, BOOK OF PROVERBS*

William Cook — *SUCCESS, MOTIVATION AND THE SCRIP-
TURES*

Cavett Robert — *HUMAN ENGINEERING*

THE END

Perhaps an unusual way to start a book — but this is an "unusual" book. It's about you, your family, your future, and how you can get more out of all of them by giving more to each of them. We believe that this is "the end," or at least the beginning of the end, of negative thinking, negative action, and negative reaction; the end of defeatism and despondency; the end of settling for less than you deserve to have and are capable of obtaining; the end of being influenced by little people, with little minds thinking little thoughts about the trivia that is the stock and trade of Mr. & Mrs. Mediocrity. In short, it is the end for you of the world's most deadly disease — "Hardening of the Attitudes."

Welcome to The Richer Life.

CHAPTER ONE
THE "MORE" WAY OF LIFE

THE 2:20 TO BOSTON

John Jones was in New York City. He wanted to go to Boston, so he went to the airport and bought a ticket. Having a few minutes to spare, he walked over to some scales, stepped on them, inserted a coin and down came his fortune: "Your name is John Jones, you weigh 188 pounds and you are going to catch the 2:20 to Boston." He was astounded because all of the information was correct. He figured this must be a trick, so he stepped back on the scales, inserted another coin and down came his fortune: "Your name is still John Jones, you still weigh 188 pounds and you are still going to catch the 2:20 to Boston." Now he was more puzzled than ever. Sensing a trick, he decided to "fool" whoever or whatever was responsible. He went into the men's room and changed clothes. Once again he stepped on the scales, inserted his coin and down came his fortune: "Your name is still John Jones, you still weigh 188 pounds — but you just missed the 2:20 to Boston."

This book was written for the people who have missed the 2:20 to Boston or for some reason decided to get off before it reached its destination. In short, **this book is for those who have been missing much of the good life**. It is designed to help you get the extras you deserve to have and are capable of getting.

Each word has been weighed, each thought has been evaluated, and each point carefully considered. I have made every effort to personalize it in a conversational manner so you would feel that you and I are in a private conference discussing you and your future. I hope you take this message of hope and optimism *personally* because that is the way it was written.

From the beginning I will plant a series of hope, success, happiness, faith, and enthusiasm seeds. I will "water" and "fertilize" these seeds and even add a few additional ones. By the end of the book the crop will be ready for harvesting to the degree, and in the amount, you have utilized or followed through on the message in this book. I stress that this is a P.M.A. [positive mental attitude] book, but it is a great deal more than that. *See You At The Top* is a P.L.A. [Positive Life Attitude] book. It's the power of positive *believing* which is the necessary ingredient for converting positive thinking into positive action. Since man is tridimensional [physical, spiritual and mental], we deal with the complete person. This is the *only* way to have complete success, which I will define as we go along.

IS ONE PICTURE WORTH 10,000 WORDS?

One man said that a picture is worth ten thousand words. Thousands have repeated his words and millions more have believed them. However, it is my personal belief that the man or woman who believes this saying has never really read Lincoln's *Gettysburg Address* or the *Bill of Rights*. Neither have they read and understood the *23rd Psalm* or prayed the *Lord's Prayer*. These works contain words — just words — but they are words which have changed the destiny of nations, the course of history and the lives of millions of people.

Here is a story about how some other words had a dramatic impact on a life. A number of years ago, the movie, *A Man Called Peter*, was produced. I shall never forget one of the scenes. The actor portraying Peter Marshall was preaching a sermon on belief and faith. When the scene was over the cameras kept grinding. Many members of the cast got up from their seats to walk down to congratulate the actor for a superb performance. One of the members of the cast who was a member of the "congregation" was an actress named Marjorie Rambeau. As she walked down to congratulate the actor, it was obvious she was emotionally involved in the situation. I say this, and add that it was fortunate the cameras were still grinding, because Marjorie Rambeau could not walk. She had been injured in an automobile accident and for over a year had been unable to take a step. But, as she listened to those words of faith and encouragement, she became engrossed in the message contained in those words. So engrossed, as a matter of fact, she believed the message, got up, walked and kept on walking.

I'm not implying that the "words" in this book will change the history of the world or that their effect will be as dramatic as the story of Marjorie Rambeau. However, I completely believe that the philosophy contained herein can make a substantial difference for you. Several thousand unsolicited testimonials from people in all walks of life attest to the fact that the "Richer Life" concepts — will work **for** you — if you work **with** them. Now let's look at a thought provoker! How many squares do you see?

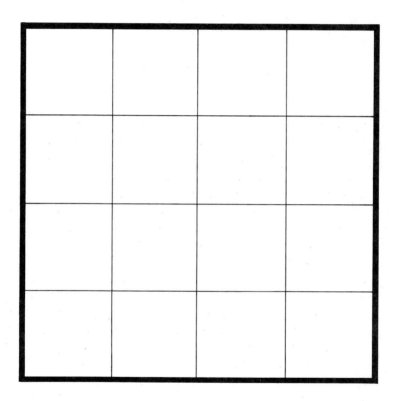

If you said 16, you have lots of company. If you said 17, you are in a much more select group, but you are still in error. Before you turn the page to see what the artist has done with these squares, why don't you take another look and see how many more squares you can find. Now, turn the page.

As you can see, there are 30 squares. Since you hold the book in your hands, no one could have added any additional squares. I simply showed you where they were. This illustrates two important concepts. First, **an in-depth look reveals considerably more than a casual glance**, doesn't it? That's true of the squares and it's also true of you, your potential and your future. Second, **most of us occasionally need someone to point out the obvious and more often, the not so obvious.**

Since to educate is to "pull out" or to "draw out," the purpose of this book will be to "pull out" the bigger, more capable person inside you. I'm convinced you will get a great deal out of this book but more importantly, the book will get even more out of you.

TRIGGERING IDEAS

As you read, I would like for you to feel you and I are together and that I am personally talking with you and asking you questions. Of necessity, most questions will be of the "Yes/No" variety. On those occasions when I do ask questions that require an answer, I hope you will pause and carefully think the answers through. Hopefully, you are not concerned with how fast you can read and "get out" of the book, but how much the book can "get out" of you. Your first reading probably will be the fastest, but subsequent readings will provide you with additional inspiration and information which will extend the immediate benefits to a richer way of life.

The chances are strong that on occasion, while listening to a speaker, reading a book or listening to a recording, you have heard or read something which really "triggered" your imagination. On those occasions you probably thought, "that reminds me," or "that gives me an idea." Try as you might at a later time, you often cannot recall the thought or idea that had been so clear in your mind a short time earlier. Since this is characteristic of most people, I'm going to urge you to get a "Trigger Page" notebook. I suggest the standard stenographic pad because it is approximately the same size as this book and will be easy to carry. Divide the pages as we have done the sample "Trigger Page." The arrows would be helpful but they are not critical.

21

COUNT THE SQUARES

Keep the "Trigger Page" notebook with your copy of *See You At The Top* because as you read the book it will "trigger" many thoughts and ideas of your own. When it does, let me urge you to stop reading, turn to a Trigger Page and carefully record each thought or idea as it occurs. This will keep you involved as an active reader, utilize more of your senses, and enable you to concentrate more completely. A poet stated it more succinctly when he wrote, "I hear and forget. I see and hear and I remember. However, when I see, hear and do, I understand and succeed." Interestingly enough, you will discover when you read the book a second time, you will get more thoughts and more ideas than you did the first time. This is especially true if you read a few minutes *every* day *before* you start your day's activities and just *before* you go to sleep.

IT'S REALLY "OUR" BOOK

I suggest you get both a red and a black felt-tip pen to record your thoughts and ideas. Start by using the red pen at the bottom of the Trigger Page in Section 1 the first time you read the book. Use the black pen and move up to Section 2 of the Trigger Page the second and subsequent times you read it. As you move up the page, you will be symbolically moving from the "red ink" to the "black ink" of life.

Let me also urge you to underline and mark the portions of the book that are meaningful to you. These markings, combined with the thoughts and ideas you record, will personalize the book and make it "your" book. It will be so personalized that you will keep it and use it as a constant source of reference.

This is quite important because **no one is smart enough to remember everything he knows.** This also means that you and I will have co-authored the book which also makes it "our" book. It should be a winner, shouldn't it?

HERE IS WHAT YOU NEED TO GET WHAT YOU WANT

The foundation stones of honesty, character, faith, integrity, love, and loyalty are necessary for a balanced success that includes health, wealth, and happiness. As you go onward and

2

An idea unrecorded is an idea often lost!

1

Trigger Page

upward in life, you will discover that if you compromise *any* of these principles you will end up with only a beggar's portion of what life has to offer. If you use dishonesty, deceit, or fraud, you might acquire money, but you will have fewer real friends and little peace of mind. *That* is not success. [I agree with the wit who said, "You climb the highest by staying on the level."] The man who earns a million, but destroys his health in the process is not really a success. The corporate executive who alienates his family in his climb to the top is not a success. He can't take it with him and to whom is he going to leave it?

The longer I live and the more successful people I meet, the more convinced I become that these foundation stones are the most critical success weapons we have in our arsenal. In any crisis or emergency, those with whom we deal, and on whom our health, wealth and happiness depends, will act more readily, and cooperate more completely, if our credibility is beyond question. **Ability is important — dependability is critical.**

I wish it were possible for me to introduce to you the scores of personable, persuasive, talented — even brilliant — people I have met in my travels who are generally just one step in front of the bill collector and often just two steps ahead of the law. They are always looking for a "deal" and the "fast buck." They *never* build very much or very high, because they have no foundation to build on. Others with the right foundation end up living in the basement or building a chicken shack on that foundation. Many times they don't take all the steps to use the talent they have to get the richer life. Others don't realize that **the real opportunity for success lies within the person and not in the job; that you can best get to the top by getting to the bottom of things** — and then climbing those stairs — one at a time. They don't realize that success and happiness are not matters of chance but choice. You literally — as you shall see — choose what you want in life.

Now let's make a list of the things you want to be, do or have in the tomorrows of your life. Later, you probably will add additional items to this list. As a starter, you probably want more and better friends, more personal growth, better health, more money, more happiness, more security, more leisure time, opportunity for advancement, more peace of mind, more true love, the ability to be more competent and to contribute more to your fellow man. On the following page is your personal stairway to the top with the things you want, or want more of, listed on the door of your executive suite of tomorrow. We will use this stairway frequently to help you stay "on track." You might not need to be told what characteristics and qualities you need to get the things you want, but I'm betting you are human enough that you need to be reminded.

There are probably some other things you want but I'm confident if you had the things we've listed you would have a rich and rewarding life. Chances are strong that at this moment you do not have everything you want and expect to have in the tomorrows of your life. Fortunately, they are all available and you can get them to a much greater degree than you ever dreamed possible. I stress their availability, but just as you must have or develop muscles if you want to be a weight lifter, so must you have or develop certain characteristics in order to open life's vault of valuables and extract the things you want and deserve to have.

SIX STEPS AND YOU'RE THERE

I'm convinced the "good" things I've described are available to *you*, but I'm even more convinced that if you really want the things we've listed you must take six specific steps to get them. It's critical that you understand this because just as a baseball player will be "out" if he doesn't touch all the bases, so will you be "out" if you skip any of the steps.

My good friend, and outstanding motivational sales technician, Dick Gardner, calls these steps "gradients" and uses these examples to emphasize the point: The boy who is introduced to a young *lady* and immediately tries to kiss her will lose any chance for serious consideration as a suitor. The student who attempts to move directly from simple arithmetic to geometry will face a hopelessly impossible situation. The salesman who introduces himself to the prospect and immediately starts trying to "write an order" will miss the sale and create ill will in the process. The suitor, the student, and the salesman would *all* have skipped too

Will you stare up the steps
or
step up the stairs?

many steps or gradients and would have failed. Each of them would have had infinitely better chances at success had they taken all the steps. Now obviously some people can take the steps faster than others, but if you take *all* the steps you will be far more certain to get the things you really want.

Next to your stairway to the top is an elevator to the top. As you can see, the elevator has an out of order sign on it. From where I stand, the elevator to the top is, has been, and always will be "out of order." In order to get to the top, according to sales executive John Hammond — you'll have to take the stairs — and you'll have to take them one at a time. Fortunately, they are directly in front of you so you know where they are, what they are and exactly how many stairs you must climb before you reach the top.

As you start on your stairway to the top, your first step will be the development of a healthy self-image. The second step is the recognition of the worth and ability of other people as well as the necessity of effectively living and working with them. The third step is a strong goal orientation. You need a plan to build a house. To build a life, it is even more important to have a plan or goal. The fourth and fifth steps are that you must have the "right" mental attitude and be willing to work. Within the pages of *See You At The Top*, you will learn that you really "enjoy" a price rather than "pay" a price. I say this because **the price of success is much lower than the price of failure.** This is obvious when you compare the failures in life to the successes in life. Don't be misled however, because you do have to work, but the difference between work being a drudgery or a joy is an adjustment in your thinking. The sixth step is that you must also have a burning desire to excel. You must have lots of "want to" — and, you must live in a free enterprise system so you can control your own destiny.

Fortunately, **you already have every characteristic necessary for success.** You have *some* character, faith, integrity, honesty, love, and loyalty. You like some things about yourself and your fellowman. You have some goals, some "right" mental attitudes, and obviously you do some work and have some desire. Really, all you need to do is use what you have and give each characteristic a chance to grow, because the more you use of what you have, the more you will have to use. Besides, it doesn't take much of a man or a woman to be successful — it just takes all of the person and you do have all of you.

The message in two stories will emphasize this point. A young couple, lost on a rural road, spotted an old farmer so they stopped the car and asked him a question. "Sir, could you tell us where this road will take us?" Without a moment's hesitation the old farmer said, "Son, this road will take you anywhere in the world you want to go, if you are moving in the right direction." [You can be on the right road and still get run over if you are standing still.]

A young business executive took some work home to complete for an important meeting the next day. Every few minutes his five-year-old son would interrupt his chain of thought. After several such interruptions, the young executive spotted the evening paper with a map of the world on it. He took the map, tore it into a number of pieces, and told his son to put the map together again. He figured this would keep the little fellow busy for a long time and he could complete his work. However, in about three minutes the boy excitedly told his dad he had finished. The young executive was astonished and asked the boy how he had done it so quickly. The little guy said, "There was a picture of a man on the other side, so I just turned it over and put the man together. When I got the man right, the world was right." Needless to say, when you get *you* right — your world will be right.

Thought: You do have to take *all* the steps to get to the top but you don't need to build a nest on them. Like the man said, "There are two ways to climb an oak tree. You can climb it — or you can sit on an acorn." This book was written to help you climb it.

CHAPTER TWO
THE TIME IS NOW

YOU CAN BE BRIGHT — AND BROKE

A number of years ago oil was discovered on some Oklahoma property that belonged to an old Indian. All of his life the old Indian had been poverty stricken, but the discovery of oil suddenly made him a very wealthy man. One of the first things he did was buy himself a big Cadillac touring car. In those days, the touring cars had two spare tires on the back. However, the old Indian wanted the longest car in the territory so he added four more spare tires. He bought an Abraham Lincoln stovepipe hat, added tails and a bow tie and completed his outfit with a big black cigar. Every day he would drive into the hot, dusty, little Oklahoma cowtown that was nearby. He wanted to see everyone, and be seen by everyone. He was a friendly old soul, so when riding through town he would turn both left and right to speak to everyone in sight. As a matter of fact, he would turn all the way around and speak to folks. Interestingly enough, he never ran into anybody or over anybody. He never did any physical damage or any property damage. The reason is simple. Directly in front of that big beautiful automobile, there were two horses — pulling it.

TURN IT ON

Local mechanics said there was nothing wrong with the car's engine, but the old Indian never learned how to insert the key and switch on the ignition. *Inside* the car were a hundred horses — ready, willing and raring to go, but the old Indian was using two horses on the *outside.* Many people make the mistake of looking outside to find two horsepower when they should look inside where they have over a hundred. Psychologists tell us this is about the ratio of the ability we have to the ability we use, 2 to 5%.

Oliver Wendell Holmes said, "The biggest tragedy in America is not the great waste of natural resources, though this is tragic. The biggest tragedy is the waste of human resources." Mr. Holmes pointed out that **the average person goes to his grave with his music still in him.** So, unfortunately, the most beautiful melodies of all are the unplayed ones.

For a long time I thought the most tragic thing that could happen to man during his lifetime would be to discover an oil well or a gold mine on his property as he lay on his death bed. Now I know that it is infinitely worse to never discover the vastly greater wealth that lies within the individual. As my good friend, Major Reuben Siverling, says, "a dime and a $20 gold piece have the same value if they are corroding at the bottom of the ocean." The difference in value is manifested only when you lift those coins up and use them as they were intended to be used. *Your* value becomes real and marketable when you learn to reach within yourself and utilize the enormous potential that is there. To help you more fully utilize your potential, I am writing this book. With it I hope to enable you to discover and utilize that gold mine or oil well inside you. **Your "natural resources," unlike the natural resources on planet Earth, will be wasted and "used up" only if they are never used at all.** So my purpose is to get more of your talent into action so you and others can enjoy what you have to offer. No doubt about your talent, you've got it in spades, and *now* you are going to start using it so that instead of being bright and broke [if you are broke] you will be bright — and prosperous.

GARBAGE-DUMP THINKING

A number of years ago I heard a philosopher say, "You are where you are because that's exactly where you want to be." I bought that idea and even repeated it to others. Then, late one night, I was in Birmingham, Alabama, driving to Meridian, Mississippi. It was important that I be in Meridian the next morning. Since the roads were under repair, I stopped at a service station for assistance. The attendant pointed out the best route for me and even drew a map. He assured me that if I followed his map, I would be in Meridian with time to spare. I followed his directions exactly and yet, one hour later I was 45 miles further from Meridian than I had been when he gave me the directions. Obviously, I was not there because that's where I wanted to be. I was there because somebody had given me the wrong directions.

I might say the same thing to you. If you're broke, despondent and down in the dumps, if you're not getting along well with your family or in your career, I just cannot believe that these are the conditions and circumstances you really want. There is a chance that maybe — just maybe you have been given the wrong directions which have influenced you negatively and caused you to suffer from garbage dump thinking. [Now don't get too cozy with the thought that any and all of your problems should be dumped into someone else's lap because as you shall see — if your past situation could possibly be "blamed" on someone else — your future growth and progress is placed squarely on your shoulders.]

Let me explain: In a large southern city there is a magnificent new shopping center which stands on the former city garbage dump. For over a century no one saw this location as anything but the "garbage dump." About twenty-five years ago, however, some progressive-minded citizens started "seeing" that location as a beautiful new shopping center. Immediately they stopped dumping garbage and started hauling good, clean fill dirt and dumping it over the century-old garbage. They did this until a solid foundation was prepared. It was on this foundation that they built a magnificent new shopping center. But really this shopping center is built on garbage, isn't it?

I tell this story because the chances are that over a period of time, people have been dumping "garbage" into your mind. What you must understand, however, is it doesn't really matter if garbage has been dumped into your mind in the past. In fact, it doesn't even matter if others, through either malice or ignorance have built low ceilings over you. You can overcome all of that "garbage," so I'm going to say to you, "Happy Birthday," because **today is the first day of the rest of your life.** The past is over and the fact you have read this far indicates you are now in the process of building a foundation for a greater future.

Warning! "Garbage" has probably been dumped into your

mind for a long time. Realistically we should understand that a person suffering from malnutrition cannot be restored to complete physical health by eating one well balanced meal, regardless of how big or good it might be. So please understand that for the moment all we can do is cover that "garbage" with a thin veneer of positive thinking and right mental attitude. The chances are good that periodically some of that "garbage" will pop through the veneer and you will suffer again from "stinkin' thinkin'." However, keep reading because every chapter you absorb will bury that "garbage" deeper and deeper, until you will eventually bury the *old* garbage. However, since we live in a negative society, we will always have the problem of fresh garbage being dumped into our minds on a daily basis. A friend, an acquaintance, or an overheard conversation can drop a couple of fast loads of garbage into our minds. We switch on the radio or the television and boom-boom, somebody else dumps fresh garbage into our minds. Now we have the problem of stinkin' thinkin' again, so what do we do now, Coach? Keep reading, the answer is spelled out in minute detail in another Segment. I'll guarantee it.

THE FUTURE IS NOW

An exciting new field of psychology has been developed which doesn't dig up all the old garbage of the past. It doesn't "saw sawdust" by harping on the problems of the past. Instead, it deals with the hope of the future. It is not problem conscious, it is solution conscious and its results have been tremendous. An exciting book entitled *Schools Without Failure*, by William Glasser, follows the same basic philosophy. In his book, Dr. Glasser describes the programs that work with youngsters who have never known anything but frustration, defeat, disappointment and failure. He deals in the hope of the future and not in the problems and personalities of the past. By taking the positive approach and giving students mountains of encouragement, his results have been astonishing.

Actually, this still puts man 2,000 years behind the advice the apostle Paul gave us in the *Holy Bible* when he said, "Forgetting those things which lie in the past I press forward toward the mark." Significantly, Paul wrote those words while on death row in a Roman prison. Paul also emphasized that he fought the battle of life to win. My approach is similar. I recognize that **winning is not everything, but the effort to win is.**

THE LOSER'S LIMP

Characteristically, when a person falls victim to Garbage-Dump Thinking, he develops an assortment of "Loser's Limps." You know what the Loser's Limp is if you've ever attended a football game or watched one on television. [Incidentally, the last time I saw the local team play I knew they were in trouble when the punter signaled for a fair catch on the snap from center.] The offensive player slips behind the defensive player, reaches up, pulls in a pass and heads for the end zone. The defensive man quickly recovers and takes out in hot pursuit. When the offensive player gets about 20 yards from the end zone, the defensive player realizes he's not going to catch the man with the ball. Everybody in the stands knows it too. So, the defensive player frequently pulls up limping and the people in the stands say, "Well, no wonder the poor guy couldn't catch him. Look, he's crippled." Now that is his Loser's Limp. What is yours?

THE NATURAL BORN

To utilize the ability you have you must start by getting rid of any loser's limp you might have. A typical Loser's Limp is, "I'm not a born salesman, or a born doctor, lawyer, artist, architect, engineer, etc." I would like to emphasize this point. In my travels, I have picked up newspapers from the rural villages of Australia to the bulging metropolises of North America and Europe. I've read where women have given birth to boys and girls, but thus far I have never read where a woman has given birth to a salesman, or a doctor, lawyer, artist, engineer, etc. However, I do read where doctors, lawyers, salesmen, etc., die. Since they are not "born," but they do "die," obviously, somewhere between birth and death, by *choice* and by *training*, they become what they wish to become. [Would you permit a "natural-born" doctor to go adlibbing through your abdomen? Or a "natural-born" lawyer to defend you in court?]

As a matter of fact, I've never seen where a woman has given birth to a success or to a failure. It's always either a boy or a girl. Occasionally, I've seen a man stand up and say, "I'm a self-made man." So far I've never seen the guy or gal who didn't make it stand up and say, "I'm a self-made failure." You know what they do? They point the index finger and say, "I'm not successful or happy because of my parents." Some say, "My wife or husband doesn't understand me." Some blame the teacher, the preacher or the boss. Some blame everything from skin color and religious beliefs to lack of education and physical deficiencies. Some say they're too old or too young, too fat or too slim, too tall or too short, or that they live in the wrong place.

Incredibly enough, some even say they were born the wrong month or under the wrong star. [Personally, I have no faith in the stars, but total faith in the One who made the stars.] I also believe that Loser's Limps are "garbage." And regardless of your "lot" in life you can build something solid on it.

Some even pull the reverse and say they are discriminated against because they are not a member of a minority group or not a female. Still others point the finger at all of society and blame everybody for their problems or lack of success. Now I want you to notice one thing. When you have your index finger pointed toward someone else, you'll discover there are three times as many fingers pointed right back at you. **Your success and your happiness start with you.** The more involved you become in the message of this book the happier you will be to know that you do control your future. Perhaps for the first time, you will recognize your own enormous potential.

PRISONERS OF HOPE

Surely, one of the saddest experiences in life is to hear someone say, "If I could talk, run, jump, sing, dance, think, concentrate, etc., like him or her," and the voice trails off into silence. The message is, "If I just had someone else's ability, what wouldn't I do?" The answer, my friend, is you would not do a cotton-picking thing with someone else's ability if you are not using the ability you already have. You're kidding yourself, and that's not even being honest. If you're not careful you will become one of the "Prisoners of Hope" that we meet in Every City, U.S.A. These Prisoners of Hope are the people who hope that some day they will walk along the street and kick a box or bag that will contain their personal fortune. They hope for the big break that will give them instant fame and fortune. You can also see them at the seashore, hoping their ship is on its way, but deep down knowing it has never left port. Yes, they are Prisoners of Hope, and so are the people who are always dreaming and wishing for someone else's ability or talent. The truth of the matter is **you already have the ability necessary for success.** The story of life repeatedly assures you that if you will use what you have, you will be given more to use. Life also tells you if you don't use it, you'll lose it.

HERE ARE THE "BEAUTIFUL" PEOPLE

The "jet set", who indulge in questionable moral practices in their international travels, featuring the "good life" complete with fun and games, are definitely not the beautiful people. From my vantage point, the truly "beautiful people" come from every walk of life and often suffer from everything from polio to total blindness. They refused to accept a Loser's Limp and became quite successful, happy and well-adjusted individuals in the process. They represent every race, creed and color. They have educational backgrounds that vary from the third grade to Ph.D. I've seen people who have succeeded sometimes because of, and many times in spite of almost unbelievable handicaps. Their stories are the most beautiful stories we can encounter. Without exception, these people believe that, **"man was designed for accomplishment, engineered for success and endowed with the seeds of greatness."** When you adopt this belief you will discover that there will be no need to blame anyone for any problem. In short, you will be on your way because you will have discovered that you can always find a capable helping hand at the end of your own sleeve. In my work I often see people who *don't* succeed, but I seldom see one who *can't* succeed. What I'm really suggesting is that you accept the fact that from this moment on, your situation — and future — is in capable hands — yours!

IT'S IN YOUR HANDS, SON

Perhaps a parable will help you see my point. High on a hilltop overlooking the beautiful city of Venice, Italy, there lived an old man who was a genius. Legend had it he could answer any question anyone might ask of him. Two of the local boys figured they could fool the old man, so they caught a small bird and headed for his residence. One of the boys held the little bird in his hands and asked the old man if the bird was dead or alive. Without hesitation the old man said, "Son, if I say to you that the bird is alive, you will close your hands and crush him to death. If I say the bird is dead, you will open your hands and he will fly away. You see, Son, in your hands you hold the power of life and death." This I say to *you* without qualification, and with no mental reservations whatsoever. **In your hands you hold the seeds of failure — or the potential for greatness.** Your hands are capable but they must be used — and for the right things — to reap the rewards you are capable of attaining.

DON'T LEAVE ME NOW

Throughout this book I'll be telling a lot of stories because I believe life itself is a continuing story. I'm also going to use every method at my disposal to hold your attention and keep you on your toes.

The reason is simple. You probably read at the rate of 200 to 400 words per minute, but your mind functions from 800 to 1800 words per minute. The normal tendency is for your mind to fill this blank time or space with a thousand unrelated thoughts. Now, combine this with the fact that your reading-learning attitude varies as much as the kind of day you are having varies, and you can easily understand how and why your mind wanders. It's actually possible to read several pages and not absorb *anything.*

For example, while reading this book you have already left me a dozen times on brief trips. You've gone everywhere and done everything from looking in on the kids to teaching a class, making a sale, attending a football game or going to the rest room. If you don't believe it, turn back to any page you have already read and *carefully* read it again. Odds are you will see several words, thoughts or ideas you missed the first time. Incidentally, this is not an insult to your intelligence. As a matter of fact, in most cases the brighter you are the more likely this will happen. I might also add that the brighter and more ambitious you are, the harder you will work to reduce the number of times it happens in the future. As the author of this book, I have to hope you were not on one of these "trips" during this paragraph. [As a matter of fact I "dare" you to re-read the last two pages.]

Knowing you may take a brief trip makes it easier for you to appreciate my earlier advice to use felt-tip pens to underline the points that grab you. Incidentally, if you also record these thoughts and ideas in the Trigger Page Notebook, you will truly be an "active" and not a "passive" reader. This will be helpful for review purposes. To re-read and review this information is extremely important. One of America's leading universities found that people exposed to new material one time will remember only about 2% of it two weeks later. If they are exposed to the same material on six consecutive days, they will remember 62% of it two weeks later. But there's something much more important than that. The more times you are exposed to the same information, the more likely you are to take action on it — and action by you is my objective. As a matter of fact, action is the manifestation of learning. Just as "faith without works is dead," learning without action isn't learning.

DON'T GET COOKED IN THE SQUAT

Many times individuals will indicate with a nod of the head that they already know or have heard the information as I start to cover a point in a talk. I'm often tempted to stop and ask what they've done about it. Unless and until you do something with what you have learned, you might as well not have learned it. The person who won't read is no better off than the person who can't read. The person who knows but won't use success principles and information is no better off than the person who doesn't know them. *You intend* to "do something," don't you? [Say yes!].

Since you answered "yes," let me say, "Congratulations, you are now successful!" I say that because **success is not a destination, it's a journey, it's the direction in which you are traveling.** Not only have you started, but you're headed in the right direction. I enthusiastically congratulate you because you're not like "most people."

Most people wait until everything is just right before they do anything. They refuse to go out on a limb because they don't understand that the fruit is always out on the limb. They refuse to bet on themselves. For them, the ball game of life is already over, and they've lost it. Their epitaph could well read, "Born 1942, died 1974, buried 1997," or whenever the heart finally stops beating. They are the people who end up like the cook's biscuits.

Let me explain. When I was a small boy in Yazoo City, Mississippi, we lived next door to some rich folks. I know they were rich because they not only had a cook, but the cook had something to cook. In the 1930's that was a sure sign of wealth. I was there for lunch one day, as I tried to be most every day. [Don't misunderstand, we had plenty to eat at our house. I know we had plenty because if I ever passed my plate for seconds, they always said, "No, you've had plenty."] On this occasion, the cook brought out a pan of biscuits. Since they were no thicker than a silver dollar, I asked, "Maude, what happened to those biscuits?" She rared back, laughed and said, "Well, those biscuits squatted to rise, but they just got cooked in the squat."

HALF-A-MINDERS AND GONNA-DOERS

Do you know someone who got cooked in the squat? Do you know someone who is "gonna do something just as soon as the kids get out of school or the kids get back in school?" Perhaps they would do it as soon as cold weather gets here or cold weather is over." Other excuses range from when Christmas arrives or Christmas is over, John fixes the car, paints the house, cuts the grass, etc." In a nutshell, those who make a list of "external" changes that must be met before they take "internal" action will always end up getting "cooked in the squat."

Well, I'll tell you about those biscuits — they squatted
to rise but they just got cooked in the squat.

Do you know anyone who is "half-a-mind" to lose some weight, go back to school, take a public-speaking course, beautify the lawn, get active in church or community affairs, etc.? Unfortunately, both the "half-a-minders" and the "gonna-doers," the people who wait until everything is "just right" before they do anything, will never do it. Those who wait until all the lights are on green before starting, will never leave home. They are the "half-a-minders" and the "gonna-doers," which means they are "never-doers" and, as I say, they get cooked in the squat.

Chances are excellent that on occasion you have said to someone that you were going to do a certain task, embark on a course of progress and development, or begin to do more things just as soon as you "get around to it." Since I encounter so many people who fit this position, and since I don't want a reader of my book to "get cooked in the squat," I utilize something that is extremely effective. My business card is round. On one side is my name, address and phone number. The other side has the word "TUIT" in large letters. Since the card is round and it is a Tuit, that makes it "a Round Tuit." Later in the book I will tell you how to get a Round Tuit. [And I guarantee that I will get around to telling *you* how to get a Round Tuit, so keep reading.] When you get your "Round Tuit," keep it with you at all times and when someone asks you to do something which you would normally promise to do as soon as you "get around to it," you will be reminded that you already have your "Round Tuit," so you can go ahead and do it.

IT JUST ISN'T SO

Throughout this book I'm going to completely refute the idea that you have to take advantage of people, abuse them and be dishonest to be successful. As a matter of fact, I'm going to prove beyond any reasonable doubt that the only way you can really be successful in all areas of your life, is to be completely honest with yourself and your fellowman. I will further establish that **you can get everything in life you want, if you help enough other people get what they want.** This is true whether you are a salesman, doctor, father, mother, businessman, student,

minister, mechanic or even an elected government official.
This story will help you understand that it's not just what you
have in your head that counts.

THE BALLOON SALESMAN

Several years ago, a balloon salesman was selling balloons on
the streets of New York City. When business got a little slow, he
would release a balloon. As it floated into the air, a fresh crowd of
buyers would gather and his business would pick up for a few
minutes. He alternated the colors, first releasing a white one,
then a red one and later a yellow one. After a time, a little Negro
boy tugged on his coat sleeve, looked the balloon salesman in the
eye and asked a penetrating question. "Mister, if you released a
black balloon, would it go up?" The balloon saleman looked at the
little boy and with compassion, wisdom and understanding said,
"Son, it's what's inside those balloons that make them go up." The
little boy was fortunate indeed to encounter a man who could see
with more than just his eyes. With good eyes you can see to run or
walk, work or play. The person who can see with his heart and his
eyes can also reach out and touch the spirit within another human
being and reveal the good that lies in him. Yes, the balloon
salesman was "right." I'm also "right" when I tell you, **it's what's
inside you that will make you go up.**

Now, my friends, whether you are in Decision Valley or on
Hesitation Hill, or even if your career or personal life is already in
high gear, let me urge you to fasten your seat belt, because you
are on a trip to the top. It's an exciting trip, with more suspense
than an Alfred Hitchcock thriller, more action than a John
Wayne western, more drama than a Shakespearian play and
more fun than a three-ring circus. It's immersed in love, filled
with laughter and offers more true reward than King Solomon's
Mines. In short, this book is actually the Owner's Manual for your
Future.

It's true, **you can get what you want instead of having to
want what you have.** Success is easy after you believe. But first,
you must believe. So stick around, and keep reading. You're on
your way to believing, which simply means, you're on your way.

SEGMENT TWO

YOUR SELF IMAGE

PURPOSE: I. TO DEMONSTRATE THE IMPORTANCE OF A HEALTHY SELF IMAGE.

  II. TO IDENTIFY THE CAUSES OF A POOR SELF IMAGE.

  III. TO REVEAL THE MANIFESTATIONS OF A POOR SELF IMAGE.

  IV. TO GIVE YOU FIFTEEN METHODS OF IMPROVING YOUR SELF IMAGE.

  V. TO ENCOURAGE YOU TO CHOOSE, AND THEN REMAIN ON, THE ROAD TO A HEALTHY SELF IMAGE.

ADDITIONAL READING MATERIAL

Robert Schuller	— *SELF LOVE*
Bruce Larson	— *THE ONE AND ONLY YOU*
James and Jongeward	— *BORN TO WIN*
Mildred Newman Bernard Berkowitz	— *HOW TO BE YOUR OWN BEST FRIEND*
David Dunn	— *TRY GIVING YOURSELF AWAY*
Og Mandino	— *THE GREATEST MIRACLE IN THE WORLD*
Jerry Lucas Harry Lorayne	— *THE MEMORY BOOK*
James Dobson	— *HIDE OR SEEK*
James Dobson	— *DARE TO DISCIPLINE*

(If you have children, both of these books are a must.)

CHAPTER ONE
THE THIEVES

GENUINE OR COUNTERFEIT

The scene is a small neighborhood grocery store and the year is 1887. A distinguished-looking gentleman in his late fifties or early sixties is buying some turnip greens. He hands the clerk a twenty-dollar bill and waits for his change. The clerk accepts the money and starts to place it in the cash drawer as she made change. However, she noticed that the ink was coming off on her fingers, which were still wet from handling the turnip greens. She was shocked and paused to consider what to do. After an instant of wrestling with the problem, she made a decision. This was Emmanual Ninger, a long-time friend, neighbor, and customer. Surely he would not give her a bill that was anything less than genuine, so she gave him the change and he left.

Later, she had some second thoughts because twenty dollars was a lot of money in 1887. She sent for the police. One policeman was confident that the twenty-dollar bill was the genuine article. The other was puzzled about the ink that rubbed off. Finally, curiosity combined with responsibility forced them to obtain a warrant to search Mr. Ninger's home. In the attic they found the facilities for reproducing twenty-dollar bills. As a matter of fact, they found a twenty-dollar bill in the process of being printed. They also found three portraits which Emmanual Ninger had painted. Ninger was an artist, and a good one. He was so good, he was hand-painting those twenty-dollar bills. Meticulously, stroke by stroke, he applied the master's touch so skillfully, he was able to fool everyone until a quirk of fate in the form of the wet hands of a grocery store clerk exposed him.

After his arrest, his portraits were sold at public auction for $16,000 — over $5,000 each. The irony of the story is, it took Emmanual Ninger almost exactly the same length of time to paint a twenty-dollar bill as it took him to paint a $5,000 portrait. Yes, this brilliant and talented man was a thief in every sense of the word. Tragically, the person he stole the most from was Emmanual Ninger. Not only could he have been a wealthy man if he had legitimately marketed his ability, but he could have brought so much joy and so many benefits to his fellowman in the process. **He was another in the endless list of thieves who steal from themselves when they try to steal from others.**

THIS THIEF WAS A SNOB

A second thief I would like to tell you about is a man named Arthur Barry. He too was an unusual thief. He was a jewel thief who operated during the "roaring twenties." Barry gained an international reputation as probably the outstanding jewel thief of all time. Not only was he a successful jewel thief, he was also a connoisseur of the arts. As a matter of fact, he had become a snob and would not steal from just anyone — not Arthur Barry. Not only must his "prospects" have money and jewels in order for him to come calling, but their name must also be listed in the top echelons of society. It became somewhat of a status symbol to have been called on and robbed by this "gentleman thief." This feeling, I hasten to add, caused the police force a great deal of embarrassment.

One night, Barry was caught during a robbery and shot three times. With bullets in his body, splinters of glass in his eyes and suffering excruciating pain, he made a not too unexpected statement: "I'm never going to do this anymore." Miraculously, he escaped, and for the next three years he remained outside the penitentiary. Then, a jealous woman turned him in and Barry served an eighteen-year sentence. When he was released, he kept his word. He didn't go back to the life of being a jewel thief. As a matter of fact, he settled in a small New England town and lived a model life. Local citizens honored him by making him the commander of a local veterans' organization.

Eventually, however, word leaked out that Arthur Barry, the famous jewel thief, was in their midst. Reporters from all over the country came to the little town to interview him. They asked him a number of questions and finally one young reporter got to the very crux of the matter when he asked the most penetrating question of all. "Mr. Barry," he queried, "you stole from a lot of wealthy people during your years as a thief, but I'm curious to know if you remember the one from whom you stole the most?" Barry, without a moment's hesitation said, "That's easy. The man from whom I stole the most was Arthur Barry. I could have been a successful businessman, a baron on Wall Street and a contributing member to society but instead I chose the life of a thief, and spent two-thirds of my adult life behind prison bars." Yes, Arthur Barry was truly the thief who stole from himself.

YOU KNOW THIS THIEF

A third thief I would like to talk about is obviously *you*. I'm going to call you a thief because any person who does not *believe* in himself and fully utilize his ability is literally stealing from himself, from his loved ones and in the process, because of reduced productivity, he also steals from society. Since no one would knowingly steal from him or her self, it's obvious that those who steal from themselves do it unwittingly. Nevertheless, the crime is still serious because the loss is just as great as if it were deliberately done.

So the question is obvious: Are you ready to quit stealing from yourself? I'm optimistic enough to believe that you have started your climb to the top. For you and many others, this book will provide the motivation, inspiration and knowledge to take you a long way. Let me warn you however, your education in this field isn't complete the minute you finish this book. Your body needs nutritional food every day and your mind needs mental nourishment just as often, so keep reading and soon, when you look into the mirror, you will be looking into the eyes of an ex-thief.

THE TELEPHONE RINGS

I'm personally convinced that a healthy self-image is the starting point — the first and most important step to reaching our objectives. After all, **if we don't start, it's certain we can't arrive.** Perhaps this analogy will sell you on that concept.

Let's play a game for just a moment. Your telephone rings and the voice at the other end says, "Friend, don't be disturbed, I don't want to borrow any money and I have no favors to ask. I just thought I would call and tell you that I think you're one of the nicest persons who ever drew a breath of air. You are an asset to your profession and a credit to your community. You're the kind of person I like to be with because every time I'm around you, I feel inspired and motivated to do a better job. I wish I could see you every day because you motivate me to be my best self. That's all I wanted to say, friend. Look forward to seeing you soon." Now, if a close friend called you and said those things to you what kind of day would you have? Remember, you know the words are sincere because they are coming from a close friend.

If you were a doctor, would you be a better doctor? If you were a teacher, would you be a better teacher? If you were a salesman, would be you a better salesman? If you were a mother, would you be a better mother? If you were a father, would you be a better father? If you were a coach, would you be a better coach? If you were an athlete, would you be a better athlete? If you were a student, would you be a better student? Would you be better? Regardless of who you are or what you do, you know in your own mind you wouldn't only be better at your job, but you would be happier, wouldn't you? [Say yes.]

One other question arises at this point. In light of the previous conversation, how much more would you know about being a doctor? Or a sales person? A lawyer? A coach? A student? An athlete? How much more would you know if you had gotten that phone call? The answer obviously is you wouldn't know any more. Still, in your own mind you know you would be better and happier in your job. The reason is simple. You've had a change of image. You would say, I'm an asset to my community and a credit to my profession. That old boy said so and he is one more smart cookie." You wouldn't argue with him for one single moment. You would see yourself in a different light. Your self-image would change and at that instant an interesting thing happens. Your confidence goes up and when your confidence goes up, your competence goes up at the same time. Simply stated, it means that **when your image improves, your performance improves.**

Since you know what this kind of phone call would do for you, why don't you do the same thing for someone else? Why don't you put this book down and pick up the telephone [unless it is 2:00 a.m. or some other ridiculous hour]. Call that person you sincerely like and respect, and tell him or her how much you appreciate who they are, what they do, and how much they mean and have meant to you. The person you call will be appreciative and you will feel good about it. Significantly, you will like yourself better as a result of helping to build up someone else. More on this later.

The next story — straight out of life — clearly demonstrates the importance of a healthy self-image and what happens when your self-image changes.

FROM "DUNCE" TO GENIUS IN ONE EASY STEP

When Victor Seribriakoff was fifteen, his teacher told him he would never finish school and that he should drop out and learn a trade. Victor took the advice and for the next seventeen years he was an itinerant doing a variety of odd jobs. He had been told he was a "dunce" and for seventeen years he acted like one. When he was 32 years old, an amazing transformation took place. An evaluation revealed that he was a genius with an I.Q. of 161. Guess what? That's right, he started acting like a genius. Since that time he has written books, secured a number of patents and has become a successful businessman. Perhaps the most significant event for the former dropout was his election as chairman of the International Mensa Society. The Mensa Society has only one membership qualification, an I.Q. of 140.

The story of Victor Seribriakoff makes you wonder how many geniuses we have wandering around acting like dunces because someone told them they weren't too bright. Obviously, Victor did not suddenly acquire a tremendous amount of additional knowledge. He did suddenly acquire a tremendous amount of added confidence. The result was, he instantly became more effective and more productive. When he saw himself differently, he started acting differently. He started expecting, and getting, different results. Ah yes, as a man thinketh.

JUST HOW IMPORTANT IS YOUR SELF-IMAGE?

Mildred Newman and Dr. Bernard Berkowitz in their book, *How to Be Your Own Best Friend*, ask a penetrating question. "If we cannot love ourselves, where will we draw our love for anyone else?" You can't give away something you don't have. The Bible says, "Love thy neighbor as thyself."

Is self-image important? Dorothy Jongeward and Muriel James wrote a marvelous book entitled, *Born to Win*. They point out that man was born to win, but throughout a lifetime, as a result of our negative society, he is conditioned to lose. They, too, stress that a healthy self-image is critical in the success parade.

You cannot consistently perform in a manner that is inconsistent with the way you see yourself. Your self-image will lead you to the top of the stairway or put you on an escalator to the basement. See yourself as a deserving person and you will be — do — and have. See yourself as nondeserving and you have not. Fortunately, regardless of how you have seen yourself in the past, you now have the motivation, method and capacity to change, and change for the better. Of all the gifts our Creator gives us, surely the gift of choosing the way we wish to be is one of the greatest.

As we delve into our self-image, let's remember that **the mind completes whatever picture we put in it.** For example, a plank 12" wide laying on the floor would be easy to walk. Place the same plank between two ten story buildings and "walking the plank" is a different matter. You "see" yourself easily and safely walking the plank on the floor. You "see" yourself falling from the plank stretched between the buildings. Since the mind completes the picture you paint in it, your fears are quite real. Many times a golfer will knock a ball into a lake or hit it out of bounds and then step back with the comment, "I knew I was going to do that." His mind painted a picture and his body completed the action. On the positive side, the successful golfer knows he must "see" the ball going in the cup before he strokes it. The good hitter in baseball "sees" the ball dropping in for a base hit before he swings at the ball, and the successful salesman "sees" the customer buying before he makes the calls. Michaelangelo clearly saw the Mighty Moses in that block of marble before he struck the first blow.

STRIKE THREE

Easily, the most puzzling and disappointing incident in the sports world occurs in baseball when a batter steps up to the plate and proceeds to let the pitcher throw three strikes without taking a single cut at the ball. Three golden opportunities to at least advance a runner, get on base himself, or maybe even hit a home run, and he never moves the bat from his shoulder. The reason is simple. He "saw" himself striking out, being put out or maybe even hitting into a double play. He left his bat on his shoulder hoping for a "walk" — a free ride to first base.

Even more disappointing is to see a person in the ball game of life step up to the plate, and never really take a cut at the ball. He is the biggest failure of all according to Larry Kimsey, M.D. — because he doesn't try. If you try and lose, you can learn from losing, which greatly reduces the loss. Obviously, **there is little you can learn from doing nothing.** These people serve as their own judge and jury and sentence themselves to a life in the prison of mediocrity. They never really get in the game of life and take an honest cut at the ball. They serve as their own worst enemy and the blindest umpire of all. Their self-image is that of falling — failing — or striking out. Unfortunately, their mind then completes the picture and another person of ability joins the scrap heap of "could have been." The late Dr. Maxwell Maltz, internationally famous plastic surgeon, and author of "self help" books that sold over 10,000,000 copies, says this is the reason the goal of any form of psychotherapy is to change the self-image of the patient.

YA GOTTA BELIEVE — IN YOU

The starting point for both success and happiness is a healthy self-image. Dr. Joyce Brothers, well known author, columnist and psychologist says, "An individual's self-concept is the core of his personality. It affects every aspect of human behavior: the ability to learn, the capacity to grow and change, the choice of friends, mates and careers. It's no exaggeration to say that a strong positive self-image is the best possible preparation for success in life."

You must accept yourself before you can really like anyone else or before you can accept the fact that you deserve success and happiness. Motivation, goal setting, positive thinking, etc., won't work for you until you accept yourself. You must feel you "deserve" success, happiness, etc., before those things will be yours. The person with a poor self-image can easily see how positive thinking, goal setting, etc., would work for others, but not for himself.

Let me stress that I am talking about a *healthy* self acceptance and not a super-inflated "I am the Greatest" ego. Of all the diseases known to man, conceit is the weirdest of them all. It makes everyone sick *except* the one who has it. [Actually the individual with a bad case of "I" trouble is really suffering from an extremely poor self image.]

THE HITCHHIKER

Since so many people are unaware of the enormous potential that lies within even an uneducated mind, I would like to share a personal experience to illustrate a point. Several years ago, I picked up a hitchhiker. As soon as he seated himself, I knew I had made a mistake because he had been drinking a little and was talking a lot. He soon revealed he had just been released from prison where he had served eighteen months for bootlegging. When I asked if he had acquired any knowledge he could use once he was released, he enthusiastically replied he had learned the name of every county in every state in the United States, including the parishes in Louisiana.

Frankly, I thought he was lying so I challenged him to prove what he was saying. I selected South Carolina as a test state since I had lived there nearly eighteen years. My rider, who had a limited education, proceeded to demonstrate that he did know the names of all the counties in that state and was anxious to prove he knew the others as well. I have no idea why he selected this particular project and spent so much time acquiring apparently useless information. The point, however, is even though he was formally uneducated, his mind was capable of acquiring and storing an enormous amount of information. So is yours, but I hope you concentrate on learning and then applying usable information to life's daily opportunities. Unfortunately, many "educated" people never succeed in life because they are not "motivated" to put their imagination to work to utilize their knowledge.

One point you need to clearly understand is that **education and intelligence are not the same thing.** Three of the most intelligent and successful people I know finished the 3rd, 5th and 8th grades. Henry Ford quit school at 14 and Thomas J. Watson, founder of I.B.M., went from a $6.00 a week salesman to Chairman of the Board. Many of the successful people I mention through the pages of this book have even less education yet they made it — and made it big in this highly technical world of the 1970's, so a limited "formal" education is no excuse and certainly no reason to have a poor self-image. Obviously education is important, but dedication is even more important. This book was not written just to "educate" or inform you, though I certainly expect you to learn a number of things from it. It was written to help you get rid of excuses for failure, give you reasons and methods to succeed while urging you to dedicate yourself to utilizing the potential you possess.

THE $50,000 FAILURE

In many ways, things are relevant. One man who earns $50,000 a year could well be judged a failure if he is capable of earning five times that amount. On the other hand, one who earns $10,000 per year could be an overwhelming success, if he is using a high portion of his talents and abilities. I know talents vary and in the ability department we are not all created equal. I also know none of us use *all* our ability. In fact, very few of us even use most of our ability. One of my goals in this book is to convince you that you have more ability than you think and then to motivate you to use more of that ability.

Earlier, I mentioned earnings as a mark of success primarily because money is a familiar yardstick by which we can measure a contribution. Regardless of what your occupation might be, there are others with the same opportunity who earn considerably less money and still others who earn a great deal more. In the final analysis, **opportunity for growth and service lies with the individual.** Almost without exception you can measure a person's contribution to society in terms of dollars. The more he contributes the more he earns.

SERVE NOW — EARN LATER

Now, before you jump more than six feet off the ground, let me hasten to add I did say "almost." I personally know some teachers who make very little money and others who earn large amounts. The same is true of doctors, lawyers, salesmen, ministers, truck drivers, secretaries, etc. As you view the individual, you discover that those who are earning the most money are *generally* making larger contributions, but there are some obvious exceptions.

The dedicated teacher who chooses to remain in a remote mountain or rural area or in a tenement area school might be an example. He or she might be the only hope many of the children have for raising the ceilings their families might have set for them. The dedicated minister might remain in a small local area because he fervently believes God chose him to serve that specific community. Generally speaking, however, the well-paid minister is rendering more service to more people. The same is true of the teacher, doctor, truck driver, salesman, etc.

The oft-repeated philosophy, **"You can get everything in life you want, if you help enough other people get what they want,"** is another way of saying if you serve more, you earn more.

From time to time some of my Christian friends ask me how I reconcile my Christian beliefs with my view on money. I always smile and tell them that I believe God made the diamonds for His folks and not Satan's crowd. All you've got to do to verify this is check the record. Read what God said in Malachi 3-10, Psalms 1-3 and III John 2, and I believe you will agree that money is scripturally okay. [Solomon was the richest man who ever lived, Abraham had cattle on a thousand hills, and Job would not have qualified for food stamps.] The *only* admonition God gives us is that we must not make money or anything else our god because when we do we will never be happy — regardless of how much we have. We know this is true because in the past two years five billionaires have died and all five of them were still trying to earn more money. Someone in Dallas asked how much money Howard Hughes had left and got this answer: "He left it all." That's the amount each of us will leave, isn't it? It's all right to get money — lots of it — as long as you get it the right *way* and you don't let the money get you.

Most people don't have money because they don't understand it. They talk about cold, hard cash and it is neither cold nor hard — it's soft and warm. It feels *good* and it's color-coordinated to go with any color you might be wearing. Not once has my redhead ever had to change outfits because what she was wearing would not go with what I was carrying.

Occasionally I will hear someone truthfully say they really do not want to earn large sums of money [ministers, teachers, social workers, etc.] but generally speaking any other person who says this will lie about other things, too.

Yes, a well-paid individual will be quite comfortable in the philosophy of this book. By the same token, the service oriented person will also find much encouragement and comfort in the "Zigmanship" philosophy. So keep reading — *regardless* of your status at the moment.

NOTES AND IDEAS

CHAPTER TWO
CAUSES OF A POOR SELF IMAGE

THE FAULT FINDERS

If self-image is so important, why do so many people have a poor one and what are the causes? I'm convinced that the beginning of a poor self-image is the fact that we live in a negative society and deal constantly with negative individuals. Any scanning of the news will verify this. Typical comments from the "average home in America" repeatedly reveal that negativism prevails. An overweight person sits down to the table and says, "everything I eat turns to fat." A housewife who is a lousy housekeeper views the "wreck" when she arises in the morning and comments, "I'll never get this mess cleaned up." [One lady *was* so bad Good Housekeeping cancelled her subscription. Her husband might have been luckier than "this old boy down home," though. His wife was so fastidious that if he got up for a midnight snack, when he came back to bed she had it made.]

The businessman walks in his office, or the laborer steps into his shop, and often comments, "Boy, I'll never get this work done today." A child comes home from school and says, "Dad, I'm afraid I flunked that arithmetic test," and his dad might say, "Don't sweat it son, you've come by it honestly. I never could learn that stuff either." A mother sends her child off to school and cautions her, "Now, don't get run over." The weatherman on TV says we have a 20% chance of rain, or that it will be partly cloudy. Why doesn't he tell us we have an 80% chance of sunshine and that it will be mostly fair? Ask the average person how he is doing and he will make such comments as "Not too bad," or "Since it is Monday or Friday, I'm doing fine." Easily the most tragic cause of a poor self image is the influence and impact of some well intentioned preachers, churches, and good Christian people who **only** preach hell, fire, and brimstone. Who preach only God's judgment with little or no mention of God's love. They stress the negative and very seldom mention the positive. They dwell on punishment and forget about rewards. Personally, if I thought God was "against" me and was out to "get" me it would definitely give me a poor self-image. The major reason I wrote **Confessions of A Happy Christian** was to bring out the positive aspects of God's love.

The second reason many people have poor self-images out of proportion to their talent and ability is simple. Their ability, appearance and intelligence have been ridiculed or questioned repeatedly by parents, teachers, friends and others in authority. In many cases, these hurts come in the form of insinuations and innuendos, but they are just as real and devastating as if they were true. Many times, even a chance or unintentional remark starts the negative slide which is then fed by hurts that are real or imagined. The net result is, we see ourselves through the negative eyes of others. If your friends, family and associates find fault like there is a reward for it, you get a distorted picture of the real you. This segment is written to give you a newer and truer picture of the remarkable person who is going to take you to the top — you.

In other cases, an unthinking or exaggerated series of statements has a negative effect on the self-image of a youngster. A little boy breaks something and one of the parents might typically shout, "Johnny, you're the clumsiest boy I have ever seen; you are *always* dropping things." What a burden for a child to carry. To begin with, it is not true. There is quite a difference in "dropping a dish" as versus "always breaking things." Other times, the child makes a mistake and the parents will make such ridiculous comments as, "Well, what else can we expect; he is *always* doing things like this." The child walks in and drops his coat or throws his shoes off and one of the parents might be inclined to say, "Johnny, you are the roughest kid in the neighborhood. You wear your shoes out faster than anybody." The child might start for school with his shirt tail out and mom fusses as she tells him, "You never look nice — you're always a mess." **The destructiveness of this approach should be obvious but unfortunately it is often anything but obvious.** This information is crucial in child-rearing as well as dealing with employees. The usual devastating put-downs imply that a person is basically bad rather than that he is a person who sometimes does bad things. [Obviously there is a vast difference between a "bad" person and a person who does something bad.]

Combine this with some phase of physical appearance,

[obesity, bad teeth, poor complexion, "weak" smile, bad eye sight, too tall — too short, "different" voice, etc.], lower I.Q., or learning difficulty and you have all the ingredients for a low self esteem. The child then reasons that since he or she is "ugly," "dumb," or inept he doesn't deserve love from others. Then it follows in logical sequence that if others cannot, or do not love him, that he cannot — even should not — love himself.

Societies emphasis on physical appearance is one of the reasons Bill Gothard, in his week-long seminar on Basic Youth Conflicts, states that no wise parent will compliment the appearance of another child in the presence of his own. This makes the child feel that the parent puts great value on physical attractiveness and that the parent feels the other child is prettier, smarter, etc., than he or she, and it tends to create a feeling of inferiority.

When commenting on another child, the wise parent will say, "My, what nice manners," or, "He is such an honest boy," or, "Isn't she helpful?" The wise parent will compliment the trait or characteristic he would like to see developed more in his own child. This is critically important because survey after survey shows that 95% of the youth of America would change their appearance if they could. In Hollywood, with its stress on physical appearance, conclusive evidence points out that nearly 100% of the "beauties" would like to alter their own personal appearance, and many of them do, through plastic surgery.

A poor self-image, more commonly known as an inferiority complex, is often carried into adulthood and if fed by a negative mate, the problem is compounded. That's the primary reason the wise husband never comments about the attractiveness of another woman in the presence of his wife. This could lead the wife to feel that he considers the other woman more attractive than she. This has a tendency to feed an already negative self-image and helps to put the marriage on shaky grounds. Comments like, "You're always late," "You never do anything right," "You never cook a decent meal," also compound the problem. They are not designed to build either confidence or love. Besides, there is a tremendous difference between "I am a failure in life," and "I did not get the raise," or "I did not get the job."

POOR IMAGES GET WORSE — WHEN FED

Poor self-images of the worst kind are created, or enlarged, when teachers, people in authority or even the general public come in contact with the underprivileged or members of a minority race in a manner that produces inferiority complexes. For example, I never fully realized the extent of the damage to the image of the black man until I saw the Xerox series hosted by Bill Cosby. One scene from a Shirley Temple movie stands out in my mind.

The scene was a birthday party five-year-old Shirley Temple was having. The party was nearly over when a 14-year-old black girl and several of her younger friends came calling with a present for "Miss Shirley." Here was a five-year-old white girl, smiling and friendly, accepting a present from a 14-year-old black girl, obviously awed at the "privilege" of just stopping by. The black girl is moved to tears when the five-year-old white girl invites her to share some of the leftover birthday cake. It doesn't take much imagination to know that the stereotype portrayed would lead to a feeling of inferiority.

Fortunately, much of this extreme treatment has disappeared. As a result, the Negro has made more progress in this generation than any people in recorded history. His progress has been in direct proportion to the change in his self-image. Unfortunately, prejudice still exists, but progress is being made daily. The complete solution will come with education, love and understanding by both black and white, that skin color and ability have no correlation. I like what Jesse Owens, the great Oympic track star says about color, "Black is not beautiful, white is not beautiful — those are skin colors and anything that doesn't go beyond skin color is not beautiful."

The third cause of a poor self-image is the tendency to confuse failure in a project with failure in life. A child who fails a subject in school or who doesn't make the team, makes the mistake of identifying a single failure with failure in life itself. This is tragically reinforced many times by teachers and/or parents.

Once the poor self-image slide starts, the natural tendency is to feed the inferiority feeling. Many people do this when they castigate themselves because they can't remember everything they hear and everybody they meet, which brings us to our fourth cause, an untrained memory. At the beginning of this Segment, I listed a marvelous new book which will help you to dramatically improve your memory in a matter of hours. It was written by Jerry Lucas and Harry Lorayne. To give you an idea of the tremendous capacity of the human mind, Jerry is now in the process of memorizing the entire Bible, and has just completed a book that will teach you how to do the same thing. Jerry, who knows where he is going here — and hereafter — is terribly convincing when he tells you that anyone — even you — can dramatially improve your memory by using his techniques.

For the moment, here are two warming thoughts which will give you a lot of comfort. First, a perfect memory doesn't indicate a great mind any more than a huge dictionary, with *all* the words in it, represents a great piece of literature. Second, the person who can't remember is infinitely better off than the one who can't forget. Those two thoughts are temporarily comforting, but don't hang your hat on them. Go buy *The Memory Book*, I did, and it's fantastic. Actually, **there is no such thing as a "good" memory or a "bad" memory; it is either trained or untrained.** The choice of whether you train it or leave it untrained is up to you.

BE FAIR — TO YOU

The fifth cause of a poor self-image is an unrealistic and unfair comparison of experiences. We generally make the mistake of comparing our experience with another person's experience. We exaggerate their successful experience and downgrade our own success. **Experience has nothing to do with ability.** [Experience can increase skill but that is another subject.] For example, there are *three million Australians* who can do something most of us cannot do. They can drive down the left hand side of the highway. On the other hand, if you can drive, the chances are good that you can do something three million Australians cannot safely do. You can drive down the right hand side of the highway. This does not mean that either is smarter than the other. It simply means you have had a different experience. There are over 200 million Chinese under twenty-one who can do something you probably cannot do. They can speak Chinese. Does that mean they are smarter than you? Not at all; it means they have had a different experience. At this moment you are doing something that over three billion people cannot do. You are reading this book in English. Obviously this does not mean you are smarter than three billion other people. It does mean you have had a different experience.

Chances are good that you stand somewhat in awe of any competent doctor as he rattles off those big words describing your condition. You undoubtedly feel he is truly a brilliant and remarkable man and he might well be. What about you? The chances are exceptionally good that your doctor would be lost in your job, and could not perform nearly as well as you. Chances are also excellent that if you were to spend the next fifteen years of your life as your doctor did, learning those big words, studying diseases, medicines and cures, you could don the white coat and stethoscope of an M.D. yourself.

ALL ARE EDUCATED AND UNEDUCATED
IN DIFFERENT AREAS

This experience will emphasize what I mean. About three years ago, following an extremely heavy rain, the alley in back of our home became virtually impassable. However, I had to go down the alley to reach our garage and in the process, I became hopelessly stuck directly behind our driveway. I spent about 45 frustrating minutes burning rubber in an effort to get out of that mud hole. I put bricks, boards, and anything else available underneath the wheels in an effort to get traction. It was all in vain, so I finally called the tow truck to pull me out [negative people would have called the wrecker]. The driver viewed the situation and asked if he could try to drive the car out of the mud. I protested that it was absolutely useless, but with a quiet confidence he asked again if he couldn't "just give it a try." I told him to go ahead, but assured him that it was no use and besides I didn't want him burning up my tires. He sat down, turned the wheels slightly, started the car, jockeyed a couple of times, and within thirty seconds, slowly but surely drove that car out of the mud. When I expressed astonishment, he explained that he had been raised in East Texas and had spent his lifetime driving out of mud holes. I'm convinced that this man was no "smarter" than I, but he did have a different experience.

Ironically, many of the people we admire for their skills and accomplishments also admire us for the same thing. Please don't misunderstand; I am not saying that some people do not have aptitudes for various jobs or professions. I am simply emphasizing that you too have a unique skill, talent, aptitude and experience. You must recognize that a different experience does not mean you are less than another, nor that he is less than you.

Instead of feeling inferior because someone else can do something you can't, why not concentrate on what you can do that others can't. Admire the skill of others but remember, in most instances, you could greatly improve your own skill by using the same amount of time and effort. Experience is often the only difference.

FOUR WINNERS

A sixth cause for a poor self-image is comparing your worst features to someone else's best features. One woman did that and ended up at age 38, a scrub woman on welfare. Then she read Claude M. Bristol's *The Magic of Believing.* She started believing and looking at her positive qualities, one of which was the ability to make people laugh. Since that time — even though she still doesn't compete with the beauties of the world — Phyllis Diller has earned as much as $1,000,000 in a single year. Eleanor Roosevelt was a sad combination of homeliness, fright and fear. Long after she was grown and the "Negative Nells" of life were quoting those old cliches about not teaching old dogs new tricks, Eleanor made a decision. She took stock of her assets, started seeing herself for her true values and became one of the most charming and persuasive women in America. Incidentally, she fainted — passed out cold — at her first public speech. Jimmy Durante and Humphrey Bogart were not exactly poster material, but they capitalized on their appearances and decided they had a place in life if they used what they had. None of these people "saw" themselves as physically unattractive. They saw the talent or good qualities they had. They did not "compare" their "worst" features to someone else's "best" features. Instead, they took their own best features or talents and used what they had to get what they wanted. I'm convinced there are hundreds of glamour girls or matinee idols who would love to have the success and admiration that these four people achieved.

USE IT — OR LOSE IT

Surely you remember the story of the talents in the Bible. One man had one, another had two, still another had five. The Lord went away for a long time into a far country. When He returned, He asked the one who had five what he had done. The man replied that he had taken the five talents, put them to work and now he had ten talents. The Lord replied, "Well done, thou good and faithful servant, because you have been faithful in using that which you have, then I will give you more talents." The one who had been given two talents, took those talents, put them to work and multiplied them. Then the Lord went to the one who had one talent, and inquired as to how he had done. The man replied, "Lord, you only gave me one talent, while you gave the others many talents. Besides, I knew you were a hard and cruel master, that you reaped where you had not sowed, and so I took the one talent and buried it."

Then the Lord said, "Thou wicked and slothful servant." [Throughout the entire Bible, Jesus Christ is not this hard on anyone else, so apparently He expects us to use our talent.] He then took the one talent and gave it to the one who had ten. Since that time, the cry-babies of the world have been saying, "The rich get richer and the poor get poorer," or "Them what has, gets." The Bible says, "To him who hath, the more shall be given." The message is clear. **Take what you have and use it and your talent will be increased which brings more rewards, etc.**

Many people have poor self-images because they set standards of perfection that are unrealistic and unreachable. This is the seventh cause of a poor self-image. When they fail — and fail they must — they never forgive themselves. They feel they must either be perfect — the best — or the worst. Since they failed, they figure they must be the worst. This affects all areas of life and is an underlying cause of job dissatisfaction, discord in the rearing of children, unhappiness in a marital relationship, etc. After all, if a person feels he is the "worst," then surely he cannot believe he "deserves" a good job, a good mate, good children, or anything of merit or value.

In my mind the greatest single cause of poor self-images within the last ten years has been the opening of the flood gates of pornography, especially child pornography which has to rate as the most degrading and despicable form of exploitation in existence. I'll deal with pornography at greater length when we look at the steps we can take to build a healthy self image.

Og Mandino in his magnificent book, *The Greatest Miracle in the World*, points out two additional causes of a poor self-image. First, Darwin's "theory" of evolution, that man is not from God but is animalistic in origin, has dealt man's self esteem a serious blow. I agree with Og. If I thought I came from a monkey, it would lower my self esteem considerably. This concept has indirectly helped create a discipline problem. If our young people act like animals and we follow the dictates of a permissive society by not disciplining them we really re-inforce the poor self image, because as Dr. James Dobson so beautifully points out in his book *"Dare to Discipline,"* discipline, or rather the lack of it, is definitely a cause of a poor self image. He points out that it is through the loving control of discipline that parents express personal worth to a child. Dr. Dobson is simply echoing what God told us 2000 years ago.

The second point concerns the damage done by Sigmund Freud. Freud gave us a built-in excuse or "loser's limp" when he told us our thoughts and actions originated from early childhood experiences deeply buried in our subconscious mind which we could neither control nor understand and we're therefore not responsible for.

With one scientist telling us we came from the lowest form of animal life and another telling us we are not responsible for our conduct, it's easy to see how we could see ourselves as "nothing." Darwin, before his death, acknowledged God as the architect of the universe and some of Freud's findings are questionable. For example, John Hopkins Psychologist, Robert Hogan, recently said: "Freud thought you could study neurotics and learn about normals. He got it backwards. You have to study the normal to understand the delinquent." Unfortunately, much damage has already been done. Einstein pointed out that incorrect input requires eleven or more correct inputs to negate the erroneous information. This is another way of saying that it takes a number of "right thinking" deposits to overcome those "stinkin' thinkin'" deposits.

When you combine all these reasons for having a poor self-image, there is little wonder that so many people are so badly crippled by this prevalent and contagious disease. Fortunately you are doing something about yours. As we explore the manifestations of a poor self-image in the next chapter, you will be able to identify some personal behavior you had not previously associated with a poor self-image. It is important to recognize the manifestations of a poor self-image so that you can more effectively deal with your own self-image problem [if you have one]. This will also give you additional insight in living and working with other people. When we can identify a problem and face the problem with confidence and enthusiasm, the solution is on the way.

NOTES AND IDEAS

CHAPTER THREE
MANIFESTATIONS OF A POOR SELF IMAGE

Those with poor self-images quickly reveal themselves by their critical and jealous nature. They resent the success and even the number of friends others have. They are jealous without cause of wives, husbands, boyfriends or girlfriends. [If a husband or wife comes in at all hours of the night smelling like a member of the opposite sex, I'd say there is cause for jealousy.] Since they don't like themselves, they can't possibly believe that a member of the opposite sex could love them above all others. Ironically, they often defend their jealousy by exclaiming to all who will listen that they love their mate "too much." In reality, they can neither love nor trust their mate because they neither love nor trust themselves. They gossip and often keep rumors alive with ugly and often untrue comments. [They haven't learned that when they're throwing dirt, they're not doing a thing but losing ground.] Their insecurity is also evident by their resentment when someone else receives praises or recognition.

Perhaps the most noticeable manifestation of a poor self-image is the way a person reacts to criticism and the way he reacts to laughter. They can't stand it if they suspect that someone else is laughing "at" them. They can't laugh at themselves and strongly feel that either laughter or criticism from others is a "put down," an effort to make them "look bad." Their reactions are completely out of proportion to the act or actions.

A person with a poor self-image is generally uncomfortable when alone or inactive. He's gotta be going somewhere and doing something all the time. When alone, he or she keeps the radio and/or TV going, even if they are not watching or listening. Some will even carry their transistor radios with them as they walk, drive, or fly around the country.

A poor self-image also reveals itself in a breakdown of motivation. Many times, when a person quits competing and puts forth the "I don't care" attitude, it is because they can't see themselves as "winning" the outstanding boy or girl because they aren't attractive or deserving enough. Then they completely "let go" and "overdo" their protest in every conceivable way. They are frequently loud, critical, vindictive and overbearing. Such people often dress unattractively, forego personal hygiene, frequently become obese, abandon morality and flaunt immorality, turn to drugs or alcohol and become vulgar and profane in speech. Ironically, they often adopt a superior attitude and try to make others, who don't share their views, feel inferior. It's distressing to see sloppy, dirty, profane and unkept individuals because the outward appearance is a dead giveaway to the self-image, and of course no one has yet established any advantage to being dirty or unkept.

Interestingly enough, the exact opposite is frequently a manifestation of a poor self-image. These individuals place too much emphasis on material things: flashy cars, money, the current fad, way-out clothes, hairdos or make-up. They also feel they could never be accepted as they are. In their insecurity they go to extremes to gain friends and acceptance. They often join gangs with an "everything goes" approach to life because they so desperately crave acceptance — "just as I am." Tragically, they generally end up with pseudo friends and many of the habits and characteristics of these "friends."

As individuals, we will consistently act according to the way we see ourselves. This is why you often see people do some incredibly ridiculous things and take unnecessary risks when they are on the brink of achieving a life-long dream. For example, a high percentage of athletes who have spent years preparing for the Olympics, often have "accidents" in training, or in a preliminary event before the competition starts. They could not "see themselves" as deserving a gold medal and subconsciously took the necessary steps to make certain they deny themselves the reward the world might confer upon them.

Many fighters, football players and other athletes injure themselves just before the big event. A student trying to gain entrance to the school of his choice gets drunk or has an all-night date the night before the entrance exam. A worker seeking a promotion has a violent argument with his wife or a co-worker which upsets him emotionally, and he "blows" his chances for promotion. He might even "accidentally" cross or antagonize the very person who must recommend him before he can be promoted. A man on probation will often commit some senseless deed and end up back in prison. This — in his mind — "proves" that society is no good and is out to "get" him. Of course, what it does prove is, he could not "see" himself as a member of a free society. His self-image was such that he knew he didn't "deserve" freedom. Since society wasn't going to adequately punish him for his misdeeds, he must punish himself to make certain he "gets what he deserves."

The husband or wife with a poor self-image seldom challenges his mate on anything. Instead, he or she just goes along, becomes a door mat for the other and builds up a resentment which inevitably leads to serious marital as well as physical and emotional problems.

The examples are endless, but I'll leave it by saying that a major cause of much senseless and erratic action is simply a manifestation of a poor self-image. These persons will read this book, agree with some of it, disagree with much of it and proceed to do little or nothing about any of it. They have made excuses in the past — and will continue to make them in the future — and they are all "justified" in their own mind. They seldom "finish" anything — a book, painting the fence, decorating the house, a growth course, or school. They say things like, "I'd go back to college and get my degree, but it would take six years and by then I'd be thirty-eight." [I wonder how old he will be in six years if he doesn't go back and get his degree?] Others have said, "I'd go to church but there are so many hypocrites there." [They don't seem to realize that if a hypocrite is standing between them and God, the hypocrite is closer to God than they are.]

Fortunately, this does not apply to you. At one time it might have but not anymore. When you acquired your copy of this book, you took a big step toward changing your image. The fact you've come this far indicates you are serious about progress for yourself. In your mind you know that the pages in front of you and the years ahead of you are going to be even more exciting — rewarding — and revealing.

GOOD IMAGE = GOOD SALESMAN/GOOD MANAGER
BAD IMAGE = BAD SALESMAN/BAD MANAGER

In the sales world a poor self-image is manifested in many ways, but three of them stick out like a sore thumb. [1] The salesman won't work nearly as hard. Here's why. He makes a sales call and is rudely invited to take his sales efforts elsewhere. The salesman with the poor self-image doesn't like himself and the prospect [in the salesman's mind] doesn't like him either. Now the salesman indulges in self-pity and goes through the "Poor little me — nobody loves me" routine and heads for the coffee shop, home or office to regroup or lick his wounds. Some take an hour off and others call it quits for the day. In cases where supervision is lax, the salesman might well fabricate a dozen things to do and procrastinate several days before he goes back to work. The salesman with the healthy self-image — who likes himself — reacts altogether differently. When he is rebuffed, he completely understands that the *prospect* has a problem, so he immediately and confidently talks to another prospect who doesn't have a problem.

[2] The salesman with a poor self-image is reluctant to try to close the sale. He talks on and on with never a suggestion that the prospect should take action and buy something. You see there is a certain risk in asking someone to buy. If the prospect says no, then the salesman's ego suffers so the salesman protects his ego by not attempting to close the sale. He just talks and hopes the prospect will finally say, "I'll take it" without the salesman having to risk an ego injury by asking for the order. I've personally seen prospects challenge the salesman with a, "You're not trying to sell me something, are you?" and the salesman protests with an enthusiastic "Oh, no, no." [If he reacts this way, as if he's not trying to sell something, then he's just a professional visitor.]

The salesman with the good self-image makes a sincere effort to close the sale because he knows the worst that can possibly happen is a refusal. He also knows that a refusal is seldom, if ever, fatal and he just might make the sale. As a matter of fact, he fully expects to make the sale. Why? He believes he deserves the sale — as well as the success. Besides, he believes in his product. With a healthy self-image he would not belittle and degrade himself by selling an inferior product. He feels strongly that he is rendering a service, so he closes the sale with confidence and conviction. He knows the Norwegian word for sell is *selje*, which literally means to serve.

[3] The salesman or office worker with a poor self-image doesn't move successfully into management. Again, he fears rejection by others. In this case, it would be the people over him, under him, or around him. He generally steps out of character and dons one of four masks as the situation demands. First, he becomes "good old Joe" and assures everyone under him that nothing has changed and he wants more than ever to be "one of the gang." Second, he might fear rejection by his former peers so he makes concessions and exceptions that go beyond the principles of good management. Or he might take just the opposite approach — an arrogant "I have arrived" approach — which causes resentment among his former peers. Third, he may be unduly concerned about his relationship to the management team. In his anxiety to please and be accepted he becomes too servile, eats too much humble pie and seeks too much advice. The paralysis of fear of failure causes him to hesitate too long before taking action. Fourth, he may assume a know-it-all attitude — seek advice from no one — and set out to show everyone how to run a ship.

The person with a healthy self-image moves into management very well. He exhibits a cautious confidence that shows he is qualified and will do the job. He is short on promises but long on fulfillment. He understands the difference between serving and being servile. He neither seeks nor avoids confrontations and meets decision-making head on. He understands that he was promoted because management has confidence in his ability to either handle the job or to grow to the job. He knows where to draw the line between confidence and arrogance. More importantly, he can be firm on principal but flexible on method. He understands that ideas don't care who have them and is secure enough within himself to recognize and give full credit to the ideas of associates and subordinates. He draws the line between being friendly and being familiar. He doesn't get "all shook up" when he makes a wrong decision, because he knows in most cases the worst decision is no decision, so right or wrong he makes decisions. Then his self-image is such that he can act decisively and yet not feel threatened when he is either mistaken, challenged, or has to ask for help on specific matters.

GOOD IMAGE = BETTER PARENT
MORE HONEST PERSON

In the business community a poor self-image is manifested by spur-of-the-moment "impossible" promises. The new coach, hoping to gain instant acceptance, promises more than is expected and more than he can deliver. The manufacturer or his agent, in order to please the customer because he can't stand even temporary rejection, will forego reality and make impossible commitments. In the sales world, we find insecure salesmen with poor self-images are the ones most guilty of over-selling, over-promising — and under-delivering. They can't take rejection and feel these steps are necessary if they are to make the sale. Once the sale is made, however, the salesman develops "guilt" feelings and avoids the customer. With no service the customer grows unhappy with the product and the salesman. The customer "tells the salesman off" which compounds the self-image problem. The office worker with the self-image problem won't assert himself and seek a raise even when he knows the caliber of his work warrants more pay. The tragedy here is that the same worker if he doesn't get the raise and recognition he deserves, will often become resentful and bitter and feel that "no one understands or appreciates him or what he does." The net result is a negative effect on his performance and a reduction in the possibility of a future raise.

In the family, a poor self-image is manifested by parental reluctance to discipline the child. The parent hides this under the mask of, "It hurts me more than him because I love him so much." Actually the parent is often fearful of turning the child away and causing the child to withdraw or withhold its love. The unfortunate truth is, this creates a problem for parents and child. The parent loses control, respect and some love. The child loses confidence in the parents and the security that goes with it. This is the first step in the loss of respect for authority which leads to rebellion against authority. This rebellion is another manifestation of a poor self-image and has been instrumental in youngsters age 18 and under being responsible for commiting 45% of the serious crime in the U.S. in 1974. The tragedy is that much of this could be averted if parents and teachers knew enough [and in some cases cared enough] about how to recognize those manifestations which so clearly say — notice me — love me — I want you to care what I do. The student who habitually comes to class late — makes a grand entrance — forgets his books — talks loudly or to other students at inopportune times — asks "silly" or unrelated questions, etc., is acting in perhaps the only way he feels he can act in order to get the attention he wants and desperately needs, to prevent even more drastic and erratic action which could put him behind bars.

COWARD—CASPER MILQUETOAST—IMMORALITY OR A POOR SELF-IMAGE!

Now let's translate these same manifestations of a poor self image into other professions and areas of life. The student with the poor self-image will not confront the teacher over a poor grade even when he knows he deserves a better one.

The manifestation with the greatest long range impact occurs in the pre-teen or early teen years when Johnny or Mary, who have not accepted themselves, first discover that boys and girls are different. The problem arises in the first relationship with a member of the opposite sex and is especially serious if either or both parties feel rejection from their own families. It is further compounded if either, or both of the youngsters, is either physically unattractive or a little short intellectually [society does put quite a premium on beauty and brains].

To move from a real or imagined "no acceptance" to an almost total acceptance from a member of the opposite sex at this critical time creates a highly volatile situation. The youngsters so desperately crave acceptance that they will do anything to keep from losing this one who accepts them "just for me." Combine this situation with a permissive society, which permits and even encourages an "honest" relationship of any kind so long as it is "meaningful", and you have a situation which lends itself to going steady at an early age. This togetherness, often in front of a television program or movie screen featuring moral laxity has all the ingredients necessary for premarital sex, promiscuity, venereal disease, illegitimate births, and/or an early marriage to a partner with nothing in common except a biological urge.

If the youngster with the poor self-image doesn't find a "steady" and "everyone else has someone" then he or she will often dress in a revealing and provocative manner to "catch" someone or anyone. Fishermen call this trolling. The problem with this technique is you generally "catch" everything from gars and turtles to snakes and stumps, and generally speaking the "catch" is harder to "throw back" than it is to reel in. Even when you catch something with this "bait" the chances are good that you will lose your "catch" to another troller who has more to show or who will show more. Any relationship primarily built on physical attractiveness is predestined to be short lived.

The youngster with a healthy self image simply will not get caught in the trap of an early and/or unhealthy relationship with members of the opposite sex. He or she is smart enough and has enough self esteem not to be "used," or fall for the oldest lines — and lies — of them all, "prove you love me" and "everyone else is doing it." This youngster understands the difference between happiness and pleasure and refuses to "sell out" a lifetime of happiness and virtue for a moment of dubious pleasure and obvious immorality.

There is evidence that "good old Joe" and his distaff counterpart actually have a problem which is a common one and is no respecter of age, sex, education, size, or skin color. He has the "I must be a nice guy and never offend anyone" kind of self-image syndrome. As a youngster, he smokes cigarettes he doesn't want — takes the drink he doesn't like — laughs at dirty jokes that actually offend him — joins the gang he secretly dislikes and goes along with conduct and participates in a dress code he secretly abhors. All because he has never accepted himself and is terribly concerned that if he asserts himself and "crosses" his peer group, he will not have any friends.

As an adult he has a tendency to tell people only what he thinks they want to hear. He would never send an overcooked steak back to the kitchen and he patiently waits an extra hour while the doctor sees other patients. He even gives up his place in the barber shop, lets others take his parking spot or even crash the line in front of him. He doesn't argue with the boss nor object when a co-worker takes credit for work he has done.

Don't misunderstand. If you are Joe and your self-image is so healthy you can conduct yourself in this manner because this is what *you* want, that's super good. If you view these incidents as minor or small stuff that mean nothing in your game plan for life, then your self-image is in excellent shape. However, if you do these things to gain acceptance then you are gaining everything but acceptance. The reason is simple. You are not presenting the real you. In fact, you are presenting a phony, and most people — including other phonies — don't like a phony.

It is safe to say that every area of life and every occupation is affected by a poor self-image. If you fit, or think you fit, into the group with a poor self-image, let me enthusiastically urge you not to fume or fret because in the next few pages we will give you some step-by-step procedures to correct a poor self-image and make a good one better. You are now ready to start stepping up the stairs to success. Happily, you will discover it's easier to move up those stairs faster when you get out of the crowd at the bottom — and friend, if you were ever at the bottom of those stairs — you are now moving up.

CHAPTER FOUR
FIFTEEN STEPS TO A HEALTHY SELF IMAGE

STEP ONE. Take inventory — you are far from bankrupt. Realistically, your net worth — if you should decide to "sell out" — is several million dollars. When you complete the inventory, you will come to the full realization that **no one on the face of this earth can make you feel inferior without your permission,** and you will like yourself too much to give that permission. I love what the immortal Booker T. Washington [the ex-slave who founded Tuskegee Institute at a time when racial prejudice was almost total] said, "I will permit no man to narrow and degrade my soul by making me hate him."

To begin with there are three reasons why you should like you as you are. First reason — *COMMON SENSE DEMANDS IT.* Recently a woman in Gary, Indiana, received $1,000,000 because a drug had caused her to lose her sight. She had taken the drug to clear up a rash on her face and it settled in her eyes, causing her to lose approximately 98% of her vision. Would you swap places with her? In California, another woman was awarded $1,000,000 because of a back injury received in an airplane accident. Doctors say she will never walk again. Would you swap places with her? The chances are a thousand to one that if your vision is normal and your back is strong, you wouldn't consider swapping places with either of these ladies. The chances are even greater that if you made the offer to either lady, they would gladly make the exchange and throw in a heartfelt thank you.

Deep down in your own mind you know that regardless of your financial position and regardless of how deep your interest in money might be, you would refuse the offer to "swap." If you are a normal human being, you would like to have the money but not in exchange for one of your greatest assets, your health.

Betty Grable, the famous pin-up queen of World War II, was best known for her "million-dollar legs," so named because they were insured for $1,000,000. How would you like to see another pair of million-dollar legs? If you will look down at your own, you will be looking directly at a pair of legs that, if they will move you around, you would not sell for the million dollar price tag placed on Betty Grable's legs. Since you would not take a million dollars for your eyes, a million dollars for your back or a million dollars for your legs, you are already worth over three million dollars and we just started on your personal inventory. Like yourself better already, don't you!

Fortunately, you don't have to swap one asset [your health] for another [money]. By developing the positive characteristics we cover in this book and building on the foundation of character, faith, integrity, love, loyalty and honesty, you can have them all. [Health, wealth, happiness, peace, friends, security, etc.]

ONE OF A BILLION!

A few years ago, I read in a Dallas paper that a Rembrandt painting had sold for over one million dollars. As I read the article I thought to myself, "What in the world would make some paint on a canvas worth so much money?" Then a couple of thoughts occurred to me. First, this was obviously a unique painting. As a matter of fact, of all the billions of paintings painted since the beginning of time, this was the only one exactly like it in existence. It was a Rembrandt original. Its rarity gave it value. Second, Rembrandt was a genius. He had a talent that occurs only once every hundred years or more. Obviously, it was his talent that was being recognized.

Then I started thinking about you. Since the beginning of time, billions of people have lived on the face of this earth. There are several billion people on earth today, but there never has been and there never will be another you. You are a rare, exclusive, different and unique being on the face of this earth. These qualities give you enormous value. Please understand that even though Rembrandt was a genius, he was a mortal. The same God who created Rembrandt created you, and you are as precious in God's sight as Rembrandt or *anyone* else. In addition to having a rare talent, Rembrandt used that talent by lifting his paint brush every day. Since his birth there have probably been hundreds of Rembrandts in every field of endeavor who have never lifted their paint brushes or gotten off their seats to make their marks.

Let's pursue this thought just one more short step. If you had the only car in town you would have an extremely valuable possession unless you parked it in the garage and left it there. Since you do have the *only* you in existence, *you* are valuable, so take you and your talent and use it. Just remember, God created you and gave you talent for you to use and not to bury.

Second reason — *SCIENCE EXPLAINS IT.* Most people have a lot of confidence in science, so let's take a look at you scientifically. You have the capacity between your ears to store more information than can be stored in dozens of man's most sophisticated computers. In your mind, you can store more information than you will find in the millions of volumes in the Library of Congress. Scientists tell us that if man were to attempt to create a human brain, it would cost billions of dollars, would be larger than the Empire State Building and would require more electricity than a city of thousands. Its construction would involve the most brilliant men in the world and yet with all of this size, cost and power requirements, this man-made brain couldn't originate a single thought, which you can do in the flash of an eye.

Your remarkable mind brings seventy-two muscles into perfect coordination each time you utter a word. [As much as I talk, some of my friends figure I have a muscle-bound mouth.] Seriously now, you wouldn't try to convince me, yourself, or anyone else that you're not a remarkable person with more than enough capability to climb the stairway to the top — would you? [I'll bet you know other people with less ability who are climbing to the top — don't you?]

SELLING YOU — YOUR MIND

You might say, "Well, if I'm so smart, how come I'm broke, or at least badly bent?" That's a good question. Here's at least a partial answer. Unfortunately, you came equipped at birth with your mind. Both of us would be better off if I owned your mind. I would sell it to you for, let's say $100,000, so I would profit enormously. However, you would have made the bargain purchase of all time. Never again would you look in the mirror and make any deprecating comments. As a matter of fact, you would give yourself quite a little pep talk. I can almost hear you say, "Now look friend, I have a hundred thousand bucks invested in you and you are really something. Yes indeed, you can do it." Never again would you say anything unkind about a mind worth so much money. Nor would you believe it if anyone else said anything unkind about your $100,000 mind. Let me again stress, as we talk about a healthy self-image, that I'm not talking about a super inflated "I'm the Greatest" ego. All I'm talking about is developing a simple healthy self-acceptance.

BEST OF ALL

Third reason — *BIBLE VERIFIES IT.* The most important reason you should like you appeared on a bumper sticker the other day. It said, **"God loves you — whether you like it or not!"** The Holy Bible tells us that man was created in God's own image, only slightly less than the angels. Jesus Christ said, "What I have done, ye can do also and even greater works than these." He put no age, education, sex, size, color, height or any other superficial qualifications as a requirement to attainment. He didn't leave you out. This is the faith we mentioned in the very beginning. Success is easy — after you believe — and since you are on your way to believing, you are on your way to succeeding.

Look at it this way. If you are a parent with growing children, how do you feel when one of your children says degrading things about himself or herself? I am a "nothing," a "nobody" or, "I can't do anything right." Do statements like that make you happy? Do they cause you to swell with pride or do they break your heart and make you shake your head in despair? How do you think our Heavenly Father feels when we who are His say ugly, deprecating things about ourselves? In reality, we have no right to belittle ourselves, or any other human being, do we? Actually, God would be pleased if you were to take one last look in the mirror before you start your day and say, now remember, _____, God loves you — and so do I.

Since you probably advise others to be a little more patient and allow more time to accomplish certain objectives why don't you take the advice Bill Gothard gives when he reminds us that

God is not through with us. Bill explains that we are prescription babies made according to God's formula. Next he reminds us that, if we are not satisfied with ourselves we should get back up on God's easel and let Him finish the job.

GOD DON'T SPONSOR NO FLOPS

I love what Ethel Waters said at the Billy Graham revival in London several years ago. Someone expressed amazement and asked why Dr. Graham was getting such a tremendous response from thousands upon thousands of Britons. Ethel just smiled that big beautiful smile of hers and answered, "Honey, God don't sponsor no flops."

Mary Crowley, well known Dallas businesswoman and an outstanding Christian, expresses it equally as well when she says, "You are somebody because God doesn't take time to make a nobody and once you learn how much you matter to God, you don't have to go out and show the world how much you matter." Then, with a twinkle in her eye she smiles and says, "God made man, took one look and said, 'I can do better than than' — and made woman." Speaking from the male side of the table, I agree with her one hundred percent.

Now that we've partially completed your personal inventory, you definitely like yourself better, don't you. [Careful now — don't get smug about it.]

STEP TWO — MAKE UP — DRESS UP — GO UP

The way you look on the outside has a definite bearing on how you feel and see yourself on the inside. The following article is taken from the February 6, 1974 edition of the Dallas Morning News. It relates this point very well.

ELDERLY LADIES BEAM
UNDERNEATH FACE CREAM

A group of Dallas' more senior women are beaming with pride over their "new look."

Once a week they file through the halls of Golden Acres in wheelchairs or with the assistance of canes and walkers to meet for their weekly facial.

"It's been such an uplift," one 81-year-old awaiting her cleansing and beautifying process claimed Tuesday. "You know you have something to do in the morning . . . you have a goal. My skin has been thriving. Would you guess that I am 81 years old?" she asked while rubbing her hand across her check. "Yet, I have the skin of a 50-year-old." The woman is in ill health and legally blind, yet fastidiously applies makeup each morning before leaving her room.

The program is funded through the Dallas Geriatric Institute with Mary Kay Cosmetics furnishing needed supplies. The average age of the participants is 83 years. After six months and more than 21,400 treatments, the institute noticed a definite improvement in the self-images of the elderly ladies.

Fifty women — ages 57 to 94 — were given weekly facials as well as makeup applications in the morning and an evening cleansing of day time cosmetics.

"The point we have tried to prove is that older women are still interested in how they look," said Marvin Ernst, director of the institute. "The better they look, the better they feel." The preliminary findings showed participants increased their self-esteem scores while non-participants remained the same. "Assistance in personal grooming has a positive effect upon how one feels about one's self and has a general effect of making people happier in their situations," Ernst said.

Every husband in America says his wife is happier, friendlier and more productive after she comes home from a trip to the beauty shop or after she has gotten all dolled up in a new outfit. Teachers will tell you that Johnny and Mary put their best foot forward when they show up for school in new clothes. Jim Moore and Joe Graham, principals at Calhoun High School in Port Lavaca, Texas and Bay City High School in Bay City, Texas, as well as many others, verify this by pointing out that conduct is considerably better on "picture taking day" when the students "dress up." The cliche that clothes don't make the man is another of those half-truths that create problems — especially if you grab the wrong half. The truth is, your outward appearance does affect your image and your performance. The outside appearance is enhancing — or crippling — the potential of the person on the inside. Employers note that employees do better work, all other things being equal, when they are neatly or sharply dressed. Even the computers agree with this. A six year study of two identical groups of male managers revealed that computer dressed business men earned $4,000 a year more than their counterparts, hold better positions and were more enthusiastic about their work.

So to improve your self-image, make up or dress up the outside. Throughout the rest of this book I will make reference to this fact, particularly in the areas of goal-setting, attitudes and habits. In the Attitude and Habit Segments the "how to" of creating that physical change will be treated.

STEP THREE. Regularly read Horatio Alger stories. Read the biographies and the autobiographies of the men and women of every race, creed and color who used what they had and got a great deal out of life by making contributions to life. It would be difficult, if not impossible, to read the life stories of Henry Ford, Walter Chrysler, Abraham Lincoln, Thomas Edison, Andrew Carnegie, Booker T. Washington, etc., and not be inspired. I challenge anybody to read the story of Eartha White, daughter of an ex-slave, which appeared in the December 1974 issue of Reader's Digest, and not be inspired to do more with their life. We relate to these stories and when we see them succeeding, we visualize ourselves doing the same thing.

STEP FOUR. Listen to the speakers, teachers and preachers who build mankind. When you hear people like Norman Vincent Peale, W. A. Criswell, Paul Harvey, Ken McFarland and Robert Schuller, you will get a lift in many ways, I'll say more about this in the attitude segment of the book. As a rule of thumb, you are safe to assume that any book, speaker, movie, T.V. program, individual or recording that builds mankind will build you and your self-image.

STEP FIVE. Build a healthy self-image with a series of short steps. **One reason many people never attempt new things is their fear of failure.** If possible, start any new venture with a phase or portion you are confident you can handle, then transfer that initial accomplishment from one area of success to another. The child who multiplies 2 x 2 transfers that to bigger success and multiplies 3 x 4, 5 x 6, etc. He "sees" himself as capable of mastering mathematics. The young girl who "survives" the first batch of oatmeal cookies "sees" herself as being capable of baking better things. The high jumper who is capable of clearing six feet starts each session with the bar considerably lower, when this is done the jumper can and will jump higher. For example, at Calhoun High School in Port Lavaca, Texas, a high jumper jumped four inches higher than ever before and their pole vaulter set the national record. All of this after our "I CAN" course for schools was introduced. Both of these young men credit an improvement in self-image with their improvement in performance. As he "warms up" he "sees" himself successfully clearing the lower heights until he "sees" himself clearing greater ones. The point I wish to make in building your healthy self-image is this: start in an area where you know you can succeed. Once success is accomplished there, move another step, and another and another. Each step gives you added confidence and your self-image improves your performance which improves your self-image which improves performance which improves . . . [Harvard Psychologist, David McClelland, calls this "accomplishment feedback."]

In the sales-training world we have simulated or practice runs in the training room before we send a salesman out to make his first call. We know if our fledgling salesman goofs or has a "sales wreck" in the classroom, the experience won't be shattering because very little is at stake. In addition, we will urge him to practice on his family and in front of the mirror. The late Maxwell Maltz called this "practice without pressure" because the salesman had nothing to lose.

One sensible word of caution about self-confidence is appropriate at this point. Remember, you have probably been making an overdraft on the bank of confidence all of your life.

Realistically, you cannot expect to bring your account up to date in one day or by reading this book just one time. The longer and more regularly you take the necessary steps and follow the recommended procedures, the bigger your account in the confidence bank of a healthy self-image will be and the bigger the confidence account the greater the accomplishment.

STEP SIX. Join the smile and compliment club. When you smile at someone and they smile back, you automatically feel better [and it definitely increases your "face" value]. Even if they don't smile back, you will feel better because you know **the most destitute person in the world is the one without a smile.** You immediately become richer by giving that person yours. Ditto for the compliment. When you sincerely compliment a person or extend him a courtesy he is going to receive a direct benefit and like himself better. It is impossible for you to make someone feel better and not feel better yourself.

One of the best ways to make anyone else feel better is to spread optimism and good cheer. You can do this almost instantly in your daily exchanges with associates and family. When someone says, "hi, how ya doing?", give them a big cheerful, "Super good — but I'll get better." If you don't feel that good it's safe to say you *want* to feel that way and even safer to say that if you *claim* the feeling you will soon *have* the feeling. In the attitude segment you will learn why this is true.

Another way is to "properly" answer the phone. Many people answer the telephone with a gruff "hello" or an even more gruff "Yes" as if the caller had committed a dastardly sin. My personal approach is this. When I answer the telephone at home, I answer it by singing a little ditty, "Oh, good morning to you," or I might say, "Howdy-Howdy-Howdy," or "good morning, this is Jean Ziglar's husband, or "good morning, we're having a great day at the Ziglar's and hope you are too." I do this because that is generally the way I feel. However, I answer my phone this way — regardless of how I feel. Again — the reason is simple, if I don't feel good, but act that way, I will soon feel that way. Also, I have a responsibility to the person who is calling. If I am optimistic and cheerful, the chances are much stronger that I will give a lift to the person calling, and the truth of the matter is, I am my brother's keeper. The Bible says, "a merry heart hath a continual feast" and this approach guarantees a "merry heart".

At our company, our secretaries answer the telephone just as enthusiastically by saying, "Good Morning, it's a great day at Zig Ziglar's." Our company is The Zig Ziglar Corporation.

I'm convinced that everyone, including you, just naturally feels better when exposed to a cheerful optimistic individual almost regardless of the nature or length of the contact.

STEP SEVEN. Do something for someone else. Visit a shut-in or someone in the hospital. Bake a cake for an invalid. Participate in a reading or visitation program for the aged or senile. Go shopping for a shut-in. Baby sit for a young mother who needs to get out of the house. Spend a few minutes on a regular basis teaching a functional illiterate to read. Become a volunteer with the Red Cross, or a den mother, or help little ones cross a dangerous intersection to and from school. Be a big brother to an orphan. Take some fatherless kids on a hike in the woods or spend time with them in a guidance role. For a hundred different ideas and suggestions along these lines, let me urge you to read *Try Giving Yourself Away* by David Dunn. There are two major considerations you must make, however. You must accept no compensation, and the person or persons you assist should not be in a position to do anything for you in return.

This I guarantee. If you will do something for someone who is unable to return the favor, you will get a lot more than you can possibly give. In so many cases, what you give will mean much to the recipient, but the feeling you get when you do something for someone who cannot do for themselves is indescribable. You will realize that you are truly fortunate, that you do have a lot to be thankful for, that you can make a contribution and that you are in fact somebody. In short, you will stand tall in your own eyes, which is the bonus you get because you took what you had and unselfishly used it for someone else's good. Charles Dickens said it best. **"No one is useless in this world who lightens the burden of it to anyone else."**

STEP EIGHT. Be careful of your associates. Deliberately associate with people of a high moral character who look on the bright side of life, and the benefits will be enormous. As an example, I'm convinced that if every doctor, teacher, lawyer, policeman, politician, civil service employee, military person, etc., had to sell for a living for three months and then had to attend an enthusiastic sales meeting once a week, our great country would be even greater. Over the years, I have seen hundreds of men and women from all walks of life enter the sales world as shy, introverted, incompetent individuals and within a matter of weeks become confident, competent, and far more productive people. Here's why. In many cases these people had lived in a negative environment, surrounded by people who dumped negative garbage into their minds and told them what they could not do. Their entry into the sales world meant a dramatic change in environment and associates. Now everyone started telling them what they could do. They heard positive statements from trainers, managers and associates. They saw daily results on all sides as a result of this approach. Since it was more fun and more profitable for them to like themselves they almost immediately started changing their self-image.

My point is this. If every person were regularly exposed to this kind of environment and to people like this, just think what it would do to their self-image and to their attitude. Obviously, we can't *require* others to change their associates, but *you* can choose to associate with people like this. Do it and the results will be fantastic. Pick out those people who are optimistic and enthusiastic about life and I'll guarantee you some of it will "rub off" on you. Remember, **you acquire much of the thinking, mannerisms and characteristics of the people you are around.** This is true whether the people around you are good or bad. Even your I.Q. could be affected by your environment and associates. [July, 1976, Success Unlimited, tells the story.] In the Kibbutz in Israel, evaluations revealed that the average I.Q. of the Oriental Jewish children was 85 and 105 for the European Jewish children. This "proves" that the European Jewish children were "smarter" than the Oriental Jewish children — or does it? After four years in the Kibbutz, where the environment was positive, the motivation excellent and dedication to learning and growth was substantial, the average I.Q. levelled off to the same thing — 115. That's exciting. When you associate with the "right" people with a positive, moral outlook on life you greatly enhance your chances of winning.

Unfortunately, your associates also affect you negatively. A youngster [and adults too] who associate with others who smoke is far more likely to take up the habit than he would if he ran with a non-smoking group. The same is true for drug usage, drinking, immorality, profanity, lying, cheating, stealing, etc. Fortunately, you can choose your associates.

STEP NINE. To build your self-image, make a list of your positive qualities on a card and keep it for handy reference. Ask your friends to list the things they like about you, and keep that list handy. As you and your friends make that list you might get to be like "this old boy down home." He was walking down the street talking to himself and someone stopped and asked him why he did this. He replied that he enjoyed talking to intelligent people, and more importantly, he enjoyed listening to intelligent people talk. I'd say he had a healthy self-image. Brag on yourself from time to time. Get in your own corner.

STEP TEN. Make a victory list to remind you of your past successes. The list should include those things that gave you the most satisfaction and confidence. This list should extend from childhood to the present time. It can cover everything from whipping the school bully to making an "A" in a difficult course. As you periodically review this list, you will be reminded that you have succeeded in the past and that you can do it again. This builds confidence, which builds image, which builds success, happiness, etc. Actually, these last two steps reaffirm the fact that you are for you instead of against you.

As you make your list, please remember, many of the qualities so vital for the balanced success we are talking about do not show up on the talent educational charts. Think in terms of your dependability, stickability, and availability for service. Accept as fact that you can be just as honest as anyone, just as conscientious and just as dedicated. Know that you too can work as hard and that you can pray as hard. Know also that you are loved by God as much as anyone else.

STEP ELEVEN. To build a healthy self-image, there are some things you must avoid. Pornography is the primary one. Literally everything that goes into your mind has an affect and is permanently recorded. It either builds and prepares you for the future or it tears down and reduces your accomplishment possibilities for that future. Psychologists say that three viewings of a Deep Throat, The Last Tango in Paris, The Exorcist or any of the "X-rated" films or television programs have the same psychological, emotional, destructive impact in your mind as one physical experience. The people who have seen these "shows" are in agreement; they were sexually stimulated and viewed themelves with less respect. The reason is simple. These films or programs present mankind at its worst and when you see your fellow man degraded, you, in effect, see yourself degraded. It is impossible to view mankind at its worst and not feel that your own value has diminished and you can neither be nor do any better than you think you can or are. Ironically most X-rated films are advertised as "adult" entertainment for "mature" audiences. Most psychologists agree they are juvenile entertainment for immature and insecure audiences.

This same imagination of yours, when applied to the daily soap opera is devastating because over the years the "soaps" have progressively featured everything from incest and adultery to trial marriage and wife-swapping. Combine this with the enormous waste of time and the "drug-like ability" to hook you into tuning in tomorrow to see what happens, and it spells bad news with a capital Bad. For your information, tomorrow the star of the soap opera, and at least one of his or her buddies, will either be in trouble, headed for trouble or just getting out of trouble. When you view life in this negative perspective over a long period of time, you identify with the situations which most nearly parallel your own. After a time you will even find yourself thinking, "I know exactly how 'he' or 'she' feels, because that's exactly the way my 'John' or 'Sue' has done me, 'the dirty dog'."

The horoscope "hooks you" in a similar fashion and with an even more devastating effect. Many people think it's "harmless" to read the horoscope because they "don't believe any of it;" it's just something to do. The truth is, you will eventually become fatalistic as a result of it. [The chapters on habits will explain why.] Incredibly enough, some people will not make decisions or take trips if their "horoscope" is not in tune. The Bible says the horoscope is Satan's, so when you read the daily horoscope, you are reading Satan's Daily Bulletin. If you don't believe in God and/or the Bible let me point out that **the "science" of astrology was founded on the assumption that the sun revolves around the earth.** Some science!

STEP TWELVE. To improve your self-image, learn from the successful failures. Like Ty Cobb and Babe Ruth. Ty Cobb was thrown out more times trying to steal than any man in baseball history. Babe Ruth struck out more times than any man in baseball history. Hank Aaron, who broke Babe Ruth's record, has struck out more times than 99% of the players who make it to the major leagues. Nobody — but nobody — considers them failures and few people even remember their failures. Virtually everyone remembers their successes. Enrico Caruso's voice *failed* to carry the high notes so many times his voice teacher advised him to quit. He kept singing and was recognized as the greatest tenor in the world. Thomas Edison's teacher called him a dunce and he later failed over 14,000 times in his efforts to perfect the incandescent light. Abraham Lincoln was well known for his failures but nobody considers him a failure. Albert Einstein and Werner von Braun both flunked courses in math. Henry Ford was broke at age 40. Vince Lombardi became the most revered coach since Knute Rockne, but at age 43 he was a line coach at Fordham University.

The odds are strong that the leading salesman in 90% of the sales organizations in America misses more sales than most salesmen with the company. Walt Disney went broke seven times and had one nervous breakdown before success smiled on him. Actually these people succeeded because they kept at it. As a matter of fact, the major difference between the big shot and the little shot is — the big shot is just a little shot who kept on shooting.

STEP THIRTEEN. One of the best, quickest and most effective ways to improve your image and your performance is to join an organization with worthwhile goals that requires you to participate by speaking. Many people can express themselves reasonably well in private conversation but are frozen with fright at the thought of standing up and making a speech to a group of any kind. They "see" themselves as falling flat on their faces and looking foolish.

One of the fastest ways to change that image is to join Toast Masters or Toast Mistresses, International, or take our four day **Richer Life Seminar** or The Dale Carnegie Leadership Course. As a former instructor for Carnegie, and now for our own company, I have seen some remarkable image changes take place as individuals acquired the ability to stand up and express themselves. It's not necessary to become an orator, though I've seen a number of former wallflowers develop considerable ability as speakers. Initially, we had difficulty getting some of these people to stand up and speak up. As their confidence grew, however, we had another problem. That's right, we had difficulty getting some of these same people to "sit down" and "shut up."

STEP FOURTEEN. Look you — and them — in the eye. Almost without exception the man on the street as well as the highly educated professional will tell you they like people who will "look them in the eye." I plead guilty to this feeling and chances are strong that you feel the same way. There are many people who are unaware of the other person's reaction to people who avoid eye contact and hence they don't look directly at another person even when engaged in direct conversation. There are even more people whose self image is such that they feel "unworthy" and "are not good enough" to look directly into the eyes of another.

To overcome this feeling [if you have it] start with the process of looking *yourself* in the eye when you have *any* occasion to be in front of a mirror. You should also set aside a few minutes each day for the sole purpose of deliberately looking yourself in the eye. As you do this, repeat some positive affirmations of the *things* you have done [use your victory list from step ten]. Then repeat many of the things other people have said to you or about you that were positive. Concentrate on comments regarding your integrity, cheerfulness, honesty, character, compassion, persistence, thoughtfulness, good nature, spirit of cooperation, etc.; and not on physical appearance *unless* you feel you are unattractive. In that event those compliments become valuable image builders.

The second phase of "eye contact" for image building involves small children. When the opportunity presents itself talk and play with the small fry and look them in the eye as you do so. One enormous fringe benefit here is that the children will love you more and their acceptance enhances your self acceptance.

The third phase of step fourteen is to concentrate on looking your peer group and associates, as well as those who might work at a lesser position, in the eye at every opportunity. This gives you even more confidence for the final phase which is to look everybody you meet or greet, directly in the eye. [I'm obviously not talking about a "staring" contest.] Overall this procedure does a great deal to build your self-image and it is a tremendous "friend maker."

STEP FIFTEEN. Alter your physical appearance when possible, practical *and* desirable. Formerly obese people constantly tell me how much their image improved with the weight loss which enabled them to wear attractive clothing, participate in group activities, get active in sports, run up two flights of stairs and escape those constant digs ["friendly" of course] about their weight. My own image improved when I lost thirty-seven pounds.

There are also occasions when plastic surgery can be quite helpful in building the self-image. This is especially true in case of an unusually large or long nose, protruding ears, hare lip, grossly oversized or undersized breasts, etc. This area, however, often involves psychological considerations which have to be dealt with on an in-depth and personal basis. Caution and counsel are the watchwords but I have seen some dramatic personality changes take place when this type surgery is performed.

As you review the do's and don'ts of the Fifteen Steps to Building a Healthy Self-Image, let me remind you that all of these steps are designed to help you accept yourself. Once you accept yourself, it will no longer be a matter of life or death for others to accept you. At that point you will not only be accepted by them, but you will be welcomed wherever you go. The reason is simple. They will be accepting the real you and the real you is much nicer than the phony conformist who tries so desperately hard to become somebody he isn't. When the real you is accepted, a lot of things happen. Your conduct changes for the better and your morals improve. Much of your tension disappears because you are secure within yourself and the little things that formerly "bugged" you will be put in perspective. In short, you "won't sweat the small stuff." Your bank account in self-confidence will grow, communication barriers will be removed and your family relationships will improve.

Once you have accepted yourself, it's so much easier to accept other people and their points of view. Please note I said "accept." This doesn't necessarily mean you agree with them. It does mean you can accept and even understand why they feel the way they do. When that happens, you will find it easier to get along with others, regardless of race, creed, color, ethnic background or occupational interest.

REMOVE THE SYMPTOM AND SOLVE THE PROBLEM

It is beyond a doubt that most problems, whether they be economic, social, marital, etc., are not problems but *symptoms* of problems. Drugs, alcoholism, pornography, homosexuality, obesity, and in most cases vulgarity, profanity and promiscuity are merely symptoms of deeper difficulties. Many other fads are also symptoms of real problems, particularly when it's obvious the fads are related to people doing "their thing" in defiance of parents or the so-called "establishment." The small boy or girl inside of each social rebel says, "You wouldn't notice me before, so I'm going to do some things that will make you notice me. They might be foolish and you might not like what I do, or me for doing them, but you'll know I'm around." In my work with the schools around the country I am constantly told that the students who are regularly late to class, "forget" their textbooks, provoke arguments, give "smart" answers, try to be "cute" in everything they say or do, etc.; are simply demonstrating or manifesting a poor self-image. What these kids are really saying is "Notice me please, love me please, accept me, recognize me — I'm a people."

In many cases, if such a person fails to gain sufficient acceptance and recognition as he is, he will start making adjustments and compromises. In fact, he may begin to act like someone else. This is unfortunate because if a person can't make it in life being himself, he will really foul things up trying to be someone else. **You will make a lousy anybody else, but you are the best "you" in existence.** Once a person accepts himself, it isn't imperative that others accept him. He is not "destroyed" if others reject him. He can be his own man or woman without being overly concerned about the reaction of others. Does this sound self-centered? Actually, just the opposite is true. Shakespeare said it, "This above all, to thine own self be true. And it must follow as the night the day, Thou canst not then be false to any man." Once you accept yourself for your true worth, then the symptoms of vulgarity, profanity, sloppiness, promiscuity, etc., disappear. There, my friend, goes your problem.

Just for an example, look at the drug problem. Almost without exception those who get hung up on drugs, or alcohol, have a poor self-image. They don't like the way they are and figure others couldn't like them that way either. They seek an easy way to change, and drugs or alcohol seems to be the answer. Thousands of cases tragically prove that drugs and alcohol compound problems, create confusion and frequently destroy life.

The new you — with your healthy self-image, will not have to worry about these problems in your future. You have done and are doing something about your image, so now let's look at a choice you can make.

THE CHOICE IS YOURS

The Japanese raise a tree. It's called the Bonsai tree. It's beautiful, and perfectly formed although its height is measured in inches. In California, we find a forest of giant trees called Sequoias. One of these giants has been named the General

Sherman. Extending into the heavens 272 feet and measuring 79 feet in circumference, this magnificent giant is so large that if it were cut down, it would produce enough lumber to build 35 five-room houses. At one time the Bonsai tree and the General Sherman were the same size. When they were seeds, each weighed less than 1/3000 of an ounce. The size difference at maturity is considerable to say the least, but the story behind that difference in size is a lesson in life. When the Bonsai tree stuck its head above the earth, the Japanese pulled it from the soil and tied off its tap-root and some of the feeder roots, thus deliberately stunting its growth. The result is a miniature; beautiful, but still a miniature. The seed of the General Sherman fell into the rich soil of California and was nourished by the minerals, the rain and the sunshine. The giant tree was the result. Neither the Bonsai nor the General Sherman had a choice in its destiny. You do. You can be as big, or as little, as you wish to be. You can be a Bonsai or a General Sherman. Your Self-Image — the way you see yourself — will determine which one you will be. The choice is yours.

ACCEPT YOURSELF

I close this chapter the same way I opened it — by reminding you that **nobody on the face of this earth can make you feel inferior without your permission.** You are fast reaching the point where you refuse to give that permission to anyone. When you reach that point you will have accepted yourself. As you accept yourself, you will see yourself as a person who truly "deserves" the good things in life. This results in your removing those limiting ceilings and obtaining the good things in life.

Before you go on to the third Segment of this book, let me urge you to do the following things:

(1) Look at the next Stairway To The Top diagram and in big bold letters, write the word "good" opposite Self-Image and draw a box around it.
(2) Close the book, and your eyes. Now relax for a moment and see yourself as already possessing that good healthy self-image and everything else necessary for success.
(3) Review this section and place emphasis on the portions

you have underlined as well as the comments you made in your Trigger Page steno pad.

(4) "It's true if you take care of your car, it will take you places, and if you take care of your self-image, it will take you places too."

Now, get ready for the next exciting step on your **stairway to the top.**

NOTES AND IDEAS

As you take this first step up the Stairway To The Top, please know that you are stepping out of the crowd at the bottom. The next step will now be easier and the view will be better.

ZIG'S STORY

I recognize it's a little unusual for the author to insert his own story. I'm doing this because I honestly believe my story is your story. I believe I have felt your feelings and that my early fears, failures and frustrations are shared by so many people that my story will give many of you real hope — with believability.

In the original edition of this book I placed my story in the Self-Image Segment. As the months went by, however, it became more and more evident that the story would "fit" better between the Self-Image and Your Relationship with Others Segments. My climb up the ladder started when my self-image changed because another person provided the spark. I'm persuaded this story will serve as a bridge between your self-image and your relationship with others.

I was one of twelve children. My dad died in 1932, the heart of the depression, leaving Mother with five children too young to work. Fortunately, Mother was a dedicated Christian who gave us unconditional love and taught us that if we trusted the Lord, worked hard and did our best, things would work out all right. She finished the 5th grade as far as formal education is concerned, but without a doubt she graduated magna cum laude from the University of Life. She became one of the most loved and respected people in the little town of Yazoo City, Mississippi. Long after she was too old to earn money, she could still go to the bank and borrow any amount she needed on her signature. She never compromised her love for the Lord or her love for the truth. It was either black or white. There were no areas of gray. She often said an egg was never "almost" fresh. It was either fresh or it was rotten. It was either the truth or it was a lie. For her there was no compromise with truth or principle. She often saturated us with little sentence sermonettes including such gems as, "It's not who's right that is important — it's *what's* right," "The person who won't stand for something will fall for anything," "Tell the truth and tell it ever, costeth what it will, for he who hides the wrong he did — does the wrong thing still." After our children were born her favorites were, "Son, your children more attention pay — to what you do than what you say," and "if you set the example you will not have to set the rules."

40 MORE CENTS

One simple story will illustrate her philosophy. As a young boy working in a grocery story on Saturdays from 7:30 in the morning until 11:30 at night, I earned the magnificent sum of 75 cents. After a few months I was offered a job at a local sandwich shop. On this job I would start at 10:00 in the morning and work until midnight. The hours would have been shorter and the pay would have been $1.15 for the day. I wanted to make the change.

In this day and time it would be impossible for you to imagine the value of that other 40 cents, but in a rural Mississippi town in 1939 it represented a lot of money to a small boy. My Mother never considered letting me make the change and I might add, I never considered going against her wishes because Mr. John R. Anderson, a dedicated Christian and a positive thinker [he once sent me to a drawing for a cow, with a rope to lead the cow home] owned and managed the grocery store. As my Mother expressed it to me, the 40 cents wasn't important. The influence of a John Anderson could never be measured in money. She emphasized the fact she did not know the man who ran the sandwich shop. He might be all right, but she loved her boy too much to let him work in a place where the boss was of unknown quality. She had also heard it rumored they sold beer in the sandwich shop. She made her decision, and it was final as far as she was concerned. Since she had demonstrated love and instilled obedience from birth, it was natural for me to respect her wishes.

A TELLER IN A GROCERY STORE

With a Mother who loved me enough to say "No" to my whims, I had the the advantage of not only having a loving Mother, but having a concerned, caring, substitute father in Mr. Anderson. This is the background from which I came. I worked in the grocery store from the time I was in the 5th grade until after I finished the 11th grade. I started in the store as a "teller." Don't be too impressed with that title, however, it just meant I "told" people to move while I swept.

During my senior year, I moved next door and worked for the man who had been the manager of the store under Mr. Anderson.

His name was Walton Haining. He too was a fine man who took a personal interest in me. He had bought the meat market in the store next door. Soon after graduation, I was headed for the U.S. Navy. The night before I left, Mr. Haining called me in for a final "Dutch Uncle" talk. He invited me to come back after I was discharged and work for him again. Frankly, I could not get too excited about the idea because I was working about 75 hours a week and earning the grand total of thirty dollars. Mr. Haining explained that if I would come back and work two years for him and thoroughly learn the business, he would help me get my own meat market. The thing that turned me on, however, was his showing me his net earnings for the previous year, $5,117. Remember, things in 1944 were not the same as they are today.

I couldn't believe anyone could earn that much money in just one year. He assured me it was true and I could do the same thing. On July 1, 1944, I left Yazoo City, Mississippi, to enter the Navy. When the war was over I was going to return to Yazoo City, open a meat market and earn $5,117 in a single year.

While in the Navy, I met and fell in love with the former Jean Abernathy of Jackson, Mississippi. She has been my wife and my life for 31 wonderful years. After I was discharged, I entered the University of South Carolina and earned money by selling sandwiches in the dormitories at night. I did quite well during the regular school year, but during the summer months business was slow. One day, Jean saw an ad in the newspaper for a $10,000-per-year salesman. I felt it was more than a coincidence that they wanted a $10,000 a year salesman because we certainly wanted the $10,000. I called for an appointment and went for an interview. I returned home extremely excited and told my wife that we had a job and would be making $10,000 a year. She got excited too and wanted to know when we started. I explained that the man said he would "be in touch."

At this stage of my life, I was so naive, I honestly believed the job was mine and did not realize that I had been "turned down." One month later, when I still had no word concerning the job I wrote a letter restating my interest and inquiring when I was going to start. Their reply was plainly stated; they didn't feel I could sell. I persisted, and finally after another month they agreed to put me through training school. However, they made it clear they weren't obligated to give me the job if at the end of the school they didn't feel I could sell. The job was selling cookware and pay was on a commission basis. After training, they gave me the opportunity. For the next two-and-one-half years, despite a lot of help from my sales manager, Bill Cranford, all I did was prove they had been right all along. Don't misunderstand; this doesn't mean I didn't sell much, because I did. I sold my car and my furniture. The only thing that keeps this last line from being truly humorous, at least to me, is its close kinship to the truth.

YOU DON'T DROWN BY FALLING IN WATER

I don't care how broke you are or have been, I honestly believe I've been "broker." I don't care how despondent or down in the dumps you are, or might have been, I honestly believe I've been more despondent and further down in the dumps. My good friend, Cavett Robert, whose ability as a speaker and sales trainer is overshadowed only by his characteristics as a human being, says much in this observation, "You don't down by falling into water, you only drown if you stay there." He also says, "It's all right to get down, but don't get down on yourself."

You're not beaten by being knocked down. You're only beaten if you stay down. Personally, I believe I quit my sales career [in my own mind] as many times as anybody who will ever read this book has thought about quitting whatever he's doing. It was discouraging to be broke, in debt, uncertain of what I was doing and not really knowing from one day to the next whether I would sink or swim. It's times like this when faith in something bigger than yourself is so extremely important. Also of infinite value to me was my Mother's example of courage, dedication, and persistence which served as a wonderful, inspirational guide.

I'll have to admit it was sometimes tough, and discouragement was a frequent companion. I often had to buy 50 cents worth of gasoline at a time and if I made a mistake in addition, I would have to return one or two items at the grocery store. When our first daughter was born, the hospital bill was only $64. The problem was, we didn't have the $64. I had to make two sales in order to get the money together to pay the bill.

We were broke because my image was poor and my skills as a salesman were questionable, at best. To illustrate the point and to give *all* floundering salespeople encourgement, here's a true incident from my book of ineptness which should give anyone with enough gumption to get out of a telephone booth without written directions, a lot of encouragement.

Some experienced salesmen were conducting dinner parties which were group demonstrations, so I decided to try the same thing. My first "dinner demonstration" was with Mr. B. C. Moore, who lived at 2210 High Street, Columbia, S.C. Two prospects, Mr. and Mrs. Clarence Spence and Mr. and Mrs. M. P. Gates, were present. When I completed the demonstration, both prospects gave a dozen reasons why they shouldn't buy, but both ended up saying, "I'll take it." At this point, any sane salesman, especially if he's broke, would have written the orders and collected his commission; but, I walked out of the house because "I had another appointment and was running late." Later I made the sale, but I just wonder how many of you, on your dumbest, greenest day, would have done such a foolish thing. Yes, my reading friend, I'm convinced that there is hope for you.

YOU COULD BE A GREAT ONE

After two-and-one-half years of less than overwhelming sales success [to be honest I wasn't even a whelming success], the picture changed dramatically and my career did a 180 degree turn. Here's the story. I attended an all-day training session in Charlotte, North Carolina, conducted by P. C. Merrell of Nashville, Tennessee. It was a good session, but I have long since forgotten the specific techniques I learned. Later that evening I drove back home to Lancaster, South Carolina, to conduct a dinner demonstration. I was late getting home and even later getting to bed; then the baby kept us up most of the night. At 5:30 a.m. the alarm sounded and force of habit rolled me out of bed. We lived in a small upstairs apartment over a grocery store. More asleep than awake, I looked out the window and saw snow falling. There was already about 10 inches of snow on the ground and I was driving a heaterless Crosley automobile. I did what any intelligent human being would do that morning, that's right, I crawled back into bed.

As I lay there, it dawned on me that I had never missed or ever been late for a sales meeting. Mother's words also came back to me. "When you work for someone — work for them all the way. If you are in something, get all the way in and if you can't get all the way in — then get all the way out." The Bible says, "I would that you were cold or hot, but because you are lukewarm, I will spue you out of my mouth." I stumbled back out of bed and made that cold drive to Charlotte, and a whole new way of life.

When the training session was over, Mr. Merrell quietly took me aside and said, "You know, Zig, I've been watching you for two-and-one-half years and I have never seen such a waste." [Now friends, *that* will get your attention.] Somewhat startled, I asked what he meant. He explained, "You have a lot of ability. You could be a great one and maybe even become a national champion." Naturally, I was flattered, but a little skeptical, so I asked if he really meant it. He assured me, "Zig, there is no doubt in my mind if you really went to work, and started believing in yourself, you could go all the way to the top."

To tell you the truth, when those words really soaked in I was stunned. You have to understand my background to appreciate what those words meant to me. As a boy I was rather small, weighing less than 120 pounds fully dressed when I entered the senior class in high school. Most of the time since the fifth grade I had worked after school and on Saturdays and hadn't been active in sports. In addition to being little and slow, I was also scared. I never dated a girl until I was 17 and that was a blind date someone else had "fixed" for me. My self-image was that of the little guy from the little town, who some day was going to go back to that little town and earn $5,117 in a single year. Now, all of a sudden, here's a man whom I admired and respected telling me, "You could be a great one." Fortunately, I believed Mr. Merrell and started thinking like a champion, acting like a champion, seeing myself as a champion — and performing like a champion.

SUCCESS IS EASY — ONCE YOU BELIEVE

Mr. Merrell didn't teach me a lot of sales techniques but

before the year was over, I was the number two salesman in America in a company of over 7,000 salesmen. I moved from a Crosley to a luxury car and qualified for a fine promotion. The next year I was one of the highest paid managers in the States. Later, I became the youngest Division Supervisor in the country.

After my encounter with Mr. Merrell, I did not suddenly acquire a whole new set of sales skills. Nor did my I.Q. jump 50 points. Mr. Merrell convinced me that I had the ability to succeed, gave me something to live up to and the confidence to use what I already had. Had I not believed him, his message would have had no impact on me. I hope you believe me when I tell you that you too are someone special. That you were put here to succeed, be happy, be healthy and accomplish worthy objectives.

Many things have happened since that long ago encounter with Mr. Merrell, but that occasion was a turning point in my life. This is not to imply that things have always gone my way since that memorable day, because they haven't. There was a time when I became a "wandering generality" with more than my share of ups and downs.

During one of my "downs" I picked up Dr. Peale's "Power Of Positive Thinking" and my career, which was in trouble again, surged forward. Dr. Peale helped me identify the real source of my problems. Needless to say it was me. Many other good books and good people have been "life savers" at other "down" times. That's why I encourage you to deliberately seek the company of good people and good books. While there have been some "downs" after Mr. Merrell there have been more "ups", especially since July 4, 1972, when I committed my life to Jesus Christ.

This book, and The Richer Life Course which is built on the book, has been the highlight of my professional life. But it has also been my privilege to see some of my works translated into French, German, Japanese, Spanish and Braille. I have traveled over two million miles speaking to audiences as large as 16,000, ranging from student groups and sales organizations to churches, professional athletic teams and Chambers of Commerce. I have appeared with such outstanding Americans as Dr. Peale, Ronald Reagan, General "Chappie" James, Art Linkletter, Paul Harvey, Olympic Star Bob Richards, Dr. Ken McFarland,

W. Clement Stone, Pat Boone and others.

I mention these things not to impress you with what God has permitted me to do, but to encourage you as to what you do with what *you* have. I don't believe there has ever been a more "average" guy as far as size, strength, intelligence or ability is concerned. I believe that if I can — you can.

Many factors and people are involved in anyone's life story but the special impact P. C. Merrell had on my life cannot be overstated. Incredibly [at least to me] our entire converstion lasted less than five minutes and involved only a few dozen words. That's one reason I know that one picture is *not* worth 10,000 words. That is also the reason I ask God before each talk to "make me a P. C. Merrell today." That was my prayer during the entire time I spent writing this book. P. C. helped me stop seeing myself as the little guy from the little town struggling to get along. He led me to see myself as somebody special who had something to offer others.

What a privilege it would be to play just a small but similar part in your life. I just happen to believe than when I share thoughts or ideas that make your life more rewarding on planet earth, I am doing God's work. It is my hope and prayer that this book — and specifically — this chapter will be the bridge that will enable you to easily move from accepting yourself to accepting others. If that happens, then my rewards will be great — my cup truly will be running over.

NOTES AND IDEAS

SEGMENT THREE

YOUR RELATIONSHIP WITH OTHERS

PURPOSE:
I. TO CLARIFY THE WAY YOU SHOULD SEE OTHER PEOPLE.

II. TO SELL THE CONCEPT THAT YOU TREAT OTHER PEOPLE LIKE YOU SEE THEM.

III. TO ESTABLISH — YOU CAN GET EVERYTHING IN LIFE YOU WANT IF YOU HELP ENOUGH OTHER PEOPLE GET WHAT THEY WANT.

IV. TO IDENTIFY GENUINE LOVE AND GIVE SPECIFIC SUGGESTIONS ON HOW TO COURT — AFTER YOU ARE MARRIED. (SINGLE FOLKS ALREADY KNOW)

ADDITIONAL READING MATERIAL

Dale Carnegie — *HOW TO WIN FRIENDS AND INFLUENCE PEOPLE*

Mary Crowley — *MOMENTS WITH MARY*

Mary Crowley — *THINK MINK*

Maxwell Maltz — *PSYCHOCYBERNETICS*

LeRoy Brownlow — *MAKING THE MOST OF LIFE*

Aubrey Andelin — *MAN OF STEEL AND VELVET (FOR MEN ONLY)*

Marabel Morgan — *THE TOTAL WOMAN (FOR WOMEN ONLY)*

Larry Christanson— *THE CHRISTIAN FAMILY*

CHAPTER ONE
THE WAY YOU SEE OTHERS

THE GOOD FINDERS

Several years ago, an analysis was made of 100 self-made millionaires. They ranged in age from about 21 to well over 70. Their educational experiences extended from grade school to the Ph.D. level. Other traits and characteristics also varied considerably. Seventy percent of them, for instance, came from towns of 15,000 people or less. Nevertheless, they did have one thing in common. All of them were "good finders." They could see the good in other people — and in every situation.

I'm confident you've heard the story of the little boy, who in a fit of anger shouted to his mother that he hated her. Then, perhaps fearing punishment, he ran out of the house to the hillside and shouted into the valley, "I hate you, I hate you, I hate you." Back from the valley came the echo, "I hate you, I hate you, I hate you." Somewhat startled, the little boy ran back into the house and told his mother there was a mean little boy in the valley saying he hated him. His mother took him back to the hillside and told him to shout, "I love you, I love you." The little boy did as his mother said and this time he discovered there was a nice little boy in the valley saying, "I love you, I love you."

Life is an echo. What you send out — comes back. What you sow — you reap. What you give — you get. What you see in others — exists in you. Regardless of who you are or what you do, if you are looking for the best way to reap the most reward in *all* areas of life, you should look for the *good* in every person and in every situation and adopt the golden rule as a way of life.

It's a universal truth that **you treat people exactly like you see them.** It's also true that all you have to do to find "good" or "ability" in a person is to look for it. Once you find that "good" or "ability" in the other person you treat him better and he performs better. So it's good "business" and good "humanness" to be a "good finder."

DON'T TAKE THE MOON DOWN

After you have "found" the good, be sure to *do* some good by spreading the word.

Many times people see the good and then keep it a secret. This isn't true at Bay City High School in Bay City, Texas. In October of 1976, with the full support of principal Joe Graham, Barry Tacker started a recognition program for students who deserved praise and recognition but generally went unnoticed even though they displayed positive, responsible behavior and attitudes. During the school year over 500 students were recognized by the teachers and "sent" to the office. Mr. Tacker reports these results: (1) Good students were recognized. (2) Students learned they could be recognized for positive behavior not just negative behavior. (3) The Principals got to know many students by first names instead of faces. (4) Student attitudes improved, they appreciated the recognition. (5) Teachers were forced to look for the positive characteristics of students in their classes.

When students came into Mr. Tacker's office the first reaction was generally, "What have I done?" expecting *bad*. Curiosity turned into smiles as he described "What they had done."

About four years ago I met Walter Hailey, a successful and dynamic man from Dallas, Texas. I will never forget our meeting, because Walter and I established an immediate rapport. After a short visit, he wanted to show me one of his unique ventures. He is in the insurance business and has conceived a new idea for merchandising insurance to thousands of independent grocers throughout the country, using grocery warehouses as a base.

We visited one of these mammoth warehouses and as we entered, he paused in front of the switchboard operator and said, "I want to tell you what a beautiful job you are doing on the switchboard. You make people feel as though you are delighted they called." The switchboard operator smiled broadly and said, "Thank you, Mr. Hailey, that's what I try to do." Next, we walked into the office section. As we passed one department, Mr. Hailey said, "Excuse me, Zig, let's go in here. I want you to meet this man." He walked in, introduced himself and said, "You know, I haven't gotten to know you, but I know your department and I just wanted you to know I'm aware of what is happening. Since you have taken over this department, we haven't had the first complaint, which is a tribute to you." The man grinned and said, "Well, thank you, Mr. Hailey, I'm doing the best I can."

We went upstairs and, as we started to walk into the inner office, he stopped and said, "Zig, I want to introduce you to the greatest secretary who ever sat behind a desk." Then to the secretary, "You know, I don't think I have ever told you this, but my wife thinks you hung the moon, and she believes you can go take it down, any time, so I'm going to ask you not to do that." She smiled and said, "Well, I appreciate hearing that." We walked into the insurance office, and he said, "Zig, shake hands with one of the greatest insurance men who ever put on a pair of shoes."

The entire trip took less than 3 minutes but Walter Hailey gave each of these people something to live up to. He left them better than he found them. He gave them some sincere appreciation, which built enthusiasm for their jobs and their company. As a result, I can assure you they worked more effectively and efficiently. I can also assure you Walter Hailey felt better as a result of the trip — and so did I. It is impossible to influence someone else for the good and give them a boost without gaining a benefit yourself.

THE PROBLEM IS

As a young salesman, I read a story that made a lasting impression. A five-year-old girl made her musical debut in a church contata. She had a beautiful voice and from the beginning a great career was predicted for her. As she grew older she was more and more in demand for church, school and social functions. Recognizing the need for professional voice training, the family sent her to a well-known voice teacher. The teacher knew his music as perhaps few others did. He was a perfectionist who demanded top performance at all times. Any time the girl would waiver a bit or miss her timing in the least, he carefully pointed out her errors. Over a period of time, her admiration for her teacher deepened. Despite the age difference and the fact he was more critical than complimentary, she fell in love with him and they were married.

He continued to teach her, but her friends started detecting changes in her beautiful natural voice. It took on a strained quality and no longer had the clear excitement that it formerly possessed. Gradually, invitations to sing came less frequently. Finally, they virtually stopped. Then her husband-teacher died and for the next few years she did little or no singing. Her talent was hardly used, and lay dormant until an exuberant salesman began courting her. On occasion, when she would hum a little tune or a melody would burst forth, he would marvel at the beauty of her voice. "Sing some more, Honey. You have the most beautiful voice in all the world," he would say. Now the fact of the matter is, he might not have known whether she was good, bad or indifferent, but he did know he liked her voice very much. So, he showered her with praise. Not too surprisingly, her confidence returned and she began to receive invitations to sing again. Still later, she married the "good finder" and went on to a successful career of her own.

Some say compliments are just so much air, but I would like to emphasize that the salesman's praise for her was totally honest, sincere and much needed. In fact, **a sincere compliment is one of the most effective teaching and motivational methods in existence.** They may seem to be just so much air, but like the air we use to fill the tires on our automobiles, they can really ease us along life's highway.

YOU ARE A BUSINESSMAN

A New York businessman dropped a dollar into the cup of a man selling pencils and hurriedly stepped aboard the subway train. On second thought, he stepped back off the train, walked over to the beggar and took several pencils from the cup. Apologetically, he explained that in his haste he had neglected to pick up his pencils and hoped the man wouldn't be upset with him. "After all," he said, "you are a businessman just like myself. You have merchandise to sell and it's fairly priced." Then he caught the next train.

At a social function a few months later, a neatly-dressed salesman stepped up to the businessman and introduced himself. "You probably don't remember me and I don't know your name, but I will never forget you. You are the man who gave me back my self-respect. I was a "beggar" selling pencils until you came along and told me I was a businessman."

A wise man said, "**A lot of people have gone further than they thought they could because someone else thought they could.**" How do you see others? The greatest good we can do for anyone is not to share our wealth with them, but rather to reveal their own wealth to them. It's astonishing how much talent and ability rests inside a human being. We devoted considerable time in the first two Segments selling you on you. Just as the first step to success is knowing your own potential, the second step is knowing the potential of others. Fortunately, as we recognize our own ability, it's easy to recognize the ability of others. Once we see it, we can help them discover it for themselves.

THE BANKERS SAID NO

By bankers' guidelines and business logic, they should have. The applicant did not have banker's collateral [she couldn't prove she didn't need the $6,000], she wanted to inject more capital into a new business, had no experience in running a company, had parted company with her former employer over a disagreement in philosophy, the economy wasn't exactly booming and besides all that she was a woman. Worse still she had the peculiar notion that you could build a business on Christian principles. Incredibly enough she even had the idea that the customer, the company, and the sales person could benefit when a sale was made. To compound the "problem" she believed in paying bills and bonuses when they came due and not when it was convenient.

But if you think that was bad [in bankers' eyes] keep reading — it gets worse. Mary Crowley even believed that you should open a sales or training meeting with prayer. Later she and her son, Don Carter, who works beside her in the business, had the revolutionary idea that it was good business to hire the handicapped. Good for them — good for you. Additionally, the business was already "out of control" with a mushrooming sales force selling, building, and recruiting so fast the company could scarcely keep up with the orders. [Interestingly enough, it is still out of control in the eyes of some of their competitors who drool with envy at the fact that Home Interiors and Gifts stops recruiting on October 10 each year because they need to "catch their breath" and be able to give continued good service through the increased Christmas business.] To the best of my knowledge, they are the *only* sales company in America who do this.

It's clear, however, that two bankers were wrong and the one who said yes was right, because Home Interiors and Gifts, formed by Mrs. Mary Crowley of Dallas, Texas, is truly one of the Horatio Alger stories of this century. Starting from scratch — and she provided the scratch — Mary Crowley through the utilization of all the principles for outstanding and lasting success has built a company that has become a model in the direct sales world. Built on a bed rock of faith in Almighty God and the conviction that not only could a business be built on faith, integrity, hard work and equal opportunity for all, but it *must* be built that way for permanence. Being a woman — and grateful for it — Mary felt the sting of prejudice and discrimination keenly enough to know that it must not exist in Home Interiors and Gifts.

The question most people ask is why and how has Mary Crowley and her company achieved such remarkable success since it was founded in December 1957. The answer is simple, but it goes far below the surface. If I had to sum up Mary Crowley and her success in a few words, I would say that she has reached the heights because of the depth of her beliefs. She believes that "one person with a belief is equal to a force of ninety-nine who have only interest." She believes in the enormous potential in everyone and is determined to give her sales ladies an unlimited opportunity for growth and financial success. She believes that if you build people mentally, morally, physically, and spiritually that they will build the business on the same foundation. By any standard, Mary Crowley is a "rich" woman, but she's rich — not because of what she has [and that's a bunch] — but because of what she gives away [that's an even bigger bunch].

Mary says it beautifully in her book, "Think Mink." A *few* of her real gems include, "don't get the rabbit habit — think mink," "people need loving the most when they deserve it the least," "worry is a misuse of the imagination," "God will mend even a broken heart if we give Him all the pieces," "don't be an 'if' thinker, be a 'how' thinker," "you may give out but never give up," "develop a swelled heart, not a swelled head," "I love God's mathmatics. Joy adds and multiplies as you divide it with others," "Be somebody — God doesn't take time to make a nobody."

The story of Mary Crowley and Home Interiors hasn't been all sunshine and roses. There has been much blood, sweat, and tears, but never any shortage in the important things — plenty of love, faith, enthusiasm, compassion, determination, and plain hard work. That, my friends, gives you *all* the good things life has to offer. Mary's story is the classic case and it's one any lawyer could use in court to prove that you can get everything in life you want if you just help enough other people get what they want.

RATS

Several years ago, at Harvard University, Dr. Robert Rosenthal conducted an intriguing series of experiments involving three groups of students and three groups of rats. He informed the first group of students, "You're in luck. You are going to be working with genius rats. These rats have been bred for intelligence and are extremely bright. They will get to the end of the maze in nothing flat, and eat lots of cheese, so buy plenty.

The second group was told, "Your rats are just average, not too bright, not too dumb, just a bunch of average rats. They will eventually get to the end of the maze, and eat some cheese, but don't expect too much from them. They're "average" in ability and intelligence, so their performance will be average.

He told the third group of students, "These rats are really bad. If they find the end of the maze, it will be by accident and not design. They are really idiots, so naturally they will be low in performance. I'm not certain you should even buy any cheese. Just paint a sign at the end of the maze that says cheese."

For the next six weeks, the students conducted experiments under exacting scientific conditions. The genius rats performed like genuises. They reaches the end of the maze in short order. The average rats — well, what do you expect from a bunch of average rats? They made it to the end but they didn't set any speed records in the process. The idiot rats, oh brother, were they ever sad. They had real difficulty and when one did find the end of the maze it was obviously an accident and not a "plan." Here's the interesting thing. There were no genius rats or idiot rats. They were all average rats out of the same litter. The difference in performance was the direct result of the difference in the attitude of the students conducting the series of experiments. In short, the students treated the rats "differently" because they saw them "differently" and **different treatment brings on different results.** The students didn't know rat language but rats have attitudes, and attitude is a universal language.

KIDS—SALESMEN—PATIENTS— EMPLOYEES—MATES

Here's a question for you. What kind of children do you have? If you're a salesman, what kind of prospects have you been seeing? If you are a sales manager, what kind of salesmen do you have? If you are a doctor, what kind of patients have you been treating? If you are an employer, what kind of employees do you have? If you are a husband, what kind of wife do you have? If you are a wife, what kind of husband do you have?

You might say, "Wait a minute, Ziglar, doggone it all, one minute you're talking about those rats and the next minute you're talking about my kids, my wife, my husband or my prospects. Can you be a little clearer?" Obviously, I'm talking about attitude and the effect your attitude has on the people whose lives you touch. Let's take our story about the rats another step, because the experiment was taken one more step and extended to a local grade school.

One teacher was told, "You're in luck. You will be working with the genius kids. These students are so bright it's frightening. They are going to be giving you answers before you ask the questions. They are extremely intelligent kids. One word of caution, however; they are so bright they will try to fool you. Some of them are lazy and will try to con you into giving them less work. Don't listen to them. These kids can turn out the work. Just put it to them. Some of them will even say, "Teacher, that's too hard."

Don't listen to them and don't worry about the problems being too hard. These kids can and will solve the toughest ones if you give them your vote of confidence along with some daily injections of love, discipline and genuine interest.

A second teacher was told, "You have the average kids. They're not too bright nor too dumb. They have average I.Q., background and ability, so we expect average results."

Naturally, the genius students did better than the average students. As a matter of fact, at the end of the year, the genius students were one full year ahead of the average students. I'll bet you don't have to be a genius to figure out the end of this story, do you? You're right. There were no genius students. They were all average students. The only difference was in the attitude of the teacher. The teacher thought the average students were geniuses, so they were treated like geniuses, expected to perform like geniuses, and they did. They were given something to live up to and not something to live down to. It's true **the way you see "them" is the way you treat them and the way you treat them is the way they often become.**

Here's another question. Have your kids gotten any smarter the last five minutes? What about the sales people in your organization? Did your employees or associates become more productive, wiser, more professional and more skillful during those few minutes? How about your wife? Has she gotten prettier and more interesting? Or, did your husband grow in stature? If these things didn't happen, let me urge you to turn back the pages and read again, because you missed the point, and your family, friends and associates have a problem — it's you.

The poet expressed it beautifully when he said, "If you take a man as he is, you make him worse than he was, but if you see him as being the best person possible, then he, in fact, becomes the best person possible." If your kids, while *you* were reading these words have suddenly gotten smarter, if a husband, wife or associate improved, let me say, "Congratulations, *you* are the one who is making progress."

An excellent example of this philosophy, of seeing the good in the other person, is retired U.C.L.A. coach John Wooden, who by the way is the perfect answer to Leo Durocher's famous and obviously wrong statement that "nice guys finish last." Wooden saw the total person in his basketball players and was just as concerned with their morals as with their quickness. He also believed and taught that everything in life was enhanced by working with consideration for the other person. Team spirit, dedication, loyalty, enthusiasm, poise and condition were all trademarks of his teams. Since his teams won 10 out of 12 national championships, including seven in a row, there isn't much way we can disagree with his philosophy. It might surprise you to learn that this winner of all winners didn't consider winning the most important thing. As a matter of fact, he never mentioned winning to his players. He stressed "best effort" for everybody and felt that a player should feel badly only if he didn't give it his all.

YOU ARE A LOUSY FOOTBALL PLAYER

During a practice session for the Green Bay Packers, things were not going well for Vince Lombardi's team. Lombardi singled out one big guard for his failure to "put out." It was a hot, muggy day when the coach called his guard aside and leveled his awesome vocal guns on him, as only Lombardi could. "Son, you are a lousy football player. You're not blocking, you're not tackling, you're not putting out. As a matter of fact, it's all over for you today, go take a shower." The big guard dropped his head and walked into the dressing room. Forty-five minutes later, when Lombardi walked in, he saw the big guard sitting in front of his locker still wearing his uniform. His head was bowed and he was sobbing quietly.

Vince Lombardi, ever the changeable but always the compassionate warrior, did something of an about face that was also typical of him. He walked over to his football player and put his arms around his shoulder. "Son," he said, "I told you the truth. You are a lousy football player. You're not blocking, you're not tackling, you're not putting out. However, in all fairness to you, I should have finished the story. Inside of you, son, there is a great football player and I'm going to stick by your side until the great football player inside of you has a chance to come out and assert himself." With these words, Jerry Kramer straightened up and felt a great deal better. As a matter of fact, he felt so much better he went on to become one of the all-time greats in football and was recently voted the all-time guard in the first 50 years of professional football.

That was Lombardi. He saw things in men that they seldom saw in themselves. He had the ability to inspire his men to use the talent they had. As a result, these players gave Lombardi three consecutive world championships at Green Bay. Later, when he moved to Washington, many people wondered how he would handle Sonny Jurgensen, the talented but undisciplined quarterback. They didn't wonder very long. On the first day of practice one of the reporters baited him with a question about Jurgensen. Lombardi called Sonny to his side, put his arm around him and said, "Gentlemen, this is the greatest quarterback to ever step on a football field." Is it any wonder that Jurgensen had his best year ever? Lombardi saw the good in others, treated them like he saw them and helped develop the "good" that was inside of them.

LITTLE ANNIE

A number of years ago, in a mental institution just outside Boston, Mass., a young girl known as "Little Annie" was locked in the dungeon. This institution was one of the more enlightened ones for the treatment of the mentally disturbed. However, the doctors felt that a dungeon was the only place for those who were "hopelessly" insane. In Little Annie's case, they saw no hope for her, so she was consigned to a living death in that small cage which received little light and even less hope.

About that time, an elderly nurse in the institution was nearing retirement. She felt there was hope for all of God's creatures, so she started taking her lunch into the dungeon and eating outside Little Annie's cage. She felt perhaps she could communicate some love and hope to the little girl.

In many ways, Little Annie was like an animal. On occasions, she would violently attack the person who came into her cage. At other times, she would completely ignore them. When the elderly nurse started visiting her, Little Annie gave no indication that she was even aware of her presence. One day, the elderly nurse brought some brownies to the dungeon and left them outside the cage. Little Annie gave no hint she knew they were there, but when the nurse returned the next day, the brownies were gone. From that time on, the nurse would bring brownies when she made her Thursday visit. Soon, the doctors in the institution noticed a change was taking place. After a period of time, they decided to move Little Annie upstairs. Finally, the day came when this "hopeless case" was told she could return home. But Little Annie did not wish to leave. The place had meant so much to her she felt she could make a contribution if she stayed and worked with the other patients. The elderly nurse had seen and brought out so much in her life that Little Annie felt she could see and help develop something in others.

Many years later, Queen Victoria of England, while pinning England's highest award on a foreigner, asked Helen Keller, "How do you account for your remarkable accomplishments in life? How do you explain the fact that even though you were both blind and deaf, you were able to accomplish so much?" Without a moment's hesitation, Helen Keller said that had it not been for Anne Sullivan (Little Annie), the name of Helen Keller would have remained unknown.

It's not too well known, but Helen Keller was a normal, healthy baby before some mysterious disease left her almost helpless and hopeless. Anne Sullivan saw Helen Keller as one of God's very special people — treated her as she saw her — loved her — disciplined her — played, prayed, pushed and worked with her until the flickering candle that was her life became a beacon that helped light the pathways and lighten the burdens of people all over the world. Yes, Helen Keller influenced millions *after* her own life was touched by "*Little* Annie?"

THE EYES HAVE IT

A number of years ago in Northern Virginia, an old man stood on a river bank waiting to get across. Since it was bitterly cold and there were no bridges, he would have to "catch a ride" to the other side. After a lengthy wait, he saw a group of horsemen approaching. He let the first one pass, then the second, third, fourth, and fifth. Finally, there was only one rider left. As he drew abreast, the old man looked him in the eye and said, "Sir, would you give me a ride across the river?"

The rider, without a moment's hesitation said, "Why certainly, get aboard." Once across the river, the old man slid to the ground. Before leaving, the rider said, "Sir, I could not help but notice that you permitted all the other riders to pass without asking for a ride. Then, when I drew abreast, you immediately asked me for a ride. I'm curious as to why you didn't ask them and why you did ask me?" The old man quietly responded, "I looked into their eyes and could see no love and knew in my own heart it would be useless to ask for a ride. But, when I looked into your eyes, I saw compassion, love and the willingness to help. I knew you would be glad to give me the ride across the river."

With this the rider very humbly said, "You know, I'm very grateful for what you are saying. I appreciate it very much." With that, Thomas Jefferson turned and rode off to the White House. It has truly been said that our eyes are the windows of our souls. In this particular case, the old man read them correctly. Question: If you had been the last rider, would the old man have asked *you* for that ride "across the river?" It's important that he would have because there is a vast difference between giving advice and lending a hand. You and your encouragement might well be, for one or more people, that all important ride across the river. Harvey Firestone, who helped people climb the mountains of accomplishment expressed it beautifully when he said, "**You get the best out of others when you give the best of yourself.**"

SEE A NEED — AND FILL IT

The story of LaVon and Vern Dragt is one of unique courage, dedication to principle and a firm belief that faith and hard work answer most of life's problems. Vern was a well paid plasterer and the father of three small children when polio struck. A valiant struggle for life itself was followed by four and a half years of convalescence. Today Vern and LaVon are managing a business which includes over 1,000 Tupperware Dealers doing over $8,000,000 annually.

What happened between the time polio struck and the situation that exists today, is quite a story. When Vern was stricken and the savings were gone, LaVon sought outside employment. However, her job drained her physically and kept her away from Vern and the children ten hours a day. She responded to the Tupperware appeal, fell in love with the business and after her second party, decided to sell on a full-time basis. The work was fun and profitable and she could arrange her schedule of work around the family instead of having to arrange her family around her schedule as she had formerly done. Almost immediately she recognized that other men and women faced similar problems so she started extending a helping hand to them. The result is the number one distributorship in the entire country, financial security for the Dragts and an opportunity to contribute to their community, to their fellowman and to their church work.

In the process of accomplishing some of their objectives, Vern and LaVon made it possible for 125 of their managers and countless dealers to drive beautiful new cars and accomplish objectives of their own. They have given the opportunity for growth to hundreds of others, including Hal Empey who is today a Vice President with Tupperware. Their remarkable success is the result of seeing the needs of others and doing something about those needs. You do treat people as you see them and if you see others as Vern and LaVon do, then you too will be getting a lot because you will be giving a lot.

FEED OTHERS — EAT WELL YOURSELF

A man was given a tour of both Heaven and Hell so he could intelligently select his final destination. The Devil was given first chance, so he started the "prospect" with a tour of Hell. The first glance was a surprising one because all the occupants were seated at a banquet table loaded with every food imaginable, including meat from every corner of the globe, fruits and vegetables and every delicacy known to man. With justification, the Devil pointed out that no one could ask for more.

However, when the man looked carefully at the people he did not find a single smile. There was no music or indication of gaiety generally associated with such a feast. The people at the table looked dull and listless and were literally skin and bones. The tourist noticed that each person had a fork strapped to the left arm and a knife strapped to the right arm. Each had a four-foot handle which made it impossible to eat. So, with food of every kind at their fingertips, they were starving.

Next stop was Heaven, where the tourist saw a scene identical in every respect — same foods, knives and forks with those four-foot handles. However, the inhabitants of Heaven were laughing, singing and having a great time. They were well fed and in excellent health. The tourist was puzzled for a moment. He wondered how conditions could be so similar and yet produce such different results. The people in Hell were starving and miserable, while the people in Heaven were well-fed and happy. Then, he saw the answer. Each person in Hell had been trying to feed himself. A knife and fork with a four-foot handle made this impossible. Each person in Heaven was feeding the one across the table from him and was being fed by the one sitting on the opposite side. By helping one another they helped themselves.

The message is clear. The way you see situations and people is extremely important because **you treat people and situations exactly as you see them.** That's one reason I keep reminding you — you can get everything in life you want — if you help enough other people get what they want.

NOTES AND IDEAS

CHAPTER TWO

GOOD OR BAD, YOU PASS IT ON

MIDDLE KIDS ARE "DIFFERENT"

Let me tell you a personal and embarrassing story. When our family consisted of three daughters, we had a problem. Our middle daughter was about five years old. As everybody knows, the middle child is "different" and is often the "problem" child. We knew in advance we would have problems with our middle daughter because all our friends and relatives assured us the middle child is "different."

This difference is supposed to be the result of not having the security and independence of being the oldest child, nor the affection and attention generally accorded the youngest. Children, contrary to what you might believe, do want to cooperate. If parents think the middle child is going to be different they invariably treat them differently. When this happens, just as certainly as God made those little green apples, the middle child "cooperates" and turns out to be different. What everyone did not tell us was that the "difference" is positive or negative depending on the way you treat the child.

In my particular case, I handled our middle daughter in a classic manner. If I commented once, I must have commented a thousand times, "Why does Cindy whine so much? Why can't she be like Suzan and Julie? Why is she different? Why isn't she happier and more cheerful?" Cindy responded in the only way she could, she whined, complained, fussed, and generally followed the detailed instructions I was giving to her. She wasn't different when she started, but we made her different. Then, the family started a study of the way the mind works. We finally learned what the Bible so clearly says, "As ye sow, so also shall ye reap." We learned you can't plant negative instructions and raise a positive child anymore than you can plant beans and raise potatoes.

We made some significant changes in our approach. Each

time we had a visitor, my wife and I would introduce Cindy in a special way: "This is the little girl everybody loves because she is so happy. She laughs and smiles all the time." Then, "Baby, tell these folks your name." she would always give us her two-front-teeth-missing grin, and say, "It's Tadpole." [What a name for a pretty little girl.] Then we would repeat, "This is the little girl who is always smiling and laughing. She's happy and friendly and cheerful, aren't you, Baby?" She would just grin and say "Yes, sir," or "Yes, Ma'am." [We believe one of the most useful and important traits you can develop in your children is genuine courtesy and respect for the authority of the parents. We believe children feel more secure knowing they have someone to respect as parents rather than just a friend or buddy. We *required* Yes, Sir and Yes, Ma'am.]

We had been following this procedure only a month when we had one of those truly exhilerating experiences that gladdens any parent's heart. Someone came to see us and, as was our custom, I called Cindy over and said, "This is our little girl that everybody loves. Tell them what your name is, Baby." She grabbed my coat sleeve and said, "Daddy, I've changed my name." Somewhat surprised, I said, "What is your name now, Baby?" Smiling bigger than ever, she responded, "I'm the Happy Tadpole."

The neighbors on both sides of us wanted to know what had happened to Cindy. Well, something had happened to Cindy, but it didn't happen *until* Mother and Dad started seeing her as a child who deserved the best we had to offer. When we saw her in a new light we treated her like the cheerful, happy girl she was entitled to be — and that's the kind of girl she became, so today we call her "Sweetning." Yes, you treat people like you "see" them so it's extremely important that we learn to "see" others properly.

THREE LITTLE GIRLS

A number of years ago, when we lived in Stone Mountain, Georgia, I had my office in the nearby town of Decatur. One day, a friend of mine in the insurance business stopped by for a visit. He brought his three daughters who were about three, five and seven years of age. They were dressed in pretty dresses and looked like little dolls. Incredibly enough, this is the way he introduced them:

"This is the one who won't eat, this is the one who won't mind her mother, and this is the one who cries all the time."

There is no question in my mind about this man's love for those three little ones. It showed all over his face and in his eyes as he petted and played with them. Unfortunately, he was giving them something to "live down to." The way he saw them was the way he was treating them. He was giving powerful, negative instructions to each one. Chances are he often lamented the fact that he had one little girl who "wouldn't eat," and one who "wouldn't mind her mother," and one who "cried all the time." Tragically, the odds are a thousand to one he never knew why. It's true we reap what we sow — as well as what others sow in our minds. That makes it doubly important to see our little ones properly, because the way we see them determines what we sow in them, which to a large degree determines what they become.

Linda Isaac's family, friends and teachers "saw" her as a "dwarf" of limited mental capabilities, so that's the way they treated her. Her teachers in the Special Education classes in Italy, Texas didn't think she could learn, so they didn't attempt to teach her much. They passed her from one grade to the next until she "graduated" from high school. Now we have a four-foot, 80 lb. black high school graduate who functions at a first grade level. Under these circumstances, Linda had two chances in life — slim and none. Then her mother contacted Carol Clapp at the Texas Rehabilitation Commission at Goodwill Industries. As a result, Linda moved to Dallas to live with a sister and start an extensive three week vocational evaluation program. She was placed in a work adjustment program where a different crop was planted or "sowed" in her mind. As a result, she quickly outgrew that program and was transferred to the Industrial Contract Center. Today she takes telephone messages, keeps time cards and checks each day's progress. Her personality changed as her confidence grew under this "new" treatment. She has joined the Little People of America and wants to be a secretary; she loves life, likes what she is doing and her image is such she no longer minds being called "Shorty." Linda Isaac's story is one that will probably have a happy ending but it does make you wonder how many people have been consigned to mediocrity by someone who "saw" them in an inferior light and treated them accordingly.

Even as late as college, many students are inhibited by some pompous professor who proudly announces that a certain percentage of his class "always fails" and no one makes an "A". It apparently never occurs to these professors that they may be hiding their inability to teach behind a false display of academic baloney. Personally, I think the professor should work harder so he could say he was such a *good* teacher many of the students would make "A's" and *everyone* would learn in his course. *Don't misunderstand.* I'm not hinting that a teacher should *brag* on the students and tell them they are doing well regardless of how they actually are doing. *That* approach leads to academic suicide. As a matter of fact, a recent study in San Francisco reveals that members of minority groups have repeatedly been told how well they are doing, when in fact the individuals involved might be doing poorly. This is the cruelest treatment of all, because it produces diploma-bearing functional illiterates who cannot compete in the market place for jobs. *This* produces a disillusioned, bitter individual who, when encouraged just slightly with some radical rhetoric, will make society "pay" for its failure to give him an education that would make him competitive.

So, what's the solution? I have no single answer to such a complex educational problem but this I do know. We need to look for the total ability of the student, develop more patience, compassion *and* firmness in dealing with them, and be more analytical of what the student *does* and not so critical of the student. **Criticize the performance — not the performer.** In short, when dealing with students, give them lots of encouragement, but don't lie to them or mislead them by telling them they are doing well when they are not. Encourage them by letting them know they can do better work — that their assignment or performance is not up to their standards. When their image changes, so will their performance.

Over 27 years of teaching experience, much of it of a highly *concentrated* nature, convinces me that this is the most effective way to get maximum performance from the individual. In short, give them something to live up to. Convince them they *can* — and they will.

122

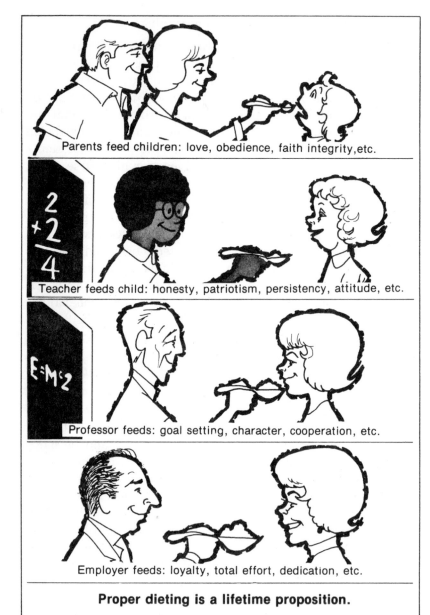

Parents feed children: love, obedience, faith integrity, etc.

Teacher feeds child: honesty, patriotism, persistency, attitude, etc.

Professor feeds: goal setting, character, cooperation, etc.

Employer feeds: loyalty, total effort, dedication, etc.

Proper dieting is a lifetime proposition.

QUEEN OF SALES

Mary Kay Ash, Chairman of the Board for Mary Kay Cosmetics, totally understands the value and importance of seeing the good and the potential in others. She knows the value from both sides of the fence. With two young children to support, she began working with Stanley Home Products. She got off to a miserable start but as she watched other girls doing well, she knew in her own mind her time would come, so she simply redoubled her efforts.

A short time later, a national convention was scheduled for Dallas. Mary Kay borrowed $12.00 to pay for her transportation and the hotel room. That was all the money she had, and the $12.00 didn't include meals. She took along cheese and crackers to eat for the three days. The convention was tremendously inspiring. On the final night, when Mr. Stanley Beverage placed the "Queen of Sales" crown on a tall slender brunette, Mary Kay made the decision that started her on the road to success.

When she walked down the receiving line to shake hands with President Beverage, she looked him squarely in the eyes and said, "Mr. Beverage, you don't know who I am tonight, but this time next year you will because I am going to be the Queen of Sales." Stanley Beverage could have casually commented on the matter, but he didn't. He apparently saw that special "something" in Mary Kay as he looked her in the eye and shook her hand, because he said to her, "You know, somehow I think you will." She did. Later, she went on to an outstanding career with that company and another one as well.

Then, one day she "retired," but her retirement lasted about a month with twelve hour work days. After a day or two of meditation to collect her thoughts, she took a yellow pad and started "figuring." She listed all the things she liked about the companies she had represented. She put down the things she considered important to a woman seeking a career in selling. She wrote down the things she wanted to do, be and have as she was building her own career. She decided to start her own company and build it on a basis that would permit her people to utilize the beauty and ability she saw in every woman. She felt it was far better and more important to reveal to the person what they already had than it was to give that person part of what she had.

Mary Kay saw women as capable of earning large sums of money and having the luxuries of life, including Cadillac automobiles. With limited finances but unlimited faith, Mary Kay Cosmetics began in August, 1963. Before the calendar year ended they had sold roughly $60,000 in retail products. In 1976, Mary Kay Cosmetics sold approximately $88,000,000 and nearly 40,000 Consultants and Directors tell the Mary Kay story in every state in the Union.

There are many reasons for this success story, but it all started when someone "saw" something special in Mary Kay. It continued and grew because she kept things in proper perspective. She teaches her people that God comes first, the family second and Mary Kay Cosmetics third. She also "saw" and "sees" enormous abilities in her people and treats them accordingly. As a result, she "sees" them all over the country, driving around in Mary Kay pink Cadillacs.

YOU KNOW HOW SCARED YOU ARE OF PEOPLE

An incident in a department store in Columbia, S.C., illustrates a similar point. It was Christmas time and the crowds were huge. A mother and her little five-year-old girl were watching a demonstration. The mother was engrossed with the event and took her eyes off the child who then drifted a few feet away. Soon the mother missed the child and glanced around for an instant before she spotted her. Then, as she leaped like an animal for her child, she exclaimed, "You come here to me, you know how scared you are of people!"

Can't you just imagine how many things the child is going to be "scared of" before she is grown? It seems so simple — after we have learned. However, as we read the words on this page, I'll have to plead guilty, as I did in the story of my middle daughter, to much of the same thing until someone taught me better. Then I was astonished that I hadn't thought of those things myself. Just good old common sense I said — *after* I learned.

Many times I've heard it said there were two things about "hindsight." No. 1, it was always right, and No. 2, it was never worth anything. That's only partially true. Hindsight is worth a lot if you learn from it and it's worth even more if it's another's hindsight you are learning from. If it wasn't this way, we would have to re-invent the wheel every generation.

IT PAYS TO SHARE

Major Anderson, of Revolutionary War fame, owned a library. He was an unselfish man who opened his library to the young men of the area who wanted to acquire more knowledge. One of the young boys who came to Major Anderson's home every Saturday morning was a Scottish lad who was extremely grateful for the opportunity to spend the day reading. Apparently, he learned a great deal in the process, because Andrew Carnegie went on to become one of the most productive and wealthy men America has ever produced. He created forty-three millionaires when millionaires were truly rare individuals. Carnegie passed this kindness on in another way. He created the Carnegie Libraries all over the United States. Untold thousands of people still benefit from his generosity.

Yes, when you see ability in others and then help nourish and develop that ability, you make some remarkable contributions. Of course, the most remarkable thing is **the more you "pass on" to others, the more you keep for yourself.** A case in point is Charles Percy, who was made president of Bell and Howell at the age of 39. He had worked up through the ranks of the company and acquired both fame and fortune. Today he is an outstanding United States Senator. Interestingly enough, the one comment most often made about Senator Percy is his uncanny ability to see the potential in another person and then persuade that person to use his ability.

Occasionally, this philosophy will temporarily move you into the shadow instead of the spotlight. A case in point is Chris Chattaway, the "pacer" who played a key role in the first four minute mile. Chattaway burned himself out the first three laps setting a fast pace for Roger Bannister, so Bannister could break the "unbreakable" 4 minute barrier. Bannister broke the barrier and achieved international fame while Chattaway dropped into relative obscurity. Since that time, however, there have been some 500 races run in less than four minutes but Chattaway is and always will be the *only* one who gave of himself by setting the pace so the unbreakable barrier *could* be broken.

TWO BIG MISSES

An obscure college professor had a wife who was hard-of-hearing. His dream was to perfect a hearing device so his wife, whom he loved very much, could hear. He devoted every spare dollar and every spare moment he had to working on his dream. History books tell us he failed in his venture, but he was far from being a failure. Alexander Graham Bell missed one goal, but mankind benefited enormously because he dedicated himself to seeking a solution to someone else's problem. He aimed to help one and missed. Instead, he helped millions.

Several years earlier, a German inventor named Wilhelm Reiss had perfected a device for transmitting sound over wires. As a matter of fact, had Reiss moved two electrodes just one 1/1000 of an inch, so they would touch each other he would have invented the telephone. Ironically, Reiss missed immortality by the slimmest of margins. His near-miss makes us wonder what might have happened if Reiss had been working with the same motive as Bell? Is there a chance those electrodes would have "accidentally" touched each other? We'll never know.

A SUBSTITUTE EMCEE

Several years ago, a friend of mine, David Smith, called and asked if I would serve as the substitute Master of Ceremonies for an Elks Club Annual Ball. I facetiously commented that I had always wanted to be a substitute master of ceremonies. "Well," he explained, "it is our big annual event and a local politician has promised to come, but we are not certain he can make it."

It was a gala event, complete with tux, tie and dance band. My wife and I arrived early for the event and as we watched David dance we were astonished at his grace and skill. He was obviously pleased, but a little embarrassed about our enthusiastic compliments. He reluctantly told us he taught ballroom dancing. It occurred to me that even though I had been seeing him for several years, I didn't really know him. With a little persuasion, he shared part of his life story.

He told how he had been forced to drop out of school at age 16 in order to help support his family. He had returned to school at age twenty-two and finished high school at twenty-five. He told us he had three daughters, two of whom were school teachers and one of them had her Master's Degree. He was obviously, and justifiably, proud of his family.

The most intriguing thing about David, however, was his age; he was 66 years old and one of the hardest-working men I have ever seen. Incidentally, he is our yard man, and his story has several lessons. It reaffirms that we can't judge a book by its cover. His story also proves **how you do what you do gives dignity to any honest labor**. Being a yard man might not be lucrative for some people, but it enabled David Smith to support himself and to educate three daughters. In addition, it establishes the fact that the **opportunity lies in the man and not in the job**. He does good work and is able to sell his service to others. The major point, however, is that David Smith wanted his daughters to have "more," so he gave more of himself for them. As a result, everybody won. It's exciting to think of the kids who will get more out of life because David Smith educated himself and then educated his daughters who educate the kids who . . .

DON'T HIRE HIM — HE'S AN EX-CON

Our society has an interesting concept of justice. We say when someone commits a crime he should pay a penalty. I agree with this approach for several reasons. However, society goes one step beyond in its treatment of those who have paid for their crimes. In spite of the fact we say to the man or woman, "Okay, we are now even, you broke the law, you have paid the price so it's all over," the truth is, in most cases it is not all over. Society continues to deal, either through malice or ignorance, with the ex-con in such a way that in many states over 80% of the convicts return to prison. I find it difficult to believe that these men and women return because they prefer life behind bars over freedom.

If an ex-con tells the truth to a prospective employer, the vast majority of them won't give him that second chance. If he doesn't tell the prospective employer the truth, inevitably the truth will come out and the man will often lose his job almost regardless of his performance. The reason for this is simple. We have a natural tendency to see the "con" and forget the "ex". We look at him or her and a message goes through our minds a thousand times: "Here is a jailbird, a thief, liar, forgerer, etc." Remember, **we treat people as we see them.** So, if we see ex-cons as thieves, we communicate that fact. Combine that with over-sensitivity to every hurt, real or imagined, and you have an explosive situation.

After a series of frustrations, when they have honestly made efforts to adjust, they frequently begin to rationalize their situations. Their reasoning goes something like this: "Everybody knows I'm an ex-con, so nobody trusts me. They think I'm going to slip again, so they're watching me very carefully. At the first stumble they're going to give me a shove back down. I can only go so long before I have to have some money and there's only one way to get it. Besides, it will serve them right." This reasoning leads them back to crime and prison.

That's the problem; now let's look at a solution. First, concentrate on preparing him for a successful return to society [I'm prejudiced but I think he should be taught The Richer Life Course based on this book], instead of just punishing him for the mistake he made while a member of society. Second, let's go to the source we can depend on to solve all problems — the Holy Bible. In the Gospel of Luke 17:3, Jesus tells us if our brother trespasses against us, we should rebuke [punish] him and if he repents [recognizes his error], we should forgive him and treat him accordingly.

The rest of the solution is found in the first few verses of the 8th chapter of the Gospel of John. The scribes and Pharisees had taken a woman in the act of adultery. They knew that Moses' law explicitly stated she was to be stoned. They brought her to Jesus to find out what he would do with her.

At first Jesus did not answer them; instead he stooped down and wrote something in the sand. The woman's tormenters persisted. They asked what he would do. Jesus then stood up and said to them, "He that is without sin among you let him first cast a stone at her." Again he stooped down and continued to write on the ground. Then, the Bible in beautiful simplicity says, "And they which heard it, being convicted by their own conscience, went out one by one." Surely you have heard **you can only see in others what is inside of you.** Look for the good in others — that's the best way to find the good in yourself.

MOST OF US HAVE DOUBLE STANDARDS

A baker suspected that the farmer who was supplying his butter was giving him short weight. He carefully checked the weight and his suspicions were confirmed. Highly indignant, he had the farmer arrested. At the trial, the judge was satisfied and the baker chagrined at the farmer's explanation. He [the farmer] had no scales, so he used balances and for a weight he used a one pound loaf of bread bought daily from the baker.

The major difference between a lot of men and women who have served time, as opposed to those who have not, lies in the matter of getting caught. Many more people would have the ex-con label hung on them if they had been caught cheating on their income tax. Many would be without a driver's license if they had been caught exceeding the speed limit [unfortunately with the aid of a C.B. radio kids are being taught the "smart" way to circumvent the law] passing on a hill or curve, running a stop sign or driving under the influence. Let me again stress that I believe the penalty should be paid when the law is broken, but in all fairness we should then mark the offender's account "paid in full". This gives him our vote of confidence which will help restore his self-confidence. When this happens, chances are much better the offender will become self-supporting and contribute to society. A lot depends on how we see him. In reality the ex-con is ahead of many of us because in some ways he has paid his debt while ours is unpaid because we were not caught.

I'm convinced that the strongest possible deterrent to a life of crime for youthful first time offenders is the imposition of a work or incarceration penalty of some kind.

This basic concept is strongly vindicated by the American Institute for Character Education. Their course, designed as an aid for teachers, is based on a theory that "school-age children who are taught to consider the likely consequences of their behavior will behave themselves." The course covers kindergarten through the fifth grade and has been tested in over 500 schools. Public School #63 in Indianapolis provides an excellent example of the effectiveness of this approach. Prior to 1970 — [U.S. News and World Report, June 14, 1976] — "the building resembled a school in a riot area. Many windows had been broken and the glass replaced with Masonite." "Most of the pupils were rude, discourteous and insolent to members of the faculty . . . The children had no school pride."

"Since September 1970, there has been less than $100 of glass breakage, and this has been accidental . . . Students are now respectful and cooperative with the teachers, and there is a feeling of one for all and all for one."

The philosophy, whether it's applied to the kindergarten child or an "older" 16 year old offender, will work. I hasten to add that this practical approach would reduce crime even further if it were started in the home, by the parents, at an early age. This can be done, as Dr. James Dobson so convincingly points out in his book, *Dare to Discipline*, by understanding that discipline is something you do *for* a child and not *to* a child.

William Glasser, the father of Reality Therapy, stresses that parents should understand that discipline is directed at the objectionable behavior of the child and is regarded as corrective love so it is accepted by the individual. Punishment is a response that is directed at the individual and is regarded as a hostile thrust so it is deeply resented. To make certain the child understands the difference, Dr. Glasser suggests a loving conclusion to the disciplinary session. This loving control enables a parent to express personal worth to the child.

You do affect others either for good or for bad, positively or negatively. That's one reason it's so important to maintain a proper perspective and a good attitude toward others. We play a role in the life of each person we touch. As a matter of fact we may well hold the key to one's future. The next story says it beautifully as it demonstrates both opportunity and responsibility.

PLEASE — THE KEY

An old man sat in a cathedral playing the organ. It was the end of the day and the setting sun shining through the beautiful stained-glass windows gave the old man an angelic appearance. He was a skilled organist playing sad and melancholy songs because he was being replaced by a younger man. At dusk, the young man rather brusquely stepped in the back door of the cathedral. The old man noted his entrance, removed the key from the organ, put it in his pocket and slowly made his way to the back of the cathedral. As the old man drew abreast of him, the young man extended his hand and said, "Please, the key." The old man took the key out of his pocket and gave it to the young man who hurriedly walked to the organ. He paused for a brief moment, sat down on the bench, inserted the key and started to play. The old man had played beautifully and skillfully but the young man played with sheer genius. Music such as the world had never heard came from the organ. It filled the cathedral, the town, and even the countryside. This was the world's first exposure to the music of Johann Sebastian Bach. The old man, with tears streaming down his cheeks, said, "Suppose, just suppose I had not given the master the key."

It's obvious the old man did give the young man the key. It's also obvious the young man made full use of that key. It's a sobering thought, because we hold the key to the future of others. We don't live alone. **Our actions and deeds affect other people, many of whom we will never know.** That's the reason our obligation and responsibility for doing the best we can with what we have goes beyond our own personal lives.

Zig and "Sugar Baby"

CHAPTER THREE
THE MOST IMPORTANT "OTHER" PERSON

ROMEO — AT HOME

Many years ago I had a friend who was constantly in hot water because of his extra marital affairs. He appeared to be a happy man about town, but in reality he was anything but happy. Our paths separated for several years and the next time we met, I saw a different man. He was happier, more relaxed, and considerably more successful. So, I asked the obvious question, "What happened?" Enthusiastically he told me about finding a beautiful but lonely and misunderstood little housewife who was married to a heel. He explained that he had "moved in," was avidly courting her and that things had never been better. Thoroughly enjoying my consternation, my friend finally explained that the girl was his wife of 15 years. Substantially relieved — but more puzzled than ever — I asked him to "explain" himself. His explanation was simple but it offers the solution to most marital problems today. He said, "You know, Zig, I discovered that if I was as thoughtful and considerate of my wife, that if I courted her as carefully, said and did as many nice things for her as I did the "other" girls, that I had both pleasure and happiness at home. He told me that the greatest thing in the world was to have someone exclusively for your own — to love, to trust, and to honor. To that I say, "Amen!"

That kind of love is demonstrated by a total, "blind" loyalty to your mate. I'm convinced that happiness, security, peace of mind, etc. is wrapped up in loyalty. My wife and I both feel that we would be completely miserable if there was any doubt about our total loyalty to each other.

Unfortunately, many husbands and wives are pleasant and considerate to associates, clerks, secretaries, postmen, and even strangers, but are often either short and abrupt with each other or take each other for granted. The question is, "Why?" I will attempt to answer the question and offer some suggestions based on the 31 wonderful years I've had with the beautiful woman God gave me to love and honor. She is the most important person in my life and we grow closer by the day. I mention this because I'm hopeful the thoughts I express will be meaningful to you and yours. It's difficult to believe that any responsible married person can be fully effective or happy without a harmonious relationship with his or her mate.

Since the marriage is the family and the family is the foundation of this country, this chapter might well be the most important one in this book. [Dr. Paul Pspense, Time Magazine, December 29, 1970 said, "It can be demonstrated from history that no society has ever survived after its family life deteriorated."] The way you see your mate, treat your mate and get along with your mate is tremendously important. As a matter of fact, this relationship has more to do with your success and happiness than your relationship with any other person. How do you see your husband or your wife? How do you see each other as a couple? Or as a family?

I don't pretend to be an expert, but from experience and observation I offer three possible reasons for most marital difficulties. First, most husbands and wives, over a period of time grow accustomed to having their mate around. They assume everything is fine and that the mate will always be with them. Obviously, they assume too much, because four marriages in ten end in divorce, while many other marriages exist in name only. Second, the environment in which we live feeds the problem. Many of our associates consider it corny or mushy to show genuine love and affection for their mates. Comedians and would-be comedians have a field day lambasting the institution of marriage, with special jabs reserved for the wife and mother-in-law. Third, the changing morality, which recognizes free love, trial marriages, extra-marital affairs, wife swapping and the shedding of a mate for no reason other than boredom, breeds insecurity and uncertainty. There is even a movement underway to give women the right to maintain their maiden name after marriage so if the couple is later divorced, the wife won't have so much "trouble" changing her bank accounts, credit cards, etc. Talk about planning for failure.

WHAT IS THIS THING CALLED LOVE?

Since love is the strong foundation upon which any good marriage is built, let's look at love for a moment. Poets write about it, singers sing about it, everybody talks about it and virtually everyone has his own idea of what it's all about. This, obviously, includes me. The thirteenth chapter of First Corinthians gives a beautiful picture of what genuine love is really like. The Book of Proverbs teaches that love covers all sins. Jesus Christ said, "First love the Lord thy God, second love thy neighbor as thyself." John 3:16 describes love at its infinite best. Psychologists and marriage counselors maintain that the most important thing a father can do for his children is to love their mother and the most important thing a mother can do for her children is to love their father. They stress that children are much more secure if they know their parents love each other even if that love is not extended to the child. This way the child feels mother and dad will be together to provide security and he will never have to face the trauma of having to choose between mother and dad.

In our generation, we see love and sex mentioned in the same breath so often, many think they are synonymous. Obviously, this isn't so. Love is a completely unselfish feeling you have for another. Lust is totally selfish. Not once does the Bible put them together, but modern man, for selfish and commercial reasons constantly makes the association.

Despite the universal recognition of the importance of love, [by theologians, scientists and the man on the street] there is very little information on the subject of how to perpetuate a marriage which God proclaimed as the ideal man-woman relationship. Many couples who proclaim their undying love at the time they exchange their wedding vows are soon at each other's throat. I'm personally convinced that many times their love in the beginning was genuine. However, **love will die through neglect just as will a flower, tree or bush.**

I believe a happy marriage makes a better teacher, doctor, minister, coach, housewife, truck driver, secretary, salesman, etc. I also believe an unhappy marriage hampers the full efforts and productivity of each member of that marriage. George W.

Crane, the imminent psychologist, says that love is nurtured by acts and expressions of love. I agree, like sterling silver, love will tarnish unless it is polished with daily applications of interest, involvement and expressions of love. Unfortunately, many couples take each other so much for granted that boredom, the greatest marriage killer of all, results.

HERE IS REAL LOVE

Dr. Crane explains that many times couples, after they reach an impasse, fall in love again. If they are morally responsible people who wish to save their marriage, they undertake a new courtship process as a feeling of responsibility. He points out that the responsibility of physically expressing and showing love will literally bring love into, or back into their lives. Dr. Crane is telling us, if we feed our love often enough, firmly enough, and long enough, the positive aspects of our marriage will grow stronger, while the negative aspects get weaker. I can enthusiastically Amen that statement. We will emphasize in later Segments, William James' statement, "You do not sing because you are happy, you are happy because you sing." He asserts that physical expressions feed mental acceptance. Dale Carnegie says, "act enthusiastic and you will be enthusiastic." What I am really getting at is this: act like you are in love and the first thing you know, you will be in love.

My first exposure to married life at its most beautiful best came about thirteen years ago in the front yard of my minister brother's home. Jewell, his childhood sweetheart who had been his wife for 33 years, was returning from a ten-day trip. She had been to Michigan City, Indiana to be with their daughter to help with her first baby. This was the first time my brother and his wife had ever been separated. When Jewell got out of the car and started toward the house, my brother, having heard the car, quickly walked out the door. They met in the front yard — warmly embraced each other — and cried like babies as they expressed their love for each other — and their determination to never again be separated.

I'll have to confess my eyes were leaking pretty badly too, as I viewed real love spontaneously expressing itself. What a shame this scene between a little country preacher and his helpmate of all those years could not have been captured on film and piped into every home in America. How beautiful it would have been to let everyone see what love — real love — is all about. Love that had been born in adolescence, nurtured in young adulthood, matured in middle age, and reached its full and beautiful zenith in the golden years of their life.

Real love is a growing and developing process that involves every emotion, problem, joy and triumph known to man. It's often harder than easy, more demanding than rewarding, more confining than freeing, and frequently involves more problems than pleasure. Such was the case with Huie and Jewell Ziglar. They started on a shoestring and often reached what appeared to be the end of their rope. When this happened — and happen it did — they just tied a knot at the end of that rope and held on. She bore his children, cooked and ironed for the family and supported him with total faith and love in everything he did. He gave her his best — his all. He loved her, respected her, petted her, and courted her like the "Jewell" she is. Five boys and a girl required lots of money, lots of time, and lots of loving discipline, but together, through their unshakeable faith in Almighty God, they raised a beautiful family.

It would be an inspiration to anyone to watch the obvious love this devoted couple and the entire family has for each other. Never have I seen so much love or so much fun in one circle. No outside entertainment is necessary when the children and grandchildren get together. Huie takes the floor and even though I'm supposed to be the word merchant in the Ziglar clan, I'll be the first to admit when brother Huie starts telling us about "Old Bullet" his "talking" dog, I take a back seat. He entertains old and young alike by the hour. Through it all comes the light of love shining like a beacon beckoning a bewildered world to re-explore its value system. It urges us to assume both the opportunity and responsibility God intended when He sanctioned the family as a unit and proclaimed that it was not good for man to be alone.

You see you truly can get everything in life you want if you help enough other people get what they want. We all want to be genuinely loved as well as genuinely loving someone else, don't we!

THIS I BELIEVE

We often see or hear a love story advertised as "the most beautiful love story ever told". Obviously all of those claims are not true, but just as obviously, someone, somewhere at sometime *has* told or will tell the most beautiful love story ever *told*. However, I am totally convinced that the really beautiful love stories have never been and never will be — told. They have been and will continue to be — lived — and lived away from the printed page, the TV set and the silver screen. The reason is simple. No husband and wife, who deeply care for each other, who put their mate above anyone and everyone else, would dream of sharing the details of their life and love. There is simply no way that a sensitive, loving husband or wife would consider revealing, to even one other person, much less the world — the countless ways they have of sharing with each other and showing to each other the depth of that love they feel for each other. To do so would make an intimate, personal and beautiful relationship a community or public property which would degrade and make common a relationship which God Almighty has decreed as holy. True love is truly beautiful and very private.

By now, you know I'm one of these old-fashioned guys who believes in God, family and country, and those vows — for better or worse — are not just words. They are opportunities to stay and grow together. Just as fine steel can be truly tempered only with the use of heat and cold, and highways can only be made safe by adding hills, valleys, and curves, so must love and marriage be built in the crucible of trials and tribulations. That's why it's so distressing to see young men and women flaunt the laws of God with trial marriage or communal living. Or for that matter, calling it quits at the first straw in the windstorm before they have time to know each other, much less to love each other. They have no concept of what love between two responsible people is all about. They haven't learned to differentiate between love and sex — they can be in the same ball park or two entirely different ones. When sex is a manifestation of love and consumated in holy matrimony it is truly beautiful and as God intended. When it is an expression of lust, it is animalistic and selfish.

Love — contrary to what the poet and the TV writer might say

— is not an instant emotion. Personally, I was attracted to my beautiful redhead the first time I saw her. I *thought* I loved her during our courtship and early years of our marriage, but to be completely honest, I didn't know what real love was until after we had been married *over* 25 years. As we head for another wedding anniversay on November 26th, that love is still growing daily. She is far and above the most beautiful, most fascinating and exciting woman I have ever seen. When I have a choice of spending five minutes with her or doing something else, she wins every time.

This is not to imply we agree on everything because we don't. Nor does it mean there are no arguments because there are. It *does* mean there is *never* any maliciousness or bitterness in our differences. It does mean each is willing to admit a mistake and apologize if he or she is wrong. It means we enjoy each other, and love each other enough to put the other one first. We never part company or go to sleep without settling our differences and reaffirming our love. We're both grateful that God has let us spend enough years together to develop a relationship and discover what real love is all about. Our prayer is that God will permit us to have many more years together before we start our walk through eternity — together.

SOME SOUND ADVICE FOR HUSBAND AND WIFE

Let's look at a step-by-step procedure we can follow in building or rebuilding a happy marriage.

1.   Remember what you did before you married each other? Remember how you kept your best foot forward at all times, showed your best side, were on good behavior, were thoughtful, courteous, considerate and kind? That is an excellent procedure to make certain your marriage stays solid. Even if it is in trouble at the moment, you can bring it back to its original bloom.

2.   Read Mary Crowley's book, *Moments With Mary*. In this beautiful little book, the author points out that marriage is not a 50/50 proposition, it is a 100%/100% proposition. Husbands give 100% to the marriage and wives do the same.

3.   Start and end every day with a declaration of love for your mate, and during that day, if it's feasible, take three minutes

to telephone just to chat and express your love. After all, the best time to express love for your mate is *before* someone else does. Occasionally drop a "love letter" in the mail. It's a small investment with great rewards.

4.   Surprise him or her with an occasional gift or card. It obviously isn't the gift itself, but the thought behind the gift. As Sir Lancelot said, "The gift without the giver is bare." Another poet expressed it rather eloquently when he said, "Rings and jewels are not gifts, but apologies for gifts. The only true gift is a portion of one's self."

5.   Spend some QUALITY time together. Remember how you courted each other so avidly and how you had so much time just for courting before marriage? Repeat the process. Go for a walk or simply turn off the TV and make your mate feel as if he or she is the most important person in your life. He or she *is*, whether or not you realize it at this moment.

6.   Be a good listener. As a wise man once said, "Talking is sharing but listening is caring." Listen to the myriads of detail and small talk that make up your mate's day. Always remember that **duty makes us do things well, but love makes us do them beautifully.** I emphasize again that what occasionally starts out as duty turns into complete love. Interestingly enough, you will be amazed at how exciting some of those details can be.

7.   Don't make your husband or wife compete with the kids for your attention. Reserve time just for him or her.

8.   When you disagree, remember, you can disagree without being disagreeable. However, you must never go to sleep at night with unresolved differences. You will not sleep as well and these differences will settle into both of your subconscious minds and will be a recurring source of problems. You can be honest and yet sensitive to each other.

9.   Remember, our creator decreed that the man is the head of the household. Perhaps this should have been step number one. A woman is infinitely more secure knowing she has a *man* to handle the major decisions. I have seldom, if ever, seen a truly happy marriage where the husband was not the head of the family. If the husband then makes certain that Almighty God is his master, then it insures the relationship with certainty.

However, the husband must remember he can fill this role with love and kindness and yet with authority and firmness. God also teaches us that man is to honor his wife and to love her as his own body (Eph 5:28). Remember God took the woman from under Adam's arm, not from his head so she could rule over him, nor from his foot so he might trample her. He took her from his side, from a secure and protected position, so husband and wife could walk down life's highway together. For an in-depth look at the true concept of what this means, read *The Christian Family* by Larry Christanson.

10. Remember, you will often have to "bend over backwards" to please or understand your mate. That position might be a little uncomfortable but it makes it difficult for you or your marriage to fall on its face.

11. Try this recipe guaranteed to cook up a happy marriage.

1 Cup	— Love	5 Spoons	— Hope
2 Cups	— Loyalty	2 Spoons	— Tenderness
3 Cups	— Forgiveness	4 Quarts	— Faith
1 Cup	— Friendship	1 Barrel	— Laughter

Take Love and Loyalty and mix it thoroughly with Faith. Blend it with Tenderness, Kindness and Understanding. Add Friendship and Hope. Sprinkle abundantly with Laughter. Bake it with Sunshine. Serve generous helpings daily.

12. Use Ephesians 4:32 (And be ye kind one to another, tenderhearted, forgiving one another) as your daily guide.

13. Pray *together*. Evidence is substantial that husbands and wives who pray together on a daily basis have a divorce rate of less than 3%.

14. Remember, when the inevitable disagreement takes place, who makes the move to "make up" isn't important. However, the one who makes the move demonstrates the greater maturity and love.

HUSBANDS — COURT YOUR WIFE

1. Show her those little courtesies which mean so terribly much to a woman. Open her car door, hold her chair, walk on the traffic side when you are going down the sidewalk holding her

hand. Stand up when she re-enters the room or restaurant when you are out to dinner.

2.   Bring her the details of the good news or the exciting things that happen in your business life.

3.   When you attend a social function of any kind, stay with her. Remember how proud you were to be with her before you married. Show her the same attention now.

4.   Never, oh never, indulge in telling wife jokes. It is in exceptionally poor taste. After you have gotten a nervous laugh from someone else, your pleasure will be ended but the hurt will linger with her. And if you think for one minute you don't "pay" for those cute little "wife" jokes it just means that you don't understand the female of the species. Take the opposite approach and compliment her as you like to be complimented.

5.   Women are security conscious to a much larger degree than men. Remind her over and over she is not only wanted but needed and appreciated. Her feeling and security is greatly increased with the repeated use of the word — love. She *needs* and wants to hear it far more often than the average man is normally inclined to use it. Use it often and she will be happier and more secure which means a better marriage.

6.   Separate some of the jobs around the house. Women's lib notwithstanding, I believe our very natures demand certain separation of responsibilities. For example, when your wife returns from a shopping trip for groceries, if you are home, bring them in for her. The man should do the heavy work around the house and if you are there, you should take out the garbage for her, cut the grass and do any work which is essentially masculine. Just remember, the home is your castle but it is not a castle without a king, and no king is complete without his queen. Your wife will be delighted to be your queen if you treat her like one.

WIVES — COURT YOUR HUSBAND

1.   Start every day by telling him how much you love him and end every day the same way.

2.   Remember that the natures of men and women are considerably different. A man needs his ego fed regularly,

especially if he is the breadwinner. A simple assured expression of your confidence in him and the way he is doing things means much. This is especially so when the one he loves praises him for what he does. Make your husband know *what he does*, is important and that *he* is important. Repeatedly tell him that you are proud of him and what he does.

3.   If you are not employed outside the home, stop a few minutes before he is scheduled to arrive. Take a quick bath, slip into a clean dress and add a touch of cologne or perfume. Devote a few minutes to catching your breath so you will be refreshed when you see him.

4.   On occasion, bake him a cake or prepare a special dish you know he enjoys. Whether you or the kids enjoy the dish or not is unimportant. Do it just because you love him. If you send him to work with a "cold" lunch, be sure to include a "warm" note to warm it up.

5.   Be agreeable and develop a good disposition [the same applies to you, husband]. Solomon, the wisest man who ever lived, said, "It is better to dwell in the wilderness than with a contenious woman." In modern society, a man who has an angry of contentious woman for a wife will make her pay for it. He spends unnecessary time on his job and wastes time at the local bar with male and unfortunately female friends.

6.   You do the jobs that are essentially feminine. I'm convinced that a contributing factor in many of our problems today is the lack of a clear distinction between male and female. Men should look, dress, act, think and talk like men. Woman should look, dress, act, think, and talk like women. Any time we have to pause and wonder if it's male or female, that's sad. I believe under normal conditions the wife should wash dishes and make up the beds. Obviously there are circumstances which dictate that the loving husband dig in and help. Generally speaking, though, I don't believe it is a good idea for a little boy to see Dad in the dish pan, nor do I believe little girls should consistently see Mom assuming a male role and performing masculine chores. As my mother often said, **"Your children more attention pay, to what you do than to what you say."** Let the little boy see the male role and he will grow up to be a man with a natural affection for the opposite sex. Let the little girl see

the role of the female and she will grow up to be a woman with the natural affection for the opposite sex.

7.   Do you want to be a queen? Treat your husband like a king and you will give him no choice, because no king is complete until he has his queen.

I repeat, marriage is not a 50/50 proposition. It is 100%/100%. I'm convinced it is impossible to make your mate happy and not benefit tremendously yourself.

Again, I wish to emphasize **you can get everything in life you want, if you help enough other people get what they want.** This is especially true between husbands and wives. Try it, you'll love it. If you really try it, you fully qualify to take that next step up the stairway. Take a good look. There you are with the biggest smile of your life on your face, ready to take step number two because you are making the most important person in your life truly happy.

NOTES AND IDEAS

This second step is truly the fun step because you discover that life is more fun when you're working, playing and living with a mate who truly cares about what happens in every area of your life.

SEGMENT FOUR

GOALS

PURPOSE: I. TO SELL YOU ON THE IMPORTANCE OF GOALS IN YOUR PERSONAL AND PROFESSIONAL LIFE.

    II. TO EXPLAIN WHY MOST PEOPLE NEVER SET GOALS.

    III. TO IDENTIFY THE KINDS OF GOALS YOU SHOULD HAVE.

    IV. TO ELABORATE ON THE CHARACTERISTICS OF YOUR GOALS.

    V. TO SPELL OUT IN SPECIFIC DETAIL HOW TO SET YOUR GOALS.

    VI. TO GIVE A DETAILED PROCEDURE ON HOW TO REACH YOUR GOALS.

ADDITIONAL READING MATERIAL

David Schwartz — *THE MAGIC OF THINKING BIG*

Dale Carnegie — *HOW TO STOP WORRYING AND START LIVING*

Robert Schuller — *MOVE AHEAD WITH POSSIBILITY THINKING*

Marie Beynon Ray — *THE IMPORTANCE OF FEELING INFERIOR*

Frank J. Bruno — *THINK YOURSELF THIN*

CHAPTER ONE
ARE GOALS REALLY NECESSARY?

THE TARGET YOU CAN'T SEE

To many people the name Howard Hill rings a bell. He was probably the greatest archer who ever drew a bowstring. He was so accurate he killed a bull elephant, a Bengal tiger, and a Cape buffalo with a bow and arrow. In newsreels I have seen Howard Hill repeatedly hit the target dead center. After sending the first arrow to the center of the bull's eye, he would then literally split that arrow with his next shot.

When I make this next statement, your eyebrows will probably shoot up about six inches. You, if your health is good, could out shoot Howard Hill on the best day he ever had. You could hit the bull's eye with more consistency than Howard Hill and you might never have shot anything other than a child's bow and arrow. Obviously, it would have been necessary to blindfold Howard Hill and turn him around a time or two. Then I guarantee that you would have hit the bull's eye more consistently than he.

I hope you think the analogy is ridiculous and that you are saying, "Of course I could; how could a man hit a target he couldn't see?" That's a good question. Now here's another one for you. If Howard Hill couldn't hit a target he couldn't see, how can you hit a target you don't have?

Do you have a target or goal? You must have a goal because **it's just as difficult to reach a destination you don't have, as it is to come back from a place you've never been.**

Unless you have definite, precise, clearly set goals, you are not going to realize the maximum potential that lies within you. You'll never make it as a "wandering generality." You must be a "meaningful specific." What about you and your goals? Are they clearly in focus, or still pretty fuzzy?

ACTIVITY — OR ACCOMPLISHMENT

A man or a woman without a goal is like a ship without a rudder. Each will drift and not drive. Each will end up on the beaches of despair, defeat and despondency. John Henry Fabre, the great French naturalist, conducted a most unusual experiment with some Processionary Caterpillars. These caterpillars blindly follow the one in front of them. Hence, the name. Fabre carefully arranged them in a circle around the rim of a flower pot, so that the lead caterpillar actually touched the last one, making a complete circle. In the center of the flower pot he put pine needles, which is food for the Processionary Caterpillar. The caterpillars started around this circular flower pot. Around and around they went, hour after hour, day after day, night after night. For seven full days and seven full nights they went around the flower pot. Finally, they dropped dead of starvation and exhaustion. With an abundance of food less than six inches away, they literally starved to death, because *they confused activity with accomplishment.*

Many people make the same mistake and as a result reap only a small fraction of the harvest life has to offer. Despite the fact that untold wealth lies within reach, they acquire very little of it because they blindly, without question, follow the crowd in a circle to nowhere. They follow methods and procedures for no other reason than, "It's always been done that way."

In this respect, they are as bad as "this old boy down home." His wife sent him to the store for a ham. After he bought it, she asked him why he didn't have the butcher cut off the end of the ham. "This old boy" asked his wife why she wanted the end cut off. She replied that her mother had always done it that way and that was reason enough for her. Since the wife's mother was visiting, they asked her why she always cut off the end of the ham. Mother replied that this was the way her mother did it; Mother, daughter and "this old boy" then decided to call grandmother and solve this three-generation mystery. Grandmother promptly replied that she cut the end of the ham off because her roaster was too small to cook it in one piece. Now grandma had a reason for her actions, what about you?

THIS WAY TO FAILURE

Do most people have goals? Apparently not. You can stop a hundred young men on any street and ask each one, "What are you doing that will absolutely guarantee your failure in life?" After recovering from their initial shock, each one will probably say, "What do you mean, what am I doing to guarantee my failure? I'm working for success." Tragically, most of them think they are. Almost every one believes he will make it, but the odds are against him. I say this with emphasis because, if we follow those hundred young men until they are sixty-five years old, only five of them will have achieved financial security. Only one will be wealthy. Odds are better than that in Las Vegas.

I can't believe that failure is caused by lack of opportunity, because America offers many unique opportunities. For example, several years ago a wealthy prisoner was released from the Federal Prison in Atlanta, Georgia. He had a built-in [pun intended] Loser's Limp. Nevertheless, he accumulated a small fortune by operating a tailor shop in prison. After his big mistake had landed him in prison, he was determined not to make a bigger one by "serving time". He made "time" serve him. In a real sense you have the same choice.

Do the people in life who don't succeed actually plan to fail? I don't think so. The problem is they don't plan anything. Since goals are so important, why do only 3% of the American people specifically commit their goals to paper? There are four basic reasons. First, they have never been "sold". Told yes — sold no. Second, they don't know how. Third, they fear they won't reach the goals they set and will be embarrassed. Fourth, poor self-image. They don't think they deserve the good things life has to offer so why bother to write down what you want since you don't "deserve" to have it, which means [in their mind] that they won't have it. Now get ready for a strong statement. The philosophy *and* procedures outlined in this book *will* take care of all four of these reasons *if* you really dig in.

Throughout this Segment I will be "selling" you on goals and telling you exactly how to set them. The second Segment, and for that matter the entire book, dealt with self image so you should already like yourself better. You have *all* the steps and

150

procedures you need to build your image to the point that you know you deserve the good things life has to offer, so it's now up to you on that one.

This brings us to fear, so let's rationally look at that one. If fear is your problem, it simply means that you do not want to be wrong in front of your friends so you do not make a commitment. By the way you are "half right" in this approach, you should never share your goals with anyone unless you *know* they not only believe you can reach these goals but they want you to reach them. Others decide not to commit their goals to paper so if they don't quite "make it", they will have the built in explanation that they didn't really fail because they never set those goals. This is a safer and even a "no risk" approach for them.

Using that line of reasoning, I could point out that it would be "safer" for a ship to stay in the harbor, "safer" for a plane to stay on the ground and "safer" for a house to stay empty because a ship encounters "risk" when it leaves the harbor, a plane encounters "risk" when it leaves the ground and a house invites "risk" when someone moves in. *But* the ship would collect barnacles and become unseaworthy even faster in the harbor. The plane will rust much faster on the ground and the house would deteriorate much faster standing empty. Yes, there is danger in setting goals but the risk is infinitely greater when you don't set goals. The reason is simple. Just as ships are built to sail the seas, planes to fly the heavens, and houses for living, so is man created for a purpose. *You* are here for a reason. That purpose is to get everything out of you that is humanly possible so you can make your contributions to mankind. Goals enable you to do more for yourself and others, too.

Since the first and most obvious step is to "sell" you on doing something *now* about *your* goals, I'm flat gonna do exactly that. [In all fairness I feel I should issue this "warning" since you are obviously interested in "buying" or you wouldn't have gotten this far in the book.]

LET'S GO TO ACAPULCO TOMORROW — EVERY DAY

Suppose you were to receive a phone call tomorrow from an old and respected friend who enthusiastically says, "Friend, I have good news for you. You can take a three-day trip to Acapulco with our group and it won't cost you a dime. We leave tomorrow morning at 8:00 a.m. and we have room for two more people. The boss is flying us down in his private jet and we will all stay at his Villa right on the beach." Your first reaction might be, "That would be wonderful, but I have so much to do, I don't see how I could get ready and do the things I need to do before I could go anywhere."

Before you can answer, your good wife tells you she has an idea and suggests you tell your friend you will call him back in a few minutes. The minute you hang up you and your wife start thinking and planning. First you ask, "What do I have to do?" Out comes pen and paper, and you commit to writing all the things you must get done. Next, you list them in order of their importance. Finally, you delegate some of the responsibilities to others. Then you call the friend back and say, "Hey, you know, I've been checking the schedule, and we can make that trip after all."

I'll guarantee that you would do more in the next 24 hours than you normally do in several days. Wouldn't you?

Since you had to say yes to that question, let me ask you another one. Why don't you go to Acapulco tomorrow — everyday? Why don't you list the things you need to do during the next *three* days. Then act as if you only had one day to do three days work. As my boss in the grocery store used to say, "that will force you to put your thinking cap on". You will use your mental capacity to think, plan and delegate before you start working. This will enable you to accomplish so much more, that you can literally go to Acapulco — or anywhere else you wish to go — in the tomorrows of your life. Reason: You will have changed from a "wandering generality" to a "meaningful specific". Your life will have direction.

People often complain about lack of time when the lack of direction is the real problem. Many "experts" say we should be arrested for murder when we kill time. Close examination, however, makes it obvious that killing time is not murder — it's suicide. Time can be an ally or an enemy. What it becomes depends entirely upon you, your goals and your determination to use every available minute.

NO GOALS — NO GAME

Let me illustrate the importance of goals by looking at a scene of the deciding game of a basketball championship. The teams have taken their warm-up shots and are physically ready for the game. The adrenalin is flowing and it's obvious the players feel the excitement that goes with a championship game. They return to their dressing rooms and the coaches give them the last "shot in the arm" before action begins. "This is it, fellows. It's now or never. We win or lose it all tonight. Nobody remembers the best man at a wedding, and nobody remembers who came in second. The whole season is tonight.

The players respond. They're so charged up they almost tear the doors off the hinges as they rush back to the court. As they get to the court they stop short and, in complete confusion which gives way to frustration and anger, they point out that the goals have been removed. They angrily demand to know how they can play a game without the goals. They know that without goals, they would never know the score, never know whether they hit or missed, never know how they stacked up against competition and never know whether they were on or off the target. As a matter of fact, they wouldn't even attempt to play the basketball game without the goals. Those basketball goals are important, aren't they? What about you? Are you attempting to play the game of life without goals? If you are, what's the score?

LIFE IS VALUABLE

An interesting phenomenon takes place in the rest homes and the homes for the aged around our country. The death rate declines dramatically before holidays and special days, such as wedding anniversaries and birthdays. Many of the people set a goal to live for one more Christmas, one more anniversary, one more Fourth of July, etc. Immediately after the event, when the goal has been reached, the will to live declines and the death rate shoots upward. Yes, life is valuable and is sustained only so long as life has something valuable as its object. Goals of life are important and virtually everyone knows this. However, by choice — or is it indifference — the average man on the street continues to meander through life following the lines of least resistance as "wandering generalities" rather than as "meaningful specifics."

The late Maxwell Maltz wrote a book, which I don't recommend you read; I suggest you *devour* it. Make it a part of you and your way of life. The title is *Psycho-Cybernetics*. That's an awesome title, but in reality it's a simple, beautifully written and easily understood book. Maltz says man is functionally like a bicycle. Unless he's moving onward and upward towards an objective — a goal — he's going to falter and fall.

A GOAL CAN BE A WINNING HORSE

Julie loved her horse, Irish, but at the moment she was mad, hurt, disappointed, frustrated, tired, discouraged and heartsick. For weeks she had cleaned, groomed, worked and trained that horse for the big show. She had gotten up at 3:00 a.m. on the big day and had groomed Irish down to the final detail. Irish's mane was perfectly braided, her tail was a work of art, her coat glistened like burnished steel and her hooves sparkled in the sunlight. The bridle, halter and saddle had been cleaned and polished and Julie, impeccably attired, looked like the little doll she is as she entered the arena for the big event. So what happened? Nothing, absolutely nothing. Irish, who was supposed to be a jumper wouldn't jump. As a matter of fact, she wouldn't even hop. Hundreds of hours of hard work and the dream of a ribbon all ended for Julie when her horse refused the first jump three times and was disqualified.

As I point out in another section, when you're frustrated, you can either wring your hands and lose what you have or roll up your sleeves and get what you want. Julie Ziglar, age 16 and weighing in at less than 100 lbs., decided to roll up her sleeves and get what she wanted — a horse that was a winner. She set a price on Irish, ran an ad in the paper, resisted bargaining and "horse trade" talk until she got her price. She put her money into a savings account and started her search for another dream horse. She visited the local stables, attended local shows, read every available horse publication until finally she found Butter Rum, a beautiful but "green" two-year-old thoroughbred gelding. It was an unadulterated case of love at first sight on the part of Julie and

Butter Rum — but there was a small problem. Butter Rum cost considerably more than Julie had gotten for Irish and she stubbornly refused to let mom and dad finance the difference. This situation only slowed her to a fast run however, because Julie is a girl who believes if you want something you must do something. She also believed the basic goal-reaching principle that you **go as far as you can see and when you get there, you will always be able to see further.** Using her money from Irish as the down payment and working out a payment plan for the balance, she bought Butter Rum. Then she got a job to earn money to make the payments. She also sought and personally paid for professional help in training Butter Rum. She worked him — and herself —hard and often. Soon Butter Rum and Julie began winning ribbons. Julie's wall is covered by ribbons of *all* colors, and she has been offered four-and-a-half times as much for Butter Rum as she paid for him.

The exciting thing about this story, aside from the fact it is about my little girl, is it tells us again that if we want something badly enough, we must make it our definite goal. When we go after it as if we can't fail, many things will happen to help make certain we won't.

HARNESS THE POWER

Several years ago it was my privilege to fly over Niagara Falls for the first time. As we approached the Falls, the captain of the aircraft announced over the intercom, "Ladies and Gentlemen, on your left is Niagara Falls. Those of you who have never seen the Falls from the air should move to the left side of the aircraft. It's an awesome sight." I took his advice and even though the Falls were several miles away, I could see and feel the enormous power of Niagara as I viewed the spray rising hundreds of feet into the air.

As I watched the spray and looked at those Falls, a thought ran through my mind. For thousands of years untold trillions of tons of water had gone over that 180 foot drop and drifted into a comparative nothingness. Then one day, a man — with a plan — harnessed a portion of that awesome power. He directed a portion of the falling water at a specific target and created billions of kilowatt hours of electricity to turn the wheels of industry. Thousands of homes have been lighted, tons of food harvested, numerous products manufactured and distributed. Jobs have been created, children educated, roads built, buildings and hospitals constructed as a result of this new power source. The list of benefits is almost endless, and it all came about because a man with a plan took part of the power of Niagara and directed it toward a specific target or goal. That's what I'm asking you to do.

GOALS? FOR WHOM?

The dictionary says a goal is an aim or purpose. It's a plan. Something you expect to do. Without any reservation, I'm going to say that whoever you are, wherever you are and whatever you do, you should have goals. J. C. Penney expressed it beautifully when he said, "Give me a stock clerk with a goal and I will give you a man who will make history. Give me a man without a goal, and I will give you a stock clerk." Mothers should have goals. Sales people should have goals. Housewives, students, laborers, doctors and athletes should have goals. You might not, like Niagara, light up a city, but **with definite goals you release your own power, and things start happening**.

To stress the necessity of goals, can you imagine Sir Edmund Hillary, the first man to climb Mount Everest, explaining how he was able to accomplish that feat? Suppose he explained he was *just out walking around one day when he happened to find himself at the top of the tallest mountain in the world.* Or the Chairman of the Board of General Motors explaining that he got his position because he just kept showing up for work and they just kept promoting him until one day he was Chairman of the Board. Ridiculous — of course — but no more ridiculous than your thinking *you* can accomplish anything significant without specific goals.

WHAT "KIND" OF GOALS

There are seven different kinds of goals: physical, financial, spiritual, career, family, mental, and social. Throughout the book I weave all the goals into the examples, but space limitations demand that I concentrate on only part of them. Since my

156

philosophy could, with some justification, be described as idealistic, you might be a little surprised at the space I give to financial goals. You shouldn't be. Money, assuming it is legitimately earned, is a yardstick that simply measures the service you have rendered. You are obligated to earn more than you need because in so doing you create job opportunities for those less talented than you. Many people, misquoting the Scriptures, as is frequently done, say money is the root of all evil. Not so, **the love of money is the root of all evil.**

Having said these things, let me now stress that God's first commandment is that we have no other God before Jehovah God — that includes money. Solomon, the wisest man who ever lived, tells us in Ecclesiastes, "he who seeks silver will never be satisfied with silver." Meaning simply, if money becomes our God, it will never satisfy us regardless of how much we have. We know this is true because in the last two years five billionaires have died and all five were striving at the end, to earn more money. Someone asked this old boy down home how much money he thought Howard Hughes left and this old boy said, "He left it all." If someone asks you how much you are going to leave, just tell them "the same as Howard Hughes."

Money, however, is a marvelous measurement of service rendered. Regardless of your profession, almost without exception, the more service you render, the greater the financial rewards. One thing you have already discovered, when money is needed, there are very few substitutes. Every thing else being equal, I can assure you it is better to have it than not to have it. Besides, it is beautifully colored and goes with anything.

THE STEEL DREAMER

For centuries "word merchants" have sold the idea of having dreams. Just a few years ago Martin Luther King gave those words added significance when in his famous "mountain top" talk he stirred America's conscience and set a million feet to marching when he exclaimed, "I have a dream." Another man who had a dream and saw it come true is a short, cigar smoking, bundle of energy, whose well-spring of love never runs dry. His name is Dexter Yager, a man with deep family ties and strong religious convictions.

Dexter turned down a scholarship to Yale because he was in a hurry to get started on the road to success. His free enterprise dream started with a jug of Kool-Aid which rapidly grew to a lucrative pop stand. This early taste of success completely sold him on the free enterprise system. Dexter was also quite successful as a car salesman, as an inside salesman for Sears and other ventures, including a stint with a construction company. However, Dexter and his devoted helpmate, Birdie, never really "hit their stride" until a series of circumstances, which they know were God directed, led them to join the Amway Corporation of Ada, Michigan on November 1, 1965. Their growth and success has been steady and even spectacular [I did not say easy]. Today they rate near the top with the rank of Triple Diamond Distributor.

Long hours of hard work with a tremendous amount of enthusiasm enabled the Yagers to realize their dream which had been stymied by broken promises in the past. Today the Yager organization is world wide and world famous and numbers in the tens of thousands. Dexter's Amway success, however, is not due just to what he did after he joined Amway. His success is due to the years of foundation building on the pillars of honesty, character, love, loyalty, integrity, and faith in Almighty God. His success had long been a reality in his own mind and his dream came into being when preparation met opportunity. It became a reality as Dexter knew it would because he had given birth to his dream as a youngster. Then he fed and watered it as a young adult until it developed and hardened in manhood.

In the success process the Yagers gave the business and life their all [effort, dedication, etc.] so it was inevitable that they would get a lot of things [financial security, beautiful 11,000 foot home with seven bedrooms, swimming pool, big cars, motor home, diamond rings, etc.] Birdie sums up their commitment and success this way. "When you set a limit on what you are going to give and do, you set a ceiling on how high you are going and what you will have when you get there." Since Dexter set no limits on what he was going to give, he has removed the ceilings on what he is getting.

It might not be original with Dexter, but if he didn't coin the phrase, "Don't let anyone steal your dream" he has come to be closely identified with it as he challenges audiences all over the country to be careful of their associating with other people so that none could or would steal their dreams. As for Dexter and Birdie Yager, they long ago set their own dreams in steel.

This philosophy will work for you as it did for Dexter Yager. His story in so many ways epitomizes the philosophy of *SEE YOU AT THE TOP* because Dexter is getting *everything* our artist identified on the Stairway to the Top pages. He made it to the top because he dealt with the physical, mental and spiritual man. He's staying there because he built on a solid foundation and because he recognizes the space limitations at the top [not enough room to sit down]. He's getting everything in life he wants because he's helping hundreds of other people get what they want. More importantly, he's closer than ever to his beautiful wife and their seven happy, healthy, well adjusted kids. That's Dexter Yager, the "steel" dreamer.

By now you should be "sold" on doing something about your own goals so let's move forward and identify the characteristics of goals, explain how to set them and how to reach them.

NOTES AND IDEAS

CHAPTER TWO

CHARACTERISTICS OF GOALS

NUMBER ONE — GOALS MUST BE BIG

When you set goals, something inside of you starts saying, "Let's go, let's go," and ceilings start to move up. In the following Segments and chapters we will look at people from virtually all walks of life who have succeeded. Each one had goals and did some fabulous things. I want you to read their stories carefully, because in each example I'm going to be speaking directly to you. You need to interpolate and put yourself in their shoes. By adopting their dedication to reach your goals, some wonderful things can and will happen to you — and that's a promise.

In order for goals to be effective they need to be big, because it takes a big goal to create the excitement necessary for accomplishment. There's no excitement in mediocrity or in keeping up with anybody. There is no excitement in making a house payment, a car payment or just getting along. The excitement comes when you do your best, which you can do only with the proper goals.

It's an established fact in the sports world that an athlete will perform better against tough competition than against mediocre competition. The golfer, tennis player, football player, fighter, etc., will have a tendency to loaf against mediocre or poor competition. This is one of the reasons so many "upsets" occur in the world of sports. The same is true in politics. Now, if the goal, which is really the "competition," you have set for yourself is big [tough], it will bring out your best effort. It will create excitement and it's that excitement which permits you to perform at your best and to reach your goals.

When you are at your best and do your best, you can lay down at night and truthfully say, "Today I did my very best." The result will be a rewarding and satisfying night of sleep, because you recognize you're doing your best toward reaching that big goal. It's exciting to know that as long as you're reaching for the stars [your big goal] you won't end up with a handful of mud. You need to see life as something big and exciting and your goals as big ones. A wise man once said, "**Make no small plans for they have no capacity to stir men's souls.**"

The way you see life will largely determine what you get out of it. Take a bar of iron and use it for a door stop and it's worth a dollar. Manufacture horseshoes from that iron and they're worth about fifty dollars. Take the same bar of iron, remove the impurities, refine it into fine steel and manufacture it into mainsprings for precision watches and it's worth a quarter of a million dollars.

The way you see the bar of iron makes the difference, and the way you see yourself and your future will also make the difference. You need to have a big goal. I don't care whether you are a beautician, housewife, athlete, student, salesperson or businessman, you must have a big goal. Obviously, the size of goals will vary with individuals. Booker T. Washington said, "You measure the size of the accomplishment by the obstacles you have to overcome to reach your goals." I agree with him, for, "Of whom much is given, much shall be required."

GUARANTEED "WORST IN TOWN"

Next door to the grocery store where I worked as a boy was a combination coffee shop and peanut stand. The owner was simply known as "Uncle Joe." The smell of roasting coffee and peanuts was very tantalizing and attracted a crowd virtually every time Uncle Joe was doing any roasting. He roasted the peanuts in a coal-burning, hand-turned roaster. When he finished roasting some peanuts, he would dump them into a large cardboard box. He filled bags with those peanuts. At that time, they sold for a nickel a bag. After he filled a bag, he would remove two peanuts and place them in a small box. When he had completed the job of filling the bags, he would always have several bags left in this "bonus box." Uncle Joe was born a poor man. He lived a poor man's life and he died a poor man. He thought a lot about peanuts, but peanuts were not his problem.

I shall never forget a sign I saw as I entered Columbia, South Carolina, to attend the University of South Carolina. The sign simply said, "Cromer's Peanuts — Guaranteed Worst in Town." Curiosity demanded I inquire about it. I was told when Mr. Cromer started his business, he had a small sign painted with that message on it. People grinned when they saw the sign, but they bought the peanuts. Later, he added the slogan to the bags of peanuts. People smiled even more broadly, but they bought the peanuts. As time passed, Mr. Cromer employed a large number of boys to sell peanuts on the streets of Columbia on a commission basis. His signs got bigger and his business got better. Soon, he acquired rights to sell his peanuts at the South Carolina State Fair and at the local athletic events, including the games played at the University of South Carolina. His fame and business grew. Today, Mr. Cromer is a successful and wealthy man. He too, thought a lot about peanuts.

Here are two men who sold the same product in essentially the same type area. One was poor and remained that way. The other was poor but wasn't content to stay that way. They sold the same product, but their individual goals for that product were seen in a different light.

IT'S NOT THE JOB

It doesn't make any difference what your occupation might be. Whether you are a doctor, businessman, lawyer, salesperson, minister, etc., there are wealthy people who do whatever it is you do for your living. I know some wealthy people who run service stations and I know some service station owners who are broke. There are wealthy people who sell and there are poor people who sell. There are rich educators and there are poor educators. There are rich lawyers and there are poor lawyers. The list is endless. The opportunity lies with the individual first and then with the occupation. The occupation provides the opportunity only if the individual does his part.

Whatever it is you do, there are many people in the same profession who are making significant contributions to that profession and are making a lot of money as a result. **It's not the occupation or profession that makes you succeed or fail, it's how you see yourself and your occupation.** Big goals *are* necessary, "You must see it big before you can make it big."

NUMBER TWO — GOALS MUST BE LONG-RANGE

Without long-range goals, you are likely to be overcome by short-range frustrations. The reason is simple. Everybody is not as interested in your success as you are. You might occasionally feel that some people are standing in the way and deliberately slowing your progress, but in reality the biggest person standing in your way is you. **Others can stop you temporarily — you are the only one who can do it permanently.**

Occasionally, circumstances arise that are beyond your control. If you don't have long-range goals, then temporary obstacles can be needlessly frustrating. Family problems, sickness, an automobile accident or circumstances over which you have no control can be big obstacles, but they need not be. In a later chapter, I will teach you how to react positively to the negative as well as to positive situations. You will learn that a setback — regardless of the severity — can be a stepping stone and not a stumbling block. When you have that long-range goal it's easier. Why? Because you **go as far as you can see and when you get there you will always be able to see farther.** Thought: If you wait until all the lights are "green" before you leave home, you'll never get started *on* your trip to the top.

OVERCOMING OBSTACLES

As I write these words, I am aboard a DC-10 from Los Angeles to Dallas. Our scheduled departure was 5:15 p.m. Unavoidable delays held us until 6:03 p.m. When we left the Los Angeles airport, we were headed for Dallas, but within 20 minutes the situation had changed. The cross-wind currents were slightly different from those predicted before takeoff, so we were slightly off course. The captain made a slight adjustment and we were again headed for Dallas. My point is this: when we were a little off our course, the captain didn't turn the plane around and return to Los Angeles to make a fresh start. Even so, **as you head toward your goals, be prepared to make some slight adjustments in your course.**

As you set your long-range goals, let me urge you not to attempt to overcome all the obstacles before you start. Nobody, but nobody would ever attempt anything of significance if all obstacles had to be removed before they started. If you had called the Chief of Police before you left for work this morning to inquire if all the lights were on green, he would have thought you were "under the influence." You know perfectly well you deal with the lights one at a time until you arrive at your destination. As you deal with obstacles of any kind in the same manner, one day you will arrive at your destination. Yes, you just go as far as you can see, and when you get there you can always see farther.

NUMBER THREE — GOALS MUST BE DAILY

If you don't have daily objectives, you qualify as a dreamer. Dreamers are fine, provided they build a foundation under their dreams by working daily towards realizing them. The late Charlie Cullen expressed this idea in a meaningful way. He said, "The opportunity for greatness does not come cascading down like a torrential Niagara Falls, but rather it comes slowly, one drop at a time."

Frequently, the difference between the great and the near great is the realization that **if you expect to make it big, you must work toward your objectives every day.** The weight lifter knows that if he is going to accomplish a big objective, he must strengthen and expand his muscles every day. The parent who would raise a disciplined, loving child of whom he can be truly proud knows that character and faith are built by daily injections of teaching by example. If the "more" way of life is our purpose, then our daily objective should include an honest effort to improve on yesterday. If we expect to change and improve our circumstances then we must change and improve ourselves — because we must *be* something before we can *do* anything.

The daily objectives are the best indicators — and the best builders — of character. This is where dedication, discipline and determination enter the picture. Here we take the glamour of the big, long-range goal or dream and get right down to the nitty-gritty of foundation building that will help make certain that your dream becomes your destiny. The chapters on habits in the next Segment will be especially helpful in building daily habits that build.

NUMBER FOUR — GOALS MUST BE SPECIFIC

Earlier I used the phrase, you had to be a "meaningful specific" and not a "wandering generality." Here's why. Take the hottest day the world has ever known, the most powerful magnifying glass you can buy in a store and a box of newspaper clippings. Hold the magnifying glass over the newspaper clippings. Even though you magnify the power of the sun through the glass, you will never start a fire — if you keep the glass moving. However, if you hold the glass still, and focus it on the paper, you harness the power of the sun and multiply it through the glass. Then you can start a roaring fire.

I don't care how much power, brilliance or energy you have, if you don't harness it and focus it on a specific target, and hold it there you're never going to accomplish as much as your ability warrants. The hunter who brings back the birds doesn't shoot the covey, he selects *one* quail as a specific target.

The art of goal setting is to focus on one specific, detailed objective. A "lot" of money, a "nice" or "big" house, a "high-paying" job, "more" education, "selling more," "doing something," "more for the community," or being a "better" husband, wife, student, person, is too broad a goal. In general, they are not specific enough.

For example, instead of a "big" or "nice" home, your goal should be spelled out in minute detail. If you don't know the exact details, then start accumulating magazines with pictures and floor plans of the homes that appeal to you. Combine ideas and concepts that are presented when subdivisions open or when builders or realtors hold an open house. Inspect a lot of "open houses," but don't mislead real estate agents into thinking you are a "now" prospect, so he will spend a lot of time showing you the different homes. That's not only unfair, it's dishonest and will slow you down in your quest for the details of your goal.

Take this assortment of ideas for your home and commit them to paper. How many square feet, what size, type and kind of lot, location, number of rooms, style, color, etc. Then get a local artist to make a sample drawing [an art student can probably handle it for a minimal fee]. This is particularly important as you will discover in a later Segment of the book.

I hope you fully understand that you must take the general information on goal setting and specifically apply it to your own situation. Later, I will give you a number of specifics which will apply to *your* situation. Whatever you want — if you expect to reach full effectiveness — must be *specific* in detail.

ANSWERING THE UNASKED QUESTIONS — CAN GOALS BE NEGATIVE

The answer is emphatically "Yes." Goals can be negative if one of three conditions exist. First, your goal can be negative if you don't accept the fact that you must be the architect of accomplishment and that "luck" is not involved. Second, your goal can be negative if it is unrealistically big. Third, it can be negative if it is outside your area of interests or was set to please someone else.

Let's deal with the biggest problem of them all — the too big or unrealistic goal. Many times the "too big" or unrealistic goal is deliberately set so the individual can have a ready-made excuse for failure. The individual who does this is instinctively planning for failure and is actually seeking the understanding of others by knowing they will not "blame him" for failing to do the impossible. The young man in this story could have had that problem.

Several years ago, while speaking in Detroit, Michigan, a young man in his twenties, poorly dressed, and with a limited education, approached me with a startling statement. "Mr. Ziglar, you've turned me on so, I want to shake your hand and tell you what you have done for me today." Naturally, I encouraged him to continue [I couldn't have stopped him if I had wanted to]. "What have I done?" I asked. He enthusiastically replied, "You made me a million dollars." "Well, that's fantastic," I responded. "I hope you will be willing to share it with me." Looking a little annoyed, he said, "No, seriously, I'm going to earn a million dollars, and I'm going to do it this year."

Now I'm faced with a small problem. Do I take a chance on killing this enormous enthusiasm now, or do I let him go on laboring under the illusion of an improbable goal and suffer complete defeat? I say improbable because a million dollars in a year is nearly $20,000 per week. This is a considerable sum of money for a broke, unskilled and uneducated young man to earn in one year, especially since he didn't have the $2,000 needed to buy the initial inventory to start his business. In approximately 25 years he had been unable to accumulate $2,000. Now, in just one year, his goal was to earn 500 times that amount.

Let me further illustrate the magnitude of the task. Had he taken just three weeks to raise the $2,000, he would already have been $60,000 behind schedule. Conservatively speaking, I figured if he had been unable to raise $2,000 in 25 years, it would probably take him three to six weeks longer to accumulate the money. In six weeks he would have been $120,000 behind. By then he would have been subjected to the laughter and ridicule of his friends and relatives. He probably would have already thrown in the towel and might well have tried to stop the world in order to step off. He possibly would feel foolish and defeated. Then he could honestly say, "Everybody is laughing at me," or "Everybody is against me." This same thing can happen to each of us when we set goals that are unbelievably and overwhelmingly big.

If the goal is unrealistically big, and you miss it by a ridiculous amount, the size of the failure would have an emotional impact for future accomplishments that could be extremely negative. It could even affect a person to the degree that he would no longer really make an effort of any kind. For this reason it is wiser to set the goal high but reachable.

A goal will also be negative if it is out of your field of interest and you are only trying to please someone else. If someone else is directing your goal setting, it is highly unlikely you would be completely free of resentment, which would definitely hamper your efforts.

Another indication of a negative goal is the belief that luck is involved. [Substitute the word "pluck" for "luck," then I'll buy it 100%.] Successful people get to the top because they identify their objectives, use their talents and constantly sharpen them by dedication and hard work. Their "breaks" come with commitment and objectives — and so will yours.

CHAPTER THREE

SETTING YOUR GOALS

WHERE ARE YOU?

By now your question should be, "How do I set goals? You've convinced me I should set them, but you haven't told me how, or what kind." Good point. Actually, as you will discover, it's easier to reach goals than it is to set them. A goal properly set is partially reached because it is a strong statement of your belief that you can and will reach it. As I stated earlier, **success is easy after you believe.**

I'm going to use a sales example at this point, but I stress again these examples and procedures can be translated to your job or profession — regardless of what it might be.

As a salesman, if you want to sell more effectively, you must set your goals. It's helpful if you have some working experience with your present company. However, regardless of your experience, you're going to need some records to set a big but sensible goal. The most complete map in the world won't take you anywhere unless you know where you are. You need to have a starting place. Records will help you establish that starting place. Keeping records a few minutes per day for 30 days will enable you to get a true picture of your production capability, your work capacity and the effective use of your time. You will discover that you will produce more the last 15 days than you did for the first 15 as a direct result of keeping records. For this 30-day period you need to be brutally honest. After all, you're dealing with your future. This record is for your eyes only.

There are several steps you must take in order to keep an adequate record. First, keep a record of when you wake up, when you get up and when you get into productive work. Second, keep a record of personal time you use during the day for lunch, coffee breaks, personal phone calls and attending to other personal matters. Third, keep a record of phone calls for appointments, unexpected drop-ins, service calls, reference calls, demonstrations, time spent in eyeball-to-eyeball contact with the buyer, and the sales volume you generate. Finally, keep a record of your "twilight" time. This is time spent in outer offices, the last 30 minutes of that sales call, the extra time you spent shuffling your prospect cards, etc. The first few days this will be tough, but it gets easier when it becomes a habit and your production starts to climb.

Once you have established your pattern, it's easy to make improvements. By studying your past records, you can find your best day, best week, best month and best quarter. Compare your best record with your new efficiency schedule. You'll probably see that you can take your best quarter and duplicate it only once and still have your best year. This will obviously vary a greal deal according to your product. "Low ticket" items will not produce the daily, weekly and monthly variations "high ticket" items produce [brushes or cosmetics as opposed to computers and commercial real estate]. Make your goal specific and in most cases bigger. But remember, it's better to revise a goal upward in a month than to have to dramatically reduce it.

A built-in competitiveness is often extremely helpful, so let's look at a "challenge" system. First, the don'ts. Don't bite off more than you can chew. Don't challenge the champ at the outset if you've been an "average" producer. Second, challenge the man in front of you and not the champion. That's a good procedure, especially if you make it a "double" challenge. A double challenge is one to beat the man ahead of you as well as your own best. With this approach, you won't win any victories by "fluke" of default. Each victory will make you stronger for the next challenge. Regardless of how many people are currently in front of you, if you are constantly striving to "beat your best," you will be making a lot of progress, a lot of sales and a lot of money. Obviously, if you continue to beat the one in front of you, it will be just a matter of time before no one will be in front of you.

WHAT IS MOST IMPORTANT

Let's look at the physical, financial, spiritual, career, family, mental and social goals. Here are some rules that will enable you to more accurately zero in on those goals. Of necessity, you should remember, these rules must be quite general in nature. Obviously, you must take these examples and translate them to fit your own situation.

You should commit to paper the things you want and expect. You might well say, "It will take me three days to write down all of the things I want." You're going to be surprised to discover it isn't going to take you nearly as long as you think. Write them down and list them in the order of their importance. Obviously, you will be working on several goals at the same time. You might have a physical goal of being the club golf champion, the company sales leader, the president of the PTA and a lay leader in your church or synagogue all at the same time. In this event, you'll have to decide the order of importance to you because each one requires time and will require adjustment as you work. You might have to compromise and settle for acquiring an 8 handicap instead of becoming club champion and being active in the PTA instead of president. At any rate, in order to accomplish these objectives, you'll have to be organized.

"STEPPING" OR "STOPPING" STONES

Once you've arranged your goals in the order of their importance, you should list the obstacles that stand between you and your objectives. If there wasn't something between you and your goals, you would already have everything you want. After you've listed your obstacles, you can formulate a plan to overcome them and set a time schedule. Most management authorities believe that when you properly identify a problem you have it half solved. You'll be amazed how much faster you overcome the obstacles once you identify them. As you overcome the obstacles on your way to one goal, the obstacles on the way to other goals will fall more easily.

In the preceding chapter I discussed a young man who had set what I considered to be the unrealistic goal of earning one million dollars in a single year. My advice to him in goal setting was, instead of challenging for the financial championship of the world that first year, why not approach it on the same basis a fighter would approach his quest for the championship of the world. When a man enters the professional ranks as a fighter, he starts by challenging the man above him. After each success, and as he gains confidence and experience, he moves up the ladder. Many promising fighters have destroyed their careers by getting over their heads against competition that was too tough before they had gained the necessary experience.

"In reaching and achieving your goals," I advised the young man, "take it on a more gradual basis." In essence, I advised him to find out what the top man was earning. This would enable him to know what his target actually was. Then I urged him to research the average earnings of the people within his company. I further advised him to select a figure slightly lower than the average and set this as his goal for the first month. I felt he could do better, but I wanted him to have the initial confidence that goes with reaching a first objective. **Confidence is the handmaiden of success.** Once success to any degree is yours, it's easier to achieve greater success [do something well, then it's easy to excel] I then urged him to select targets within the organization and start beating the man above him. Following this procedure he would eventually be the number one producer and could then set much higher monetary goals. To accomplish this he had to lay out his schedule on a daily basis.

Whether or not he would have reached his target of $1,000,000 in a single year is academic. With the proper approach to goal setting, I'm convinced the young man will go farther, faster and be happier in the process. Having said these things, let me remind you that I did not say his goal was impossible. I have a certain amount of courage but not enough to place an absolute ceiling on the potential of a dedicated man.

THE CONFIDENCE OF IGNORANCE

Several years ago in Columbia, South Carolina, a young cookware salesman sat in my office. It was in early December and we were talking about plans for the next year. I asked him "How much are you going to sell next year?" With a big grin on his face he said, "I'll guarantee you one thing; I'm going to sell more next year than I sold this year." My comment and question was, "That's wonderful. How much did you sell this year?" He smiled again and said, "Well, I don't really know." Interesting, isn't it?

It's also quite sad. Here was a young man who didn't know where he was and had no idea where he'd been but, *with the confidence that generally goes with ignorance, he knew where he was going.*

Unfortunately, most people are in about the same condition. They don't know where they are, have no idea where they've been, but they invariably think they know where they're going. Am I talking about you? If I am, then you might have acquired this book just in time.

I challenged the young salesman with a question: "How would you like to become an immortal in the cookware business?" Now, the word immortal is a pretty challenging word. He took the bait and responded enthusiastically. "How?" "Easy," I answered, "just break the all-time company record." This time his response was considerably less enthusiastic. He said, "That sure is easy for you to say, but nobody, including me, will ever break that record." Naturally I was curious, so I asked what he meant by "no one will ever break that record." He informed me rather emphatically that the record was not "honest" because the man who set it had his son-in-law selling cookware in his name.

INCENTIVE — THE SOUL OF SUCCESS

This young man's Loser's Limp was, "I can't do it because the record isn't honest." I reassured him the record was legitimate and challenged him by saying, "If one man set the record another can break it." Since **incentive is the soul of success**, I dangled some rewards before him. First of all, I assured him that if he broke that all-time record the company would hang his picture in the home office along with the president's. He liked that. Then, I told him his picture would be used in national ads and articles and he would become famous as the best "pot" salesman in the world [that was before marijuana was a problem, and "pot" was something you used for cooking]. He really liked that. Finally, I told him they would make him a "gold pot" or at least one that looked like gold. That did it as far as motivation was concerned, but he still had some doubt about how much he could sell.

I reminded him he could break the record by taking his best week and multiplying it by 50. He grinned and said, "Boy, that's easy for you to say ..." I interrupted, "Yes, and it's easy for you to do, if you believe you can." He still wasn't convinced he could, but he promised to give it serious thought. That's an important point, because **a goal casually set and lightly taken is freely abandoned at the first obstacle.**

NO "IF" DECISIONS

On December 26th, he called me from his home in Augusta, Georgia. Never before, nor since, have I participated in a telephone conversation that could compare with this one. The wires must have gotten hot. You could feel the excitement from Augusta to Columbia, South Carolina. He brought me up to date. "You know, since our visit earlier this month, I've kept exact records of everything I've done. I know how much business I get when I knock on a door, make a telephone call, conduct a demonstration or open my sample case. I know how much I sell every week I work, every day I work and every hour I work." With a tremendous burst of enthusiasm, he added, I'm going to break that record!" I squeezed a word in to the conversation to say, "No, you're not 'going' to break the record. You just broke the record."

I did this because not once did he use the word "if." It wasn't an "if" decision. Take the word "life" and look at it. The two center letters in the word "life" are "if." Many people go through life making nothing but "if" decisions. These are not decisions for success but preparations for failure. Not this guy. He didn't say, "I'm going to break this record *if* I don't wreck my car." It's good he didn't because that's what happened. He didn't say, "I'm going to break this record *if* there is no illness in my family." There was. He didn't say, "I'm going to break this record *if* there are no deaths in my family." He buried two loved ones, including a brother. He didn't say, "I'm going to break this record *if* I don't lose my voice." It's good he didn't because in December, with the goal literally within his reach, his voice was in such bad shape his doctor ordered him to stop talking so he did the only thing he could do — he changed doctors. No, his decision was laboriously arrived at but simply stated: I'm going to break that record, period."

We need to look at his target in order to really appreciate the size of the undertaking. Never before had he sold over $34,000 in a single year, which wasn't too bad at the time. However, the next year, selling the same product, in the same area, at the same price, he delivered and paid for, after all cancellations and credit rejections, over $104,000 worth of cookware. He sold over three times as much as he had ever sold in a single year. As a result, he broke the all-time record. Incidentally, the company did follow through on the reward he and I had discussed. He got the publicity and the gold "pot."

SMARTER AND HARDER

Many people ask if he got that much smarter. I pointed out he did get some smarter because he now had eleven years experience instead of ten. Many ask if he worked that much harder. I assured them he worked some harder and certainly smarter. He organized his time and learned the value of a minute. He found that 10 minutes here and 20 minutes there soon added up to from one to two hours per day. This was eight to ten hours per week or, incredibly enough, 400 to 500 hours a year. That was the equivalent of over fifty full eight-hour days in a year. In short, he discovered that everyone doesn't have 60 minutes in every hour, 24 hours in every day or even seven days in every week. Each man only has as many minutes, hours and days as he uses. When **he quit counting time and started making time count,** he was able to produce considerably more business and still have more time for himself and his family.

He started by finding out, through keeping records, *exactly* where he was. [You — if you're a salesman, *must* do the same thing. Find out how many prospects you must approach to secure an appointment. How many appointments you must make in order to tell your story. How many presentations you must make in order to make a sale. Combine this information with the knowledge of how much *time* it takes to secure an appointment that sticks. How much *time* it takes to make a presentation and complete a sale, including driving time, service time, paper work time, etc. With this information you will know where you are. Then it's simply a matter of arithmetic. With this information you will *know* what happens for every hour you work, but hold the phone. You will almost immediately have to revise your goal upward — and often dramatically, because your confidence, bolstered by these facts, will make you much more productive.]

As we break this story into parts, we realize the young man involved all the principles of goal setting as well as the principles of "goal reaching."

(1) He kept records to find out where he was.
(2) He committed to paper the goals he wanted to achieve on a yearly, monthly, and daily basis.
(3) He was very specific [$104,000].
(4) He set the goal big — but reachable — to create excitement and a challenge.
(5) He made the goal long-range [1 year] so he would not be overcome by daily frustrations.
(6) He listed the obstacles between him and his goal and formulated a plan to overcome the obstacles.
(7) He broke his goal into daily increments.
(8) He was mentally prepared to discipline himself to take the necessary steps to reach his goals.
(9) He was absolutely convinced he could reach his goals.
(10) He visualized himself as already reaching his goal before the year started.

To reinforce an idea expressed earlier in this Segment, you should be careful about sharing your goals with others. If you are confident and *need* to put yourself on the spot by sharing your goal with others, then go ahead. However, you will be wise to be very selective about sharing your goals. It's helpful if you have associates or loved ones who will share your optimism and give you added confidence that you can reach your goals. It's definitely harmful if you share your dreams with a wet blanket who ridicules your ideas and belittles your efforts.

The young man in the story [I'll identify him later] shared his goals with his family who believed in him and gave him support. He also shared his goals with other people because he knew himself well enough to know that he would be more likely to reach his objective if he put himself on the spot.

I recognize the examples I use in goal setting will not fit each individual case, but the principles will fit your situation. At some time in the future perhaps you will be in one of our Richer Life classes or courses around the country and can work direcly with one of our instructors in setting your specific goals. In the meantime, here are some other thoughts which should be helpful.

GOOD TODAY — BETTER TOMORROW

Let's take the case of the mother who said, "How can I set a series of goals?" First of all, a mother should have a big goal. One of the biggest goals any mother can have is to teach her children how to live in a complex society and pay their own way. To raise her children to be happy, healthy, morally and emotionally sound is a big goal for any mother. A long-range goal could be to teach her children to be contributing members of society. She can also teach them enough by word and deed that they will have an honest shot at spending eternity with Jesus Christ.

One of the finest daily goals we can set is to teach our children how to do things for themselves. The Chinese say it well, "If you give a man a fish, you feed him for the day, but if you teach him how to fish, you feed him for life." Teach your children how to do things, how to be self-supporting and self-sustaining. What could be a better daily goal for a mother than that?

Everybody's daily goals should be to do the best they can today while preparing for a better tomorrow. The future is the place where you're going to spend the rest of your life. Daily accomplishments are bricks leading to that place. If you regularly and firmly put the bricks into place with proper goal setting procedures, you will eventually build your stairway to the top. In order for you to properly set your lifetime goals as stated earlier, you must clearly understand that the elevator to the top is "out of order." You're going to have to take the stairs — one at a time. Fortunately, they are clearly marked and are beckoning you to climb them — all the way up.

CHAPTER FOUR

REACHING YOUR GOALS

BE HONEST WITH YOU

When I started this book, the words were flowing easily and coming out well, at least in my mind. When I wrote the words, **"You can go where you want to go, do what you want to do, have what you want to have, and be what you want to be,"** I'll have to confess I held those words out in front of me and with a degree of satisfaction said to myself, "That's good." Unfortunately, I had to hold the words some distance away, because there was a 41″ waistline and 202 lbs. between me and those words. As I read the words, I started thinking and talking to myself. [It's not bad to talk to yourself. It's not even bad to answer — however, if you ever catch yourself saying "Huh?" to the answer, you're in trouble. That's the position I found myself in.]

The thought occurred to me that eventually some reader would ask if I really believed what I had written. Since honesty starts within, I was led to re-evaluate every word I wrote. In a nutshell, it boiled down to this — if I believed it, I should live it and if I didn't believe it, I shouldn't write it. With this in mind I asked myself, "Are you really like you want to be, Zig?"

As I wrestled with this question, it became more and more obvious that I was either going to have to delete this portion of the book or have difficulty living with myself. It was also inevitable that I would be confronted with people who ask embarrasing questions. In addition, my son was eight years old and I felt very strongly that a father should be able to whip his children until they are at least 12 years old. At the rate I was going, I wasn't even going to be able to catch mine. The thing that sent me looking for help though, was my redhead who kept telling me to hold my stomach in — and I already was.

Fortunately, Dallas is the home of the world famous Aerobics Center founded by Dr. Kenneth Cooper. Dr. Cooper is variously described as either the Air Force Doctor or the Running Doctor.

He has done considerable research into the effect of Aerobic conditioning on the body. When you see anyone jogging, he is probably jogging because of the direct or indirect influence of Dr. Cooper. I secured an appointment and went down for the five hour examination. They started by taking two quarts [at least it looked like two quarts] of blood. They just kept filling those little vials. I thought they were starting a blood bank with me as the major supplier. Next they dunked me into a tank of water and completely immersed me three times to determine the amount of body fat I had. They discovered I was 23.9% pure lard, which wasn't exactly ideal. Next, they put me on a treadmill and wired me to a machine so they could monitor my heart and check my pulse as I walked. The length of your walk revealed your physical condition, so I was chagrined when I only walked long enough to get four seconds out of "horrible" into "just awful."

When the examination was completed and the figures compiled, Dr. Randy Martin, the examining physician, had me come into his office to go over the results. With a big smile on his face, Dr. Martin explained to me that they used computers to compile their information and the figures proved I was not overweight. However, I was exactly five and one-half inches too short. I commented that this was really bad, but Dr. Martin explained that actually I was in remarkably good physical condition — for a 66-year-old man. When I reminded him that I was 46, his expression made a dramatic change. "You're in awful shape," he said, "As a matter of fact, if you were a building, I'd condemn you." Naturally, I wanted to know what I should do, so Dr. Martin laid out a precise schedule, detailed in black and white and threw in a "pep" talk for a bonus. Before he finished telling me what I should do, I was kinda like the little boy who asked his daddy a question. His dad responded, "Why don't you ask your mother?" The little boy replied, "I just didn't want to know that much about it."

A BLOCK AND A MAIL-BOX

When I got home, my wife commented, "Well, I suppose you're going to be out running all over the neighborhood." I replied in the affirmative so she said, "If I'm going to have a 46-year-old fat boy running all over the neighborhood, I want to have you looking as good as possible." Down to the store she went to buy me some fancy running shirts and shorts to go with the running shoes Dr. Martin had advised me to buy.

While in Dr. Martin's office, I did something that was ugly, but I'll use the excuse that I had not read Ann Landers at the time. Ann says it is not nice or honest to take pages out of magazines belonging to someone else. Actually I knew that, so I can't honestly hide behind her. I took the page advertising jockey shorts. If you don't read the jockey short ads, let me suggest that you at least look at the picture the next time you see one. You will discover they don't put jockey shorts on fat boys. At least they don't have a "Good-Year."

The next morning when the alarm sounded, I hopped out of bed, slipped on those fancy running clothes and shoes, tore out the front door — and ran a block, all by myself. The next day, however, I did considerably better. I ran a block and a mailbox. The third day it was a block and two mailboxes, then a block and three mailboxes, until finally one day I ran all the way around the block. When I passed that milestone I woke up the entire family and told them what "Dad had done."

Then one day I ran a half-mile, then a mile, then a mile-and-a-half, then two miles. I started on the calisthenics bit. I did 6 push-ups, then 8, then 10, then 20, then 30, then 40. Today I can even do the G.I. push-up, which simply means I push myself into the air and slap my hands at the same time. I started doing sit-ups and the first day I did 8, then 10, then 20, then 40, then 80, then 120. The net result was the weight and waistline started coming down. I was also dieting religiously during this period of time [I quit eating in church]. Seriously, I did diet and I'll have more to say about that in a moment. My weight came down from 202 — first to 200, then 190, 180, 170 and 165. My waistline dropped from 41 to 40, 39, 38, 37, 36, 35, 34. Ten months from the day, after I had written that I weighed 165 and had a 34-inch waistline, it came to pass.

THE PRINCIPLES OF GOAL SETTING

I give you these details because this story involved every

principle of goal setting and goal reaching. The goal was mine and since my credibility was at stake, the incentive for reaching the goal was built in when I set the goal. The goal was big. Big enough that it represented a real challenge and forced me to reach deep into the wellspring of my resources to reach the objective. Yet it was neither irresponsible nor impossible. Had I elected to lose only five pounds, then no one, with the possible exception of my redhead, would have known I had lost any weight. As the pounds melted off [actually when you are sweating them off, you don't think they are melting] and my waistline started moving down, my family and friends bragged on me a lot. That really helped. I started feeling better and my energy level rose. The time I spent on the running program was returned with a bonus in the form of greater work endurance.

The size of the goal is enormously important. In a preceding chapter, I emphasize that a goal can be too big, but please remember this one was under the direction of a skilled physician. The goal was clearly defined — very specific. The target was in distinct focus. The goal was long-range. [As a practical matter it was actually an intermediate one but for purposes of illustration I'm going to use it as a long range one.] Ten months was the time remaining from the day I made the decision until the book was to be published. Thirty-seven pounds is a lot of weight to lose — maybe an impossible amount — until you divide by ten, and realize it is only 3.7 pounds per month. With this realization, I became quite optimistic, which is important if you expect to reach your goal. Unfortunately my optimism turned to confidence and then to overconfidence with the net result that I didn't bother to get started the first 28 days. [You're right — I was about to get cooked "in the squat."]

This weight loss goal really became reachable when I broke it into daily increments. When it dawned on me that in order to lose 37 pounds in ten months all I had to do was lose 1.9 ounces a day, I really got excited. Thirty-seven pounds is a lot, 3.7 pounds is not really that much, but 1.9 ounces is such a little bit. I put the weight on a bite at a time and I had to take it off the same way. The old adage that by the mile it's a trial but by the inch it's a cinch, is certainly true because of what the psychologists call "achievement feedback." Each step forward — each accomplishment — or in my case, each bit of measurable weight loss increased my enthusiasm and bolstered my confidence that I could succeed again and again. Yes — success begets success. That's why it is so important as you set and seek *any* goal, to arrange it so you can enjoy some success of some kind virtually every day. This "positive feedback" increases your confidence so you begin to "expect" and "see" yourself as accomplishing more and more, which means you will do and be more and more. The only way to reach your long-range goals is through achieving short-range objectives. Keep your eye on your major objective, but remember as you reach your daily objectives you are getting closer and closer to those long-range ones.

In order for the goal to have significance I had to set a reasonable time limit. Had I planned to lose 37 pounds in 37 years or even 37 months, the time involvement would have been too lengthy. On the other hand, had I attempted to lose 37 pounds in 37 days, that would have been even more ridiculous. Not only would it have bordered on the impossible, but the effect on my health could well have been disastrous. My time schedule was ambitious yet reasonable and attainable.

THE MARTYR

Before we continue I have a question for you. Have you ever seen a living, breathing, real, live martyr? At one time I at least felt like one. Let me explain. When the alarm sounded off each morning I would often think to myself, "What's a 46 year old fat boy doing getting up and running all over the neighborhood while his buddies are sound asleep." Then I would look down at my 41″ waist line and ask a question, "Ziglar, do you want to look like you or like the guy in the jockey shorts?" Since I didn't want to look like me, I'd hop out of bed and start running.

However, just because I had made the commitment to run and lose the weight didn't mean I had to like it. As a matter of fact, I "fussed" every step I took. I ran in the snow of Winnipeg, the sand of Acapulco, the rain of Minneapolis and the orange groves of Florida. And don't you think for one minute that I ever missed an opportunity to tell friend, foe, family and even complete strangers about this enormous "sacrifice" I was making because I had made this commitment to lose the weight. I must have been quite a bore and am a little surprised that I was able to keep either friend *or* family. Incidentally, this was in character, because for years I had told audiences literally hundreds of times that if you wanted to accomplish anything worthwhile that you had to "pay the price." [I could even put a strain in my voice and a pained expression on my face when I said you had to "pay the price" that would bring tears to the eyes of all but the strongest.]

Then one day I was running on the Portland State University campus in Portland, Oregon. It was a beautiful spring day. The temperature was about 75° and many of the students were relaxing, studying or courting and here comes Zig jogging along. The sweat was running down my back and legs, but on this day as I felt the ground and concrete flowing beneath my feet, it dawned on me that this run was "different". Suddenly I knew that I was having the time of my life. Today at age 50, armed with the knowledge that I am physically in better shape than I was at age 25, that I can out-run 98% of the college students in America over a two mile run, it is obvious to me that **you don't "pay the price" you enjoy the price.**

To emphasize my point, when I was within seven pounds of reaching my goal my gall bladder ruptured. It was four days before the doctor discovered the problem. During those four days, I probably hurt as much as I had all my life combined. By the time they got inside to correct the problem, an abscess had formed under the liver and I was full of poison. My doctor told me my excellent physical condition at that time played an important part in my recovery. As a matter of fact, my redhead was somewhat astonished that I was not even sore as a result of the operation. No, I am totally convinced *you don't pay a price, you enjoy a price.* This is applicable to all areas of life. You don't *pay* the price for, success [now remember, success is acquiring a reasonable *or* large amount of *all* the good things], you enjoy the price. You *pay* the price for failure.

TAKE IT OFF — PERMANENTLY

Now — if you have a weight problem you would like to *permanently* solve, here are some basics to follow. First, make certain it is *your* idea and *your* decision to lose the weight and that you have not been pressured into action by someone else. Second, go to a skinny doctor for an examination. An overweight one either doesn't know, doesn't believe, or doesn't understand the devastating effect of carrying a lot of excess weight. He cannot convey the conviction nor give you the psychological reinforcement you will need to sustain a weight reduction program. Third, don't use pills as a crutch to lose weight. You didn't get fat [doesn't sound good, does it? — doesn't look good either] taking pills, and you won't get permanently slim by taking pills. [If "pills" worked there would be no overweight doctors, would there?]

Fourth, make certain your doctor is a positive thinker and doesn't tell you what you can't eat. Why should you clutter your mind with negatives? Your concern and concentration should be on what you can eat. Make that list and keep it in front of you. Use the good old C.S. [Common Sense] diet principle. Don't — oh, please don't get involved in the roller coaster "fad" diets that promise dramatic weight loss "without getting hungry." [All you will permanently lose on those 30 day diets is a month.] In most cases one thing put that weight on: [Habit — a bad one]. You ate too much, and one thing is going to take it off: [Habit — a good one]. Eat less food, and maintain a balanced diet over a period of time. You didn't gain "forty 'leven' " pounds in one weekend. It was "one more bite" that "done you in."

My next observation is not scientific but I advise you to stay away from cottage cheese. Based on my personal observation, I have come to the conclusion that cottage cheese is fattening. I say this because nobody but fat folks eat cottage cheese. [Dr. Martin told me I could eat anything I wanted — then he gave me a list of the things I was going to want.]

On the serious side, there are two things wrong with roller coaster dieting. First, to lose weight and then gain it back is destructive to your self-image. Second, it is hard on your physical body and puts a strain on your entire system [ask your skinny doctor why].

Let me also tell it like it is. If you are going to lose weight you are going to get hungry — and that's a fact. It will help if you guys will take a 3x5 card and print these words on it. "Hungry? You bet I am, but it's worth it to change from 'lard' to 'hard'." The girls should print: "Hungry? You bet I am, but I'm changing from 'poundcake' to 'cheesecake'." You will still be hungry, but you'll be laughing about it instead of crying.

Dr. Bruno's book, *Think Yourself Thin*, will be helpful as you get serious about doing something about you — for you. I also urge you to turn back to the Self-Image section and remind yourself that you deserve to be slender and healthy. Remember, pleasure [eating too much for you] is very short lived, but happiness [being pleased with your slimmer, healthier, extended life — five to twenty years longer] is of much longer duration.

The fringe benefits that go with weight loss are too numerous to enumerate, but this I stress. When you reach the weight loss goal you set, your self-image and self confidence will grow by leaps and bounds and will spread to many other areas of your life. Remember — success begets success.

Don't get the wrong idea. I tell the story in detail, not in an effort to get you to lose weight but because it involves every principle of goal setting and goal reaching. First of all, the goal was mine. Neither my red head nor my doctor had "talked" me into going on a diet or losing weight. Second, my credibility was at stake since I had said you could be like you wanted to be and I obviously wasn't like I wanted to be. Third, it represented a strong commitment which you must have if you are to reach your goal. I committed to paper the fact that I weighed 165 when in reality I weighed 202. This was ten months before we went to press and since no publisher would publish the book [until the fourth printing when they decided it would sell], I financed and published it myself. My initial order was for 25,000 copies. [Can you imagine me with 25,000 copies in my warehouse saying I weighed 165 and I go waddling around at 202? Now friends, that's a commitment.] Fourth, the goal was big — lose 37 pounds. The rule is simple. If the goal is to be effective it must affect change. Fifth, the goal was specific [37 pounds] because you must be a "meaningful specific" and not a "wandering generality." Sixth, it was long range — 10 months [or as explained earlier, intermediate]. Seventh, it was broken into a daily goal of losing 1.9 ounces. Eighth, I had a plan to overcome the surplus weight [diet and jogging]. Ninth, a thorough physical examination had established precisely where I was [37 pounds overweight], which you must know in order to start in the right direction.

BE A FLEA TRAINER

In Chapter Three of this Segment on Goals, I shared with you the story of the cookware salesman who jumped from $34,000 to over $104,000 in sales in just one year. Here is the rest of the story on how he reached that objective.

The thing that made the difference is the reason I tell the story. He learned one thing that enabled him to multiply his business. He learned how to "train fleas." Do you know how to train fleas? I'm serious. It's critically important that you know how, because until you do, you will never make it big. I'll emphasize that statement. You are not going to make it big, success-wise or happiness-wise, until and unless you know how to train fleas. [Talking about fleas, did you hear the one about the two fleas at the bottom of the hill trying to decide if they should walk or — take a dog?] That is a fact. Now, I'll bet you want to know how to train fleas, don't you? Say Yes.

You train fleas by putting them in a jar with a top on it. Fleas jump, so they will jump up and hit the top over and over and over again. As you watch them jump and hit the top, you will notice something interesting. The fleas continue to jump, but they are no longer jumping high enough to hit the top. Then, and it's a matter of record, you can take the top off and though the fleas continue to jump, they won't jump out of the jar. I repeat, they won't jump out because they can't. The reason is simple. They have conditioned themselves to jump just so high. **Once they have conditioned themselves to jump just so high, that's all they can do.**

ARE YOU A SNIOP?

Man is the same way. He starts out in life to write a book, climb a mountain, break a record or make a contribution. Initially, his dreams and ambitions have no limits but, along the roadway of life, he bumps his head and stubs his toe a few times. At this point his "friends" and associates often make negative comments about life in general and him in particular and as a result he becomes a SNIOP. A SNIOP is a person who is Susceptible to the Negative Influence of Other People. That's the reason we suggest you be careful about who you share your goals with. Interestingly enough, we can also be "snioped" by the most positive people in the world. For example, when Joe Louis was Heavyweight Champion of the world, he "snioped" his opponents time after time. They were often so paralyzed with fright they were easy victims for his awesome skills. When John Wooden sent his UCLA Bruins onto the basketball court, his opponents were so "snioped" that the issue was often settled before the opening buzzer sounded. That's part, but just part, of the reason UCLA won 10 national championships in 12 years.

That's also one of the reasons coaches repeatedly teach an athlete to fight his own fight or play his own game and not let the opposition force him to play their game.

I have a close friend with the Kirby Company whom I often accuse of "snioping" his fellow Divisional Supervisors into fighting for second place. He just grins, but Jim Sperry has been first for fifteen consecutive years and every year he has had an increase in business. Fortunately, Jim is aware of the fact his fellow Supervisors have taken dead aim on his spot and are after him. Actually Jim encourages the other Supervisors in every way possible because he knows the tougher the battle for first place — the more productive his own Division will become.

The "sniop" listens to the negative garbage from the "prophets of doom," who give him excuses for failure instead of methods for success. In the process, he acquires his own Loser's Limp. Not so with our enthusiastic cookware salesman. Not only was he not a "sniop," but he had gotten rid of his Loser's Limp and had set a big goal. He had a long-range goal: to break the record and become the best "pot" salesman in the world. He had a daily goal: to sell $350 per working day. He also had a result: he tripled his business in one year. Incidentally, I know the young man's story quite well because he's my younger brother, Judge Ziglar. I'm also proud that he applied these same "goal reaching," flea training principles to become one of the top speakers and sales trainers in America. He now teaches others how to reach their goals, in seminars all over America. As an officer in our company and as an instructor for The Richer Life Course he is busy teaching others how to set records — and train fleas.

THE UNBREAKABLE BARRIER

The most outstanding example of a flea trainer is Roger Bannister. For years athletes tried to run a mile in less than four minutes. The barrier seemed unbreakable because the athletes were "sniops." An athlete might say to the world, "I'm going to run a four-minute mile." But when he would toe the mark the voice of the coach would echo in his ear, "The best you've ever done is 4:06. You can't break the barrier. As a matter of fact, I've figured it out scientifically and I doubt if the barrier will ever be broken." The voice of the doctor with stethoscope in hand would also haunt him saying, "You run a four-minute mile? Why, your heart will come right out of your body. You can't do it." The news media speculated at length over the four-minute mile and the general opinion was that the four-minute mile was beyond the physical capacity of a human being. As a result, the athlete was "snioped" right out of the four-minute mile.

Roger Bannister wouldn't be "snioped." He was a flea trainer. So he ran the first four-minute mile. Then athletes the world over started running four-minute miles. John Landy of Australia ran it less than six weeks after Bannister broke the barrier. To date there have been over 500 races run in less than four minutes, including one by a 37-year-old man. At the NCAA track meet in Baton Rouge, Louisiana in June 1973, eight athletes ran the mile in less than four minutes. The four-minute barrier was broken, but *not* because man became that much faster physically. It was broken because the barrier was a mental obstacle and not a physical impossibility.

In case you missed the point, **a flea trainer is a person who jumps out of the jar.** He's driven from within and is not "snioped" by the negative outside influences. To fully explain and identify flea trainers, I'm including a "Flea Trainer" certificate in the book. The only way you will succeed in all areas of your life is to become a full-fledged flea trainer, so I want to make certain you know what a flea trainer is. Incidentally, if you would like a beautiful autographed parchment Flea Trainer Certificate suitable for framing, and the plastic "round tuit" we mentioned earlier, just send your request to: The Zig Ziglar Corporation, 12011 Coit Road, Suite 114, Dallas, Texas 75251.

START WITH ONE

Goals in *all* areas of life might be overwhelming for an individual who has never set even one goal to do anything significant. To make certain we don't overwhelm you, let's look at the advice Judge Ziglar gives to sales people in his seminars. "If you have never set goals before, let me suggest that you start with *one* goal of a short-range nature. Select the best month you have had, add ten percent and make that your one-month goal. Take your best day during that month, write it down and keep it in front of you. Underneath that best day, put the average you will have to reach each day to break your one-month goal. Your 'average' day will be so much smaller than the best day you have had that you will be confident you can reach your one-month goal."

At the end of the month *if* you reached your goal, then you should set a quarterly goal. If you did not reach the one-month goal, then set the monthly goal again. It is important that you reach the first goal before you move to the second one. After reaching your monthly goal, then multiply that goal by three and add ten percent for your quarterly goal. This time keep your best sales week in front of you, divide the quarter into thirteen segments and place the average you must maintain each week in front of you in order to break your quarterly record. Your average week will be substantially lower than your best week, but by maintaining the average, you will reach your goal.

At the end of the goal reaching quarter, you will be in position to set your yearly goal by taking your quarterly results, multiply by four and add ten percent. This ten percent procedure is reasonable and reachable but the consistency gives you substantial increases. Basic procedure is the same as before. Take your best month, write it boldly on a card, then take the average you must produce each month in order to reach your yearly goal. This will represent a substantial increase in business and yet the monthly average is so much less than your best month, that you will have the confidence that you can do the job.

I am aware of the fact that there are circumstances over which you truly have no control. For example, the toy, swimsuit, nursery, lawn furniture business, etc., are to a large degree seasonal. You will have to make adjustments to compensate for these changes over which you have no control. Once you have made your commitments, however, you will discover that many of the "seasonal" businesses are not quite as seasonal as you thought and you will be producing more business during "the off season" than ever before.

By the time the first quarter is well under way you will be motivated to set some goals in other areas of your life. Success begets success, so getting started is obviously the first step in getting there.

UNLOCKING DOORS TO REACH YOUR GOALS

In order to reach your goals, you must understand the story of Houdini. Houdini was a master magician as well as a fabulous locksmith. He boasted that he could escape from any jail cell in the world in less than an hour, provided he could go into the cell dressed in his street clothes. A small town in the British Isles built a new jail they were extremely proud of. They issued Houdini a challenge. "Come give us a try," they said. Houdini loved the publicity and the money, so he accepted. By the time he arrived, excitement was at a fever pitch. He rode triumphantly into town and walked into the cell. Confidence oozed from him as the door was closed. Houdini took off his coat and went to work. Secreted in his belt was a flexible, tough and durable ten-inch piece of steel which he used to work on the lock. At the end of 30 minutes his confident expression had disappeared. At the end of an hour he was drenched in perspiration. After two hours, Houdini literally collapsed against the door — which opened. You see it had never been locked — except in his own mind — which meant it was as firmly locked as if a thousand locksmiths had put their best locks on it. One little push and Houdini could have easily opened the door. Many times a little extra push is all you need to open your opportunity door.

In the game of life you will discover, as you set your goals and unlock your own mind, that the world will unlock its treasures and rewards to you. Realistically, **most locked doors are in your mind.** Oops, I should have said *were* in your own mind because you are opening yours wider by the page — aren't you?

Flea Training Certificate

DALLAS, TEXAS_____19____

Read This Well ∾ Here's A Story To Tell

Let the whole world know that _____is a fully qualified — dedicated — "Flea Trainer." By jumping out of the jar and refusing to get cooked "in the squat," he is earning the rights and privileges this world has to offer.

Flea Trainers are people who are driven from within and are not "SNIOPS" [Susceptible to Negative Influence of Other People]. They have removed their own ceilings and are teaching others to do the same.

Flea Trainers work at seeing people through — instead of seeing through people. They teach others how to "get on" — instead of telling them where to "get off." They are confident but not arrogant and know how to serve without being servile.

Flea Trainers seek "total" success and a well balanced life by building on honesty, love, character, loyalty, faith and integrity. They know that dedicated effort is its own reward and that what you get by reaching your objective is not as important as what you become by reaching that objective.

_____is going up with the knowledge that "he climbs highest who helps another up."

Žig Žiglar
America's No. 1 Flea Trainer

Ⓟ ZIG ZIGLAR 1977

SEE THE REACHING

Major Nesmeth was a week-end golfer who generally shot in the nineties. Then he completely quit playing for seven years. Amazingly enough, the next time back on the course he shot a sparkling 74. During the seven-year sabbatical, he took no golf lessons and his physical condition actually deteriorated. As a matter of fact, he spent those seven years in a small cage approximately four-and-one-half feet tall and slightly over five feet long. He was a prisoner of war in North Vietnam.

His story illustrates that we must "see the reaching" if we expect to "reach the reaching," and accomplish our goals in life. Major Nesmeth was in isolation for five-and-one-half years of the time he was confined as a prisoner of war. He saw no one, talked to no one and was unable to perform a normal routine of physical activities. For the first few months he did virtually nothing but hope and pray for his release. Then he realized he had to take some definite, positive steps if he was going to retain his sanity and stay alive. He selected his favorite golf course and started playing golf in his cage. In his own mind, he played a full 18 holes every day. He played them to the last minute detail. He "saw" himself dressed in his golfing clothes as he stepped up to the first tee. He completely visualized every weather condition under which he had played. He "saw" the exact size of the tee box, the grass, the trees, the birds and all of the embellishments on a golf course. He "saw" in minute detail the exact way he held his left hand on the club and the way he put his right hand on the club. He carefully lectured himself on keeping his left arm straight. He admonished himself to keep his eye on the ball. He cautioned himself about taking the back swing slowly and easily while remembering to keep his eye on the ball. He instructed himself about a smooth down swing and follow through on his shot. He then visualized the flight of the ball down the center of the fairway. He watched it fly through the air, hit the ground and roll until it came to a stop at the exact spot he selected.

He took the same length of time in his own mind he would have taken on a golf course, taking each step to the ball he had just hit. In other words, he decided to become a meaningful specific rather than remain a wandering generality.

PRACTICE WITHOUT PRESSURE

Seven days a week for seven full years he played 18 holes of perfect golf. Not once did he ever miss a shot. Not once did the ball ever stay out of the cup. *Perfect.* In the process of shooting mental golf the Major was able to occupy four full hours of every day and maintain his sanity as a result. He was also able to do a great deal with his golf game. His story illustrates the point I want you to see. **If you want to reach your goal, you must "see the reaching" in your own mind before you actually arrive at your goal.**

If you want a raise, a bigger opportunity with your company, better grades, a better cake, a better mouse trap, the home of your dreams, etc., then let me urge you to reread this story very carefully. Follow the *exact* procedure a few minutes every day and the day will come when you will not only "see the reaching," you will have "reached the reaching" — you will be there.

As we mentioned earlier this is "practice without pressure." This is a situation where little or nothing is at stake before the main event. It occurs with the basketball player shooting practice goals, the field-goal kicker kicking field goals before the game, the young doctor practicing on the cadavers in medical school and the salesman going through his demonstration in a training class. Enough "practice without pressure," regardless of your field of endeavor, will lead to a better performance when there is pressure.

In my own case, as far as losing weight is concerned, I "saw the reaching" by taking a picture of a skinny guy and fixing it clearly in my mind. I was determined to look like him. I quit seeing myself as a friendly fat man, I became a friendly slim man.

The same principle applies in our business and professional lives. Bette Sundin, the only female Zone Manager with World Book Encyclopedia, epitomizes this "Flea Training" and "See the Reaching" philosophy. Early in her business career, Bette was told by her employer, a major steel company, that despite her competence and dedication to the job, she could never be promoted because she was a woman. For a person who was destined to jump "out of the jar," this was unacceptable, so without malice, but without hesitation or regret, she resigned.

Bette worked two years with the Girl Scouts of America before her mother saw the ad in the newspaper that was to change her life. The ad was for a person of good character who was ambitious to perform a service and it was placed by Marshall Field of Field Enterprises. Bette answered the ad and after vacillating several times, she agreed to take the training to sell World Book Encyclopedia.

She started like a house-a-fire and has been successful in every phase of the business. She became a Branch Manager in 1960. At that point, Bette had no ambitions to go any higher. She had a superb income, was home every night, doing exactly what she loved to do [share opportunity and build people] and she did not want to "hit the road" and work out of the home office.

Her goals changed because in 1974 the company restructured their field force and moved the Zone Vice Presidency to the field. This excited Bette because it meant she could work in the field with a minimum amount of travel. She took dead aim on the position of Zone Manager which is a field Vice Presidency. Not just *any* Zone, but Zone 5, which was the Midwest. Less than a year later, she got the job she had "aimed" for.

Bette Sundin points out two things that are especially significant. She deals with life with less tension and more confidence because she has her hand — in *The* hand that rules the world. Also, in *every* case she "saw herself" in the next position *before* she got there. She stresses that she was a Branch Manager for 15 years because she *saw herself* as a Branch Manager and *not* as a Zone Manager. After she *saw* herself as a Zone Manager — she became a Zone Manager. Yes, you must "See the Reaching" *before* you can — "Reach the Reaching."

RUST AND STINKWEED

Heartsell Wilson, a top platform speaker, tells how as a boy in East Texas he played on an abandoned section of railroad tracks with two friends. One friend was average size. The other friend's weight indicated that he had seldom, if ever, missed a meal. The boys would challenge each other to see who could walk the track the farthest. Heartsell and one friend would walk a few steps and fall. The overweight boy would walk and walk and not fall off the track. Finally, in exasperated curiosity, Heartsell demanded to know the secret. His overweight friend pointed out that Heartsell and his other buddy were looking down at their feet and, hence, they kept falling. He then explained he was too fat to see his feet, so he picked out a target down the tracks [a long-range goal] and walked toward that spot. As he got close, he selected another target [go as far as you can see and, when you get there, you'll always be able to see farther] and walked toward it.

Here's the irony. The fat boy-turned-philosopher pointed out that if you look down at your feet, all you see is the rust and stinkweed. On the other hand, when you look for a distance down the track you will actually "see the reaching." How true it is.

I would like to make one other point. Had Heartsell and his friend joined hands from opposite tracks, they could have walked indefinitely without falling. That's cooperation — not only with a fellowman, but with the laws of the universe. As George Matthew Adams said, "He climbs highest, who helps another up." **You can get everything in life you want if you help enough other people get what they want.** I'll say this many times throughout the book, because many young people have been sold the garbage-dump idea that you have to step on, abuse and take advantage of others in order to get to the top. In reality, just the opposite is true.

Canadian geese instinctively know the value of cooperation. You have undoubtedly noticed that they always fly in a V formation and one leg of the V is longer than the other. [In case you've wondered, I should explain that the reason one leg of the V is longer than the other is because it has more geese in it.] These geese regularly change leadership because the lead goose, in fighting the head wind, helps create a partial vacuum for the geese on his right as well as the geese on the left. Scientists have discovered in wind tunnel tests that the flock can fly 72% further than an individual goose can fly. Man, too, can fly higher, further and faster by cooperating with, instead of fighting against, his fellowman.

One of the best sources of help [and unfortunately the most neglected one] is the family, especially the mate. If the wife or the husband is "working with you" instead of just "going along for the ride," you can reach your goals faster and easier and have more fun on the trip. Don't be too surprised or disappointed if your mate doesn't initially share your enthusiasm. However, if you do a good job of selling your idea and let your mate know how important it is to have his or her cooperation and interest, both of you will gain considerably in the process. This close association and mutual interest is extremely important because it will enable you to establish a more meaningful relationship. That in itself is a beautiful goal within the goal. As the two of you start toward your goal, neither of you may be able to see the end of the tunnel. But the world has a way, not only of stepping aside for men or women who know where they are going, but it often joins and helps them reach their objective.

YOU NEED A "FIX"

During World War II, the United States developed a torpedo with a brain in it. It was a powerful weapon of destruction. Our nation was in a life-and-death struggle for survival, so this torpedo created a lot of excitement. When the torpedo was aimed at the target and fired, it would establish a "fix" on that target. If the target moved or changed directions, the torpedo would change its direction. Interestingly enough, the torpedo was designed after the human brain. Inside your brain there's something that enables you to "zero in" on a target. Even if the target should move, or you should be side-tracked, once you have gotten your "fix" you will still hit the target.

The "professional" in every field of endeavor will tell you he "see's the reaching" before he — shoots the basketball — putts the golf ball — makes the sales call — etc. In short, he gets a "fix" on the target before he fires the shot.

If you're a mother and want to be a better mother, then get a "fix" and "see the reaching." See yourself doing those things that make you a better mother. If you're a doctor and want to be a better doctor, see yourself doing those things that will make you a better doctor. If you're a Christian and want to be a better Christian, the same thing applies. If you're a student and want to be a better student, start seeing yourself as a better student. If you want to be a top salesperson, then see yourself as already being that top salesperson. By doing this, the unseen forces inside of you start "putting it all together" and they propel you toward your destination.

"I WILL"

A few years ago an international expedition was organized to climb the north wall of the Matterhorn, a feat never before accomplished. Reporters interviewed the members of the expedition who came from all over the world. A reporter asked one member of the troop, "Are you going to climb the north wall of the Matterhorn?" The man replied, "I'm going to give it everything I have." Another reporter asked a second member, "Are you going to climb the north wall of the Matterhorn?" The climber answer, "I'm going to do the very best I can." Still another was asked if he were going to climb the north wall. He said, "I'm going to give it a jolly good effort." Finally, a reporter asked a young American, "Are you going to climb the north wall of the Matterhorn?" The American looked him dead center and said, "I will climb the north wall of the Matterhorn." Only one man did climb the north wall. It was the man who said, "I will." He "saw the reaching."

In every field of endeavor, whether we seek a better job, more material goods, a closer walk with God, more loving children, a permanent and happy marriage or *all* of these things, we must "See the Reaching" before we can "Reach the Reaching."

WHAT DO YOU SEE

I think it's significant that Muhammad Ali, earlier known as Cassius Clay, had lost only two fights at the time of this writing. I think its also significant that in only two fights did he ever use the word "if." "If I should lose this fight" — there was something prophetic in what he said. He prepared the way in the event he failed. From a negative point of view he "saw the reaching."

The Apostle Peter walked on water for a short distance before he started to sink. The Scriptures clearly state, "When he saw the wind boisterous he was afraid. At that instant, he started to sink." Why did he see the wind? Why did he sink? Obviously, because **he took his eyes off the goal, which was Jesus Christ.** When you take your eyes off your goal, you too will start to sink. Yes, when you "see the reaching," whether it is positive or negative, you will then "reach the reaching."

When you keep your eyes on the goal, the chances of reaching that goal are immeasurably better. This is true whether you see victory [climbing the north wall of the Matterhorn] or defeat [Muhammad Ali or the Apostle Peter].

LOOKING UP

Back in the days of sailing ships a young sailor went to sea for the first time. The ship encountered a heavy storm in the North Atlantic. The sailor was commanded to go aloft and trim the sails. As the young sailor started to climb, he made a mistake and looked down. The roll of the ship combined with the tossing of the waves made for a frightening experience. The young man started to lose his balance. At that moment, an older sailor underneath him shouted, "Look up, son, look up!" The young sailor looked up and regained his balance.

When things seem bad, look to see if you're not facing the wrong direction. When you're looking at the sun, you see no shadows. Look back and you build an Edsel, look forward and you build a Mustang. When the outlook isn't good, try the uplook — it's always good. Apply the principles I have already presented, add to them the ones I will discuss, and you will reach your goals.

IT TAKES ACTION

I want to emphasize — **what you get by reaching your goals is not nearly as important as what you become by reaching them.** What about you? Are you sold on the necessity of having goals? Have you started your record keeping so you can find out where you are? Have you taken the first step toward setting your goals? Have you started listing the obstacles that stand between you and your goals? Can you at least partially "see the reaching?" If you answered, "Yes," to all of these questions, draw a bold square around the word "goal" on the "stairway" page. Then, make a note on your Trigger Page to complete the record keeping on your goal setting commitments in thirty days. At that time turn again to this page and encircle the word "goal."

Commit your goals to writing on one or more 3x5 cards. Make certain you print or type clearly so you can easily read every word in every line. Seal the card or cards in plastic [it costs a quarter] and keep these goals with you at all times. Review them daily. In a later chapter you'll understand more fully why this is so important. For the present, *action* is our objective. Remember, the largest locomotive in the world can be held in its tracks while standing still simply by placing a single one-inch block of wood in front of each of the eight drive wheels. The same locomotive moving at 100 miles per hour can crash through a wall of steel reinforced concrete five feet thick. That's the way you are when you're in action. Start now and get up that head of steam. Crash through those obstacles that stand between you and your goals.

With the completion of this Segment you are on step number three. As you can clearly see it is not designed for sitting. You hold your foot on it only long enough to step up to step number four. With this in mind take your felt-tip pen and on the third step write in big bold letters: "**ME — ON MY WAY.**"

NOTES AND IDEAS

When you *know* where you are going, you are half way there.

SEGMENT FIVE

ATTITUDE

PURPOSE:
  I. TO DEMONSTRATE THE IMPORTANCE OF A RIGHT MENTAL ATTITUDE.

  II. TO IDENTIFY SOME OF THE MANY CHARACTERISTICS OF ATTITUDE.

  III. TO INSURE YOUR ATTITUDE AGAINST STINKIN' THINKIN.'

  IV. TO GIVE YOU A FOUR STEP FORMULA ON HOW TO CONTROL YOUR ATTITUDE SO THAT REGARDLESS OF THE CIRCUMSTANCES, YOUR ATTITUDE FOUNDATION IS SOLID.

  V. TO POINT OUT THAT WHEN YOU CHOOSE A HABIT, YOU ALSO CHOOSE THE END RESULT OF THAT HABIT.

  VI. TO TEACH YOU HOW TO AVOID AND/OR ELIMINATE DESTRUCTIVE HABITS AND ACQUIRE GOOD ONES.

ADDITIONAL READING MATERIAL

Norman Vincent Peale — *THE POWER OF POSITIVE THINKING*

W. Clement Stone and Napoleon Hill — *SUCCESS THROUGH A POSITIVE MENTAL ATTITUDE*

Charlie Jones — *LIFE IS TREMENDOUS*

Sammy Hall and Charles Paul Conn — *HOOKED ON A GOOD THING*

G. Z. Patten — *YOU TOO CAN STOP DRINKING*

CHAPTER ONE

IS THE "RIGHT" ATTITUDE IMPORTANT?

30,000 SCHOOLS FOR MEDIOCRITY

Would you like to make more money, have more fun, enjoy life more, reduce fatigue, increase effectiveness, get along better with your neighbors, contribute more to society, enjoy better health and improve your family relationships? No, you are not reading the script from your daily soap opera. Nor is it Hadicol reborn. Nevertheless, all of these things are not only possible but entirely probable with the *right mental attitude*.

In America today, there are over 30,000 schools that will teach you how to do everything from trimming toenails and operating heavy machinery to removing tonsils and curling hair. However, there is not a single school in existence that will teach you how to be any better than mediocre unless you have the *right mental attitude*. This is one thing about which everybody agrees, whether they are doctors, lawyers, teachers, salespeople, parents, kids, Democrats, Republicans, coaches or athletes. They all share the opinion that your attitude, as you undertake a project, is the dominant factor in its success. **In short, your attitude is more important than your aptitude.**

Despite the overwhelming evidence which supports the importance of the right mental attitude, our entire educational system from kindergarten through graduate school virtually ignores or is unaware of this vital factor in our life. 90% of our education is directed at acquiring facts and figures with only 10% of our education aimed at our "feelings" or attitudes. And even than 10% is a little misleading because much of it is aimed at athletic events and their related activities [band, pep squad, cheerleader, etc.]

These figures are truly incredible and distressing when we realize that our "thinking" [facts] brain is only 10% as large as our "feeling" [emotion-attitude] brain. Keep reading — it gets worse. A study by Harvard University revealed that 85% of the reasons for success, accomplishments, promotions, etc. were because of our attitudes and only 15% because of our technical expertise [facts]. Simply stated this means we are spending 90% of our educational time and dollars developing that part of us which is responsible for 15% of our success. We spend 10% of our time and finances developing that part of us which accounts for 85% of our success. And this doesn't take into account the happiness and enjoyment factors. That is the prime reason *See You At The Top* and the course based on the book [The Richer Life Course], which deals with this tremendous need in our educational system, has been so effective. Students *and* teachers are literally starved for guidance in building the proper attitude foundation.

As a matter of fact, William James, the father of American psychology, stated that the most important discovery of our time is that **we can alter our lives by altering our attitudes.**

In layman's language we are not "stuck" with the attitude we have. Whether it's good, bad, or indifferent, it can be — it will be changed — and this book provides some of the answers about how to change to the P.L.A. [positive life attitude.]

THE MILLION DOLLAR DIFFERENCE

There are many facets to this fascinating subject we call attitude. One of them concerns optimism. **An optimist, as you probably know, is a person who, when he wears out his shoes just figures he's back on his feet.** I love the way Robert Schuller differentiates between the optimist and the pessimist. The pessimist says, "I'll believe it when I see it." The optimist says, "I'll see it when I believe it." The optimist takes action — the pessimist takes a seat. An optimist takes a look at a half glass of water and says it's half full. The pessimist looks at the same half glass of water and says it's half empty. The reason is simple. The optimist is putting water in the glass. The pessimist is taking water out of the glass. It's almost a universal truth that the person who is taking from society with no real effort to contribute to society is pessimistic and often fatalistic because he fears there won't be enough for him. The person who is doing his best and is making a contribution is optimistic and confident because he is personally working on the solution. *In life the difference between success and failure is often only an inch or two.*

For example, the great race horse Nashua won over a million

dollars on the race track in less than one hour of actual racing. Hundreds of hours of training were involved, but only an hour of competitive racing on the track. Obviously, Nashua was worth at least a million dollars and a million-dollar horse is truly a rare animal. You can buy 100 ten-thousand-dollar race horses for a million dollars, and that's a mathematical fact. The reason is obvious. The million-dollar horse can run 100 times as fast as a ten-thousand-dollar horse. Right? Wrong! He can run only twice as fast. Right? Wrong again! As a matter of fact, he can run only 25%, or is it just 10% faster or 1% faster? Wrong on all accounts.

How much faster can a million-dollar horse run than a ten-thousand-dollar horse? Several years ago at the Arlington Futurity, the difference between first and second place was $100,000. The Arlington Futurity is a race of one and one-eighth miles, which as you well know is 71,280 inches. [You did know that, didn't you?] The difference between first place and second place was just one of those 71,280 inches. That's right. There was 1/71,280th difference between first and second place, and I might repeat that other inch was worth $100,000.

The winning jockey in the 1974 Kentucky Derby was paid $27,000. Less than two seconds later, the jockey who brought his horse home in fourth place crossed the finish line. He was paid $30. Now whether that is right or wrong is beside the point. That's the way the game of life is played and we cannot change the rules of the game. What we can and must do is learn the rules well and then play them to the best of our ability.

Attitude is the "little" thing that makes the big difference. The story of life proves that it is often the minute things that spell the differences between triumph and tragedy, success and failure, victory or defeat. For example, if you call a girl a kitten, she will love you. Call her a cat and you're in trouble. Say she's a vision and you score points. Call her a sight and you've got a problem. It's the part of the blanket that hangs *over* the bed that keeps you warm. [If you don't believe this, it just means that you've never been in the service and been "short sheeted."] A watch that's four hours off is no problem because anyone will instantly know the watch is wrong and make the necessary corrections. One that is four minutes wrong — especially if it's slow — can create all kinds of problems. For example, if I'm scheduled to catch a flight at 10:00 a.m. and I get there at 10:04 I'm in serious trouble because of the arrangement I have with the airline. The deal is simply that if I'm not there when they get ready to go that they are just to go ahead without me. I found out last summer that they live up to their end of the agreement. I also found out that airplanes are much easier to catch — before they leave the ground.

ALMOST IS NO FUN

In your race to the top in the game of life, the difference between success and failure is frequently measured in minute amounts. The difference between happiness and unhappiness, making or missing a sale, being champion or an also ran is often measured in inches, but the difference in the rewards for the winner and the also ran is enormous.

There is no commission on the sale you almost make, no fun on the trips you almost take and no security in the promotion you almost get. There is no thrill in "almost" doing anything in the game of life. The thrill comes from the accomplishment, and many times the difference between accomplishment and failure is having the *right mental attitude.*

Attitude has many facets, and that's one of the reasons we cover it in such detail in this book. Take, for instance, your own attitude. If you are a student and you study for grades, you will get them, but if you study for knowledge, you will get even better grades and considerably more knowledge. If you strive to make a sale, you will probably make it. Strive to make the sale in such a way that you build a career and you will sell even more and build your career in the process. If you work only for a salary, you will get one, but it will probably be small. If you work for the betterment of the company you represent, not only will you get a bigger salary, but you will get personal satisfaction as well as respect from your colleagues. Your contribution to your company will be infinitely greater which means that your personal and professional rewards will be greater. This story says it quite well.

Several years ago on an extremely hot day, a crew of men were working on the road bed of the railroad when they were interrupted by a slow moving train. The train ground to a stop and a window in the last car — which incidentally was custom made and air conditioned — was raised. A booming, friendly voice called out, "Dave, is that you?" Dave Anderson, the crew chief called back, "Sure is, Jim, and it's really good to see you." With that pleasant exchange, Dave Anderson was invited to join Jim Murphy, the president of the railroad, for a visit. For over an hour the men exchanged pleasantries and then shook hands warmly as the train pulled out.

Dave Anderson's crew immediately surrounded him and to a man expressed astonishment that he knew Jim Murphy, the president of the railroad as a personal friend. Dave then explained that over 20 years earlier he and Jim Murphy had started to work for the railroad on the same day. One of the men, half jokingly and half seriously asked Dave why he was still working out in the hot sun and Jim Murphy had gotten to be president. Rather wistfully Dave explained, "twenty-three years ago I went to work for $1.75 an hour and Jim Murphy went to work for the railroad."

POSITIVE THINKING

Say the word "attitude," and most people think in terms of the positive and negative mental attitude. Although there are many facets to attitude, as you are discovering, I would like to discuss the most familiar one for a moment. Let's look together at the positive aspect of attitude. The best definition of "positive thinking" I know came from my daughter, Suzan, when she was ten years old. I had just returned from Pensacola, Florida, where I conducted a series of seminars for the U.S. Navy. The family had picked me up at the Atlanta Airport and we were driving toward our home in Stone Mountain, Georgia. I was quite excited about the trip and was giving my redhead some of the details. I overheard Suzan's girl friend ask her what her daddy did for a living. Suzan told her I sold that "positive thinking stuff." Naturally the little friend wanted to know what that "positive thinking stuff" was. Suzan explained, "Oh, you know, that's what makes you feel real good even when you feel real bad." I've never heard positive thinking explained any better. How you think does determine what you become.

WOULDN'T IT BE FUNNY

I'm confident you have known someone who has been married anywhere from ten to twenty-five years and have no children. Then they adopted a baby, and within a year or two they had one of their own. Don't misunderstand; there are thousands of people who for physiological reasons cannot have children, but there are even more who for psychological reasons do not have children.

Many times, if a baby is not immediately forthcoming, the couple grows unduly concerned and are soon expressing the fear that they cannot have a family. Then they decide to adopt a baby "before it is too late." When the baby arrives, they are invariably approached by numbers of "friends" and relatives who tell them essentially the same thing, "Wouldn't it be funny if the same thing happened to you that happened to my cousin, sister, friend, neighbor, acquaintance, etc.? The doctor told them they could not have children so they adopted a baby, and within a few months they discovered they were going to have one all on their own."

The mind is a dutiful servant and will follow the instructions we give it. For years the couple had been negatively instructing their minds, "We cannot have a baby," and the body followed the mind's instructions. Later when their friends gave them positive examples of others with the same situation, invariably the husband and wife said to each other, "Wouldn't it be funny if that happened to us?" Now you can finish the story, can't you?

THE "STRIKE" IS ON

A few years ago I was in Flint, Michigan speaking at a luncheon for the Flint Board of Realtors. I'll never forget the experience. Before I spoke, I was visiting pleasantly with the gentleman on my left, when I made the most serious mistake of the day. I asked him about his business expecting to get an enthusiastic response, but for the next ten minutes he elaborated on how bad business really was. He informed me General Motors was on strike and when General Motors was on strike, nobody bought anything from anybody. He assured me things were so bad that the people were not buying shoes, clothes, cars, or even food so they certainly were not buying houses. "I haven't sold a house in so long I honestly don't believe I would know how to fill out the contract," he said. "If it doesn't end in a hurry, I'm going to go bankrupt." He really labored the point. His attitude was so contagious and he was so negative he could have brightened up the whole room — by leaving it. As "this old boy" down home would say, "He is the kind of guy who can be frequently overheard saying nothing."

Finally, somebody saved my day by diverting his attention with a question. I quickly turned to the little lady on my right and asked, "Well, how is everything?" Now, I think you'll agree a question like that gave her all kinds of leeway. She could go in any direction she desired and talk about any subject she wished. Guess what she said? "Well, you know, Mr. Ziglar, General Motors is on strike . . ." I thought to myself, "Oh no, not again." Then she broke out in a big beautiful smile and finished the sentence by saying, "So business is fantastic. For the first time in months, these people have plenty of time to go shopping for the home of their dreams." "Why," she said, "some of them will spend half a day looking at one house. They start in the attic and check the insulation. They measure every square inch and check everything from closets and cabinets to the foundation. I even had one couple do their own title search on a piece of property. These people know the strike is going to end and they have faith in the American economy, but the most important thing is this, they know they can buy a home cheaper right now than they will ever be able to buy one again. So, business is really booming." Then she got quite confidential as she said, "Mr. Ziglar, do you know anyone in Washington? [Now remember, this was before Watergate.] I said, "I sure do. I have a nephew in school down there." Then she said, "No, no, I mean do you know anyone in Washington who has some political influence?" I said, "No, I'm afraid not, but why do you ask?" She replied, "I was thinking. If you knew someone who could keep this strike going for six more weeks, that's all I would need — just six more weeks and I could quit for the year."

One person was going broke because of the strike and another was getting rich because of it. The external conditions were the same, but their attitudes were enormously different. I'm convinced your business is never either good or bad — out there.

Your business is either good or bad between your ears. If your thinkin' is stinkin', your business is going to be the same. If your thinking right, your business is going to be right.

IT'S JUST A PILE OF WOOD

In the 1930's, minor league baseball was truly outstanding, and it was especially so in the Texas League. In those years, for instance, the San Antonio team had seven batters who hit over 300. During the 1976 major league season, only 10 American League batters hit that well and only 14 were able to accomplish it in the entire National League. At any rate, everybody was confident San Antonio would win the pennant, especially with its abundance of outstanding hitters. However, as is often the case on "sure things," a funny thing happened on the way to the pennant. San Antonio lost its first, second and third game. They lost the fourth and the fifth and the sixth games, too. As a matter of fact, at the end of 21 games, the San Antonio baseball team, power laden though it was, had lost 18 games.

The pitcher was blaming the catcher, the catcher was blaming the shortstop, the shortstop was blaming the first baseman, the first baseman was blaming the outfielder. As a matter of fact, everybody was blaming everybody else and the results were obviously and understandably disastrous.

And then one day — this talent-laden, but slump ridden San Antonio team played Dallas, the weakest hitting team in the league, in an afternoon game and Dallas won the game, 1—0.

San Antonio got only one hit. Josh O'Reilly, the outstanding manager of the San Antonio team knew that his team was physically sound. The problem was *"a lousy mental attitude."* In short — they were suffering from "stinkin' thinkin'," so O'Reilly looked around for a "cure" for the disease. At this time there was a faith healer in Dallas named Slater who had gained a reputation as a miracle worker, so O'Reilly devised a plan.

The second game of the series was just one hour away when O'Reilly took action. He came into the clubhouse with a burst of enthusiasm and said, "Fellows, I've got the answer to our problems. Don't worry about a thing. Give me your two best bats and I'll be back with you before game time. We're going to win

210

this game today and we're going to win the pennant." He took each man's two best bats, put them in a wheelbarrow and left. He returned about five minutes before game time afire with enthusiasm as he spoke to his team. "Fellows," he said, "we've got the problem solved. Don't worry about a thing. I've been to Mr. Slater, and he's put his blessings on these bats. He says all we have to do is step up to the plate, take a cut and we'll hit the ball. We're going to win this game and we're going to win the pennant. Don't worry about a thing. Just "go get 'em tigers."

And what did his tigers do? Remember now, this is the team that had been beaten a day earlier by a score of 1 to 0. But as the song goes, "What a Difference a Day Makes." The San Antonio team that had only gotten one hit the day before scored 22 runs and got 37 hits, including 11 home runs. I don't think it's necessary to point out that they won the game. Not only did they win the game, but they also won the pennant.

Some intriguing thoughts come to mind from this story, especially since Slater bats sold at a high premium throughout the Texas League for several years. First of all, no one ever established whether Slater had actually seen those bats. But suppose he had, what could Slater do to the pile of wood from which the bats were made. I'm sure you'll agree there was nothing Slater could have done to that pile of wood. However, I'm personally convinced there was a great deal he could do with the attitude of the men who were swinging the bats. Yes, indeed, something did happen to the minds of the men, and that's why they got all the hits that won the game and the pennant.

ENTHUSIASM IS AN ATTITUDE

A positive attitude will have positive results because attitudes are contagious. One such attitude is enthusiasm. Elbert Hubbard said, "Nothing great has ever been accomplished without enthusiasm." The difference between the good preacher and the great preacher, the good mother and the great mother, the good speaker and the great speaker or the good salesman and the great salesman is often enthusiasm. The word "enthusiasm" comes from the Greek words *en theos* and simply means "God within." If you look at the word "enthusiasm" the last four letters form an acrostic, "Iasm," which can stand for *"I am, sold, myself."* If you are sold yourself and if you truly believe in your cause, your company and your product, then you don't have a "teeth-out" enthusiasm. You have an enthusiasm that comes from the wellspring of all the resources within you.

Real enthusiasm is not something you "put on" and "take off" to fit the occasion, it is a way of life and not something you use to impress people. It has nothing to do with being loud or noisy; it is an outward expression of an inner feeling. Many extremely enthusiastic people are fairly quiet, yet every fiber of their being, every word and action, attest to the fact they love life and what it means to them. Some people who are enthusiastic are obviously loud, but loudness is neither a requisite for, nor is it necessarily an indication of enthusiasm.

THE MAD BUTCHER

According to Allan Bellamy, who personifies enthusiasm, most people let conditions control their attitude instead of using their attitude to control conditions. If "things" are good, their attitude is good. If "things" are bad, their attitude is bad. Allan believes that's the wrong approach. He believes you should build a solid attitude *foundation* so when "things" are good your attitude is good and when "things" are bad your attitude is still good, which means that soon "things" will be good. His own story supports this point.

When Allan returned from the Korean War, his mother invited him to join her in a "Mom & Pop" grocery store. Allan says it was so small, when you opened the front door it bumped against the meat counter — which was at the back door. Business was good — real good for Allan and his mother in Pine Bluff, Arkansas. This wasn't surprising because any mother who can raise her family from the dirt floor of a tent, when left on her own during the depression, and give them an education, has a lot going for her.

Since he was raised on the "someday we'll make it big" philosophy, Allan wasn't the least bit bashful about talking to the local banker about a loan — a big one, to expand the store. With limited capital but unlimited enthusiasm he persuaded the bank to loan them $95,000 to build a supermarket. Opening day was chaotic — [lots of rain on an unpaved parking lot] but highly successful. His business grew and prospered — and then word leaked out that Pine Bluff, Arkansas was the place to build a supermarket. During the next six months, ten major chain competitors opened a store in the area. Every opening took a little more of the Mad Butcher's business. [He got that name when a salesman told him it was madness to buy neck bones for 15 cents a pound and sell them for 10 cents. Allan assured him it was all right because he was the "Mad Butcher" — and the name was born.] Pretty soon Allan was doing less business in the big store than he had in the little one; and things looked pretty bleak. Then Allan and four of his people signed up for a public speaking course which places considerable emphasis on the right mental attitude. The fifth session was on enthusiasm which is, after all, an attitude. After that night Allan decided he and his people would be five times as enthusiastic as ever before. Now everyone in Pine Bluff *knew* he was mad. His customers were met at the door with an enthusiastic welcome and the entire attitude from top to bottom and front to back changed dramatically — and so did the results. In just four weeks the business jumped from $15,000 per week to $30,000 per week — and it hasn't fallen below that amount since.

Please understand, Pine Bluff didn't suddenly increase its population nor did the competition close their doors [though seven of them have now thrown in the towel.] The only change was the addition of enthusiasm. Since it worked so well on a temporary basis, Allan decided to leave it in permanently. Since that date, nearly seventeen years ago, the Mad Butcher has expanded into 26 highly successful stores. In 1974, in the face of a declining economy, The Mad Butcher, Inc. had the largest dollar and percentage increase in its history. 1976 was even better with sales in the neighborhood of $35,000,000 [that's a *nice* neighborhood]. The enthusiasm is so contagious that personnel turnover is practically zero. Since people are the prime reason for any business success or failure, Allan Bellamy — The Mad Butcher — is enthusiastically in the people-building business. He believes — as do most successful business people — that if you build your people, your people will build your business.

THE "GO GIVE" ATTITUDE

In today's world we hear so much about the go-getter we often overlook the go-giver. Don't misunderstand. I'm 100% for the go-getter. I feel "this old boy down home" was right on target. In the days of yesteryear, he ferried passengers across the Yazoo River which flows along the outskirts of Yazoo City, Mississippi. It was on this river — within the city limits, that the first torpedo was used in actual warfare. It happened in the War of Northern Aggression which is referred to in some Yankee history books as the Civil War. [That lump you see in my cheek is my tongue.] This old boy charged ten cents for each trip across the river. Once when asked how many trips he made each day, he answered, "As many as I can because the more I go, the more I get and if I don't go, I don't get."

Yes, I believe in the go-get attitude *and* the go-give attitude. As a matter of fact, I don't believe you can separate them, as the story of Israel, which is the most exciting story of the 20th Century, so clearly demonstrates. Born in adversity in 1948 — as the Bible had prophesied — the Israeli have created prosperity and a veritable oasis, in a sea of sand and poverty, among their Arab neighbors. [Don't be misled by those wealthy oil sheiks, the vast majority live in unbelievable poverty and ignorance.] Although Israel was terribly short in many resources, the Israeli did not let what they did not have, prevent them from using what they did have. When you've waited 2,000 years to come back home and have suffered persecution and discrimination all over the world, you can rest assured that every man, woman and child returned to his homeland with a tremendous amount of zeal and determination. Each came bringing the pent-up frustration of 2,000 years of being denied freedom and equal opportunity. Each one came to carve for himself a place in his homeland, and he was not only willing, he was anxious to give something in return.

The results have been the wonder of this century. He added water by irrigating the desert — and created high producing vineyards. He added ingenuity to hard work and attracted business and tourists from all over the world. He added commitment, pride, and the go-give spirit to a population of less than 3,000,000 people. This commitment and dedication in building a free and prosperous land, has enabled Israel to more than hold her own against the combined forces of the 100,000,000 Arab people who surround her. Yes, Israel is quite a story. They came to give — and get. They did both. Incidentally, Israel has the lowest crime rate in the Western world and vandalism is virtually nonexistent.

It's universally true, when you build something with your own blood, sweat and tears, it's highly unlikely you will turn around and tear it down. Builders are not destroyers — and destroyers are not builders.

LOST — AND FOUND

Even before Ed and Pam Jansen bought the philosophy of See You At The Top, they had a lot going for them. Happy marriage, beautiful kids, successful business, etc. But as Ed put it, they both felt that life could be even better. So when they saw the immediate personal benefits from the philosophy, they decided to share it with their sales people every Saturday morning. [They have the second largest furniture store in Kansas City.] The warehouse employees almost immediately wanted to get involved so Ed set aside two hours on Monday morning [8:00 a.m. to 10:00 a.m.] to teach the philosophy to all who were interested. When three of the employees did not participate, Ed discovered they could not read and the fear of embarrassment kept them from participating. Ed immediately assured them that they would not be embarrassed and urged them to attend. Since that time [February, 1977] two of the three have started learning to read and one got a much better job which pleased Ed a great deal.

A person with "tunnel" vision would react negatively to losing a good worker and valuable employee, but Ed Jansen plans to seek more people who can't read and write, teach them this philosophy, and maybe lose them too. Some would say that's a funny way to build a business, but when the employees saw Ed's deep personal interest in them, they took a much more personal interest in the business. Results: the best month in history — the following month, with every indication that it is going to get better and better. It truly "pays" to be genuinely interested in others because employees "don't care how much you know until they know how much you care." Yes, Ed "lost" a valuable employee — but he "found" a bigger business and better life — and a store full of better employees. Ed and Pam are reaching their goals by helping others reach theirs.

TOO BIG TO HIT OR
TOO BIG TO MISS

The way you see things — your attitude — is the most important factor in its success. It's always been that way as this story which happened thousands of years ago, proves.

I love the Bible, and believe it should be made available as a course in every school, because God so clearly demonstrates the difference between positive and negative thinking. The story of David and Goliath is one of my favorites and clearly emphasizes the point. The 9-foot, 400 lb. Goliath is challenging the children of Israel and blaspheming Almighty God. David, a 17-year-old, fuzzy-cheeked lad who came to see his brothers, demanded to know why they weren't accepting the challenge. [The rest is scripturally accurate but slightly Ziglarized.] The brothers explained that you could easily get hurt by fighting fellows like Goliath. They felt certain Goliath was just too big to hit. David *knew* Goliath was too big to *miss*. Next, David wanted to know where the King was and the brothers explained that the King didn't feel so good. When David told the brothers he would fight Goliath, they figured he was crazy. Obviously, the brothers were comparing their size to Goliath's and that made the 9 ft. Goliath pretty big. David was comparing Goliath's size to God — and that quite obviously made Goliath pretty small. [In case you haven't heard — David and God won.]

I also love the Bible because of its beautiful simplicity and clarity. Many people say they don't read the Bible because they don't understand it. I'm convinced their problem is not what they *don't* understand but what they *do* understand. Personally, I feel God speaks quite clearly. I'm sure you've noticed He didn't call the Ten Commandments the Ten Suggestions.

The "right" mental attitude encompasses so many areas that it would be difficult to decide which is the most important one. The next story zeroes in on one of the most neglected areas.

GREEN — AND GROWING

When I was an instructor for the Dale Carnegie Institute in New York City, it was my privilege to meet an outstanding salesman who was over 60 years of age. His name was Ed Green, and he sold real "pie in the sky" advertising. His income was reputed to be in excess of $75,000 a year, which would be the equivalent of something like $125,000 in today's economy. One night, after one of the classes, I engaged Ed in conversation and asked him quite frankly what he was doing in a class being taught by three men who had a combined income less than his. He smilingly replied "Zig, let me tell you a little story. When I was a boy, my dad took me on a trip through our garden. Dad was probably the best gardener in the community. He worked at it, loved it and was proud of it. After we finished the trip, Dad asked what I learned from the tour." Ed smiled as he continued, "The only thing I could see was that Dad had obviousy done a lot of work in the garden. At this point Dad became somewhat impatient and said, "Son, I had hoped you would observe that *as long as the vegetables were green, they were growing, but when they got ripe, they started to rot.*"

Ed finished the story by saying, "And you know, Zig, I've never forgotten that story. I came to this class because I figured I would learn something. To be completely honest, I did learn something in one of the classes that enabled me to close an account worth many thousands of dollars in commissions. I'd tried for over two years to make that sale. The commission from it has paid for all of the sales training I've taken all of my life."

Naturally, it was exciting to get a testimonial from a man like Ed Green. We continued the conversation, and I pointed out how pleased I was at his response. I also mentioned that one of the younger members of the class complained he "had heard all of these things and wasn't getting a thing out of the class." Ed observed that the young man had an attitude problem. Then he drew an interesting analogy, "Zig, I've been married over 40 years and when my wife puckers up for me to kiss her, I know exactly how it is going to be, but I still enjoy it."

In the game of life, you retain that zest for living and for learning by constantly seeking to put into your mind the things which will result in growth. Peter Drucker expressed it this way, **"Knowledge has to be improved, challenged and increased constantly or it vanishes."**

ACTION — REACTION

The next example might make the most important point in this book.

Mr. B wasn't satisfied with the way things were going in his company. He called a meeting and said, "Now, folks, we have to get organized. Some of you come to work late and some leave early. Why, some of you don't even accept the full responsibility of your jobs. Now, as President of this company, I am going to reorganize it.Since I should set the example for you to follow, here's what I'm going to do. From now on, I will be here early, I will stay late. In everything I do, I intend to be an example. If my example is good, you'll be expected to follow it. If it isn't good, I would understand if you followed it. We have a fine company and the future looks great if each of us properly handles his job and does his "best."

Like a lot of people, Mr. B's intentions were good, but a few days later he became engrossed in conversation during a luncheon at the country club and forgot the time. When he finally looked at his watch he was so startled, he almost dropped his cup of coffee as he said, "Oh, my goodness, I'm due back at the office in 10 minutes." He hopped up, made a mad dash to the parking lot, jumped in his automobile, scratched off and burned rubber like nobody you have ever seen. He was doing about 90 miles per hour down the freeway when the long arm of the law entered the picture and gave him a blistering tongue lashing and a ticket. [Hope this doesn't bring back painful memories.]

Mr. B was furious. Muttering to himself, he said, "This is really something. Here I am, a peaceful, tax-paying, law-abiding citizen, minding my own business, when this guy comes along and gives me a ticket. What he should be doing is spending his time looking for criminals, thieves and robbers. He should leave us tax-paying citizens alone. Just because I was going fast doesn't mean that I wasn't safe. This is ridiculous."

OH, HE WAS UPSET

When he got back to the office, to divert attention from the fact that he was late, he called his sales manager in for a conference, Angrily, he asked if the Armstrong sale had been finalized. The sales manager said, "Mr. B, I don't know what happened but something did and we lost the sale." Now, if you think Mr. B was upset before, you should have seen him now. He hit the ceiling as he read the "riot act" to the sales manager. "You know, I've had you on the payroll for eighteen years. During that time, I've depended upon you to produce business. Now, at last, we have an opportunity to make the big deal that would have enabled us to expand our product line, and what do you do? You blow it. Well, let me tell you something, friend. You are either going to replace that business, or I'm going to replace you. Just because you've been here 18 years doesn't mean you have a lifetime contract." Oh boy, he was really upset.

SO WAS HE

But, if you think Mr. B was upset, you should have seen his sales manager. He charged out of the office muttering under his breath, "Isn't this something? For 18 years I've given this company my 100% effort. I'm the one responsible for the success and growth of the company because I create all the new business. I'm the one who holds the company together and keeps it functioning. Mr. B is just a figurehead. This company would go down the tube in nothing flat if it weren't for me. Now, just because I miss one sale, he uses a cheap, lousy trick and threatens to fire me. This isn't right."

Still talking to himself, the sales manager calls his secretary in and demands, "Did you finish those five letters I gave you this morning?" She said, "No, don't you remember, you told me the Hillard account took precedence over everything else? That's what I've been doing." Now the sales manager exploded. "Don't give me any lousy excuses," he barked, "I told you I wanted those letters out, and if you can't get them out, I'll get someone who can. Just because you have been here seven years doesn't mean you have a lifetime contract. I want those letters mailed today, and I want them mailed without fail." Oh my, he was upset.

SHE WAS UPSET

But if you think he was upset, you should have seen the secretary. She really blew her stack as she stomped out of the sales manager's office talking to herself. "How about that? For seven years I've given this job my very best. Hundreds of hours of overtime work and never a dime in overtime pay. I do more work than any three people around here. As a matter of fact, I'm really the one who has kept the company together. Now, just because I can't do two things at the same time, he threatens to fire me. This isn't right. Besides, with all the things I know about him, who does he think he's kidding?" She walked out to the switchboard operator and said, "I have some letters I want you to type. Now, I know that ordinarily this isn't your job, but you don't do anything anyway except sit here and occasionally answer the telephone. Besides, this is an emergency and I want these letters mailed today. If you can't get them, let me know and I'll get somebody who can." Oh, she was upset and she let everyone know it.

SHE WAS UPSET TOO

But if you think she was upset, you should have seen the switchboard operator. She just about hit the ceiling. "This is really something," she said, "Here I am, the hardest-working member of the staff and the lowest paid. I have to do four things at once and they don't do a thing in the back but drink coffee, gossip and talk on the telephone. Only occasionally do they do any work, and every time they get behind they call on me to bail them out. It just isn't fair. This garbage about replacing me is really a joke because I'm the only one who has any idea about what is going on around here. If it hadn't been for me the company would have gone down the tube long ago. Not only that, but they know they couldn't find anyone to do my work at twice my salary." She got the letters out, but she really was burning as she did.

When she got home, she was still fuming. She walked into the house, slammed the door and proceeded into the den. The first thing she saw was her 12-year-old son lying on the floor watching television. The second thing she saw was a big rip across the seat of his britches. Highly provoked she said, "Son, how many times have I told you to put on your play clothes when you come home from school? Mother has a hard enough time as it is just supporting you, sending you through school and running this entire household. Now, you go upstairs right now. There's going to be no dinner for you tonight and no television for the next three weeks." Oh, she was upset.

KICKING THE CAT

But if you think she was upset, you should have seen her 12-year-old son. He stomped out of the den saying, "This isn't fair. I was doing something for mother, but she didn't even give me a chance to explain what happened. It was an accident, and could have happened to anybody." About that time, his tomcat walked in front of him. That proved to be a mistake. The boy gave him a big boot and said, "You get out of here! You've probably been up to some no good yourself."

Obviously, the tomcat was the only principal involved in this series of events who couldn't have altered the events, and this leads me to ask a very simple question. Wouldn't it have been much better if Mr. B had just gone directly from the country club to the switchboard operator's house and kicked that cat himelf?

Now, for a more important question. Whose cat have you been kicking lately? In order to help you answer my question, let's look at a series of reactions to situations. How do you react to humor? How about a smile? A compliment? How do you respond to agreeable people? How do you react when you make a sale or when people are nice, pleasant and courteous to you? How do you respond to a beautiful day or to a waitress who looks after your needs in a courteous manner? I'll bet you're pleasant, smile back and are courteous. I'll bet you appreciate all these things and they make you a friendly person. But for this you don't get a nickel's worth of credit. You see, anybody can respond favorably to circumstances like those we just described.

YOU — AND THE BUM IN THE BOWERY

How do you react to rudeness, anger, sarcasm, rejection or a slow, rude waitress? How do you respond to a traffic delay or a

Don't be a cat kicker.
React positively to negative situations.

cold, dreary day? When somebody gives you an undeserved verbal blast, do you blast right back? Do you let others pull you down to their level or do you recognize that the incident probably has *nothing* to do with you; someone else may have just stopped by and "kicked their cat." You just happened to be the next one in line. When the driver behinds you lets go with a blast of the horn, despite the fact traffic is stalled a mile in either direction, what do you do? Do you turn around and shake your fist at him while giving him a dirty look? Do you let him pull you down to his level, or do you smile and say, "Just because somebody kicked his "cat" is no reason for me to let him kick mine." When your wife, or husband, takes some pent-up frustration out on you, how do you react? How do you react to being passed over for a promotion, getting a "C" instead of an "A," missing a big sale, being slighted by Mr. Big, not being invited to the senior prom, failing to make the team or being elected to the club presidency? Your response to the negative "cat kicking" situations will largely determine your success and happiness in life.

The bum in the Bowery, the community leader, the top student, the self-made millionaire and the Mother of the Year all have a great deal in common. Each one faces frustration, heartache, disappointment, despondency and defeat. The difference in accomplishment is the result of a different *reaction* to the negatives of life. The bum reacted by saying "poor me" and in an effort to drown his problems *by* drinking — drowned *in* his drink. The successful person took similar and often greater problems — reacted positively — sought the benefit in the problem and came out stronger and more successful as a result. **We can't tailor-make the situations of life, but we can tailor-make the attitude to fit them — before they arise.** That's attitude control, and you will learn "how" in this book. You will learn in most cases, when somebody gives you an undeserved verbal blast it is because somebody else kicked his "cat." You will learn that it has nothing to do with you. More importantly, you will learn how to react positively to that negative and to other negatives as well.

As a starter, let me suggest the next time someone [start with a loved one] lowers the boom on your innocent head [be careful now and *know* you are innocent], smile and say, "Honey, has anyone been kicking your "cat" today?" If you survive that one [you will], you can move to the general public with a slight variation. When a stranger or casual acquaintance "chews you out" for no reason [again be careful and know you are innocent], just smile and say, "I have an unusual question to ask you — has anybody been kicking your "cat" today?" This brings on a variety of responses, but remember at this point you are behind in the ballgame. [Don't be surprised if he tells you, probably with some disgust, that he "doesn't have a cat."] This really means you are reacting positively to the negative and pleasantly to the unpleasant. It's natural and human to feel that the other person doesn't deserve such nice treatment from you. And you might be right, but this response is best for you and *you deserve the best treatment you can give you.*

WHEN YOU GET DOWN — GET UP

Now, let's take a positive look at some negative thinking. My friend and colleague, Cavett Robert, takes a philosophical, refreshing and common-sense approach to a journey into Negativeville as he observes, "Nobody fails by falling down or getting despondent. They only fail if they stay down or negative." Cavett stresses that you should be like a leaky tire. A defeat should take something out of you and deflate you a bit. If it didn't, it would be a strong indication you not only didn't mind losing, but you weren't emotionally involved in wanting to win.

Let me add, however, I'm talking about your internal reaction to defeat. Obviously, I don't feel you should pout, throw a temper tantrum, be a poor sport or indulge in any other childish behavior. Be gracious and mature and remember, **if you learn from a defeat, you haven't really lost.** With this new attitude, the chances are good you will enter the winner's circle after the next encounter.

You must be capable of getting emotionally high in order to fully utilize the talent you have. Frankly, it's always been a puzzle to me why anyone would think they've done something terribly wrong and have feelings of guilt, doubt and self-incrimination whenever they get a little despondent. This is a natural state of affairs, and it's perfectly all right. Let me emphasize, however, while it might be normal and all right to "get down," it is neither normal nor all right to stay that way.

Sooo — how do you get up when you are down? First — recognize that you are "down." Second — understand that **there are seldom, if ever, any "hopeless" situations.** Third — *know* that the condition is temporary and fourth — set a time limit on how long you plan to stay down. Example: I'm not a member of an organized political party — I'm a Republican. When Jimmy Carter defeated Gerald Ford for President, I was terribly disappointed. I was confident Mr. Ford would be a better president. After the election I had to decide whether I would try to help — or hurt Mr. Carter, America, and myself. I knew what I should do and what my Bible told me to do, *but* I was disappointed and felt that I had "earned" a few days of misery so I set November 15 as my "get up" day. In the interim period I said and thought negative things about Mr. Carter. On November 15, I started reading "good things" about Jimmy Carter. I listened to Carter fans, sought background material, followed his thinking on cabinet appointments, and studied some of his procedures for trimming fat from the bureaucracy. In a matter of days, I was amazed at how much *he* had changed.

On matters of lesser significance surely two hours is long enough to stay "down," but you follow the same procedure. In most cases your contacts with others will probably go like this: Other person — "How ya doing?" You — "Super good after 11:30." Other person — "Why *after* 11:30?" You — "I just suffered a disappointment and I'm being negative until then." Other person — "You mean you are going to be negative until 11:30 and then you will be positive?" You — "That's right." Other person — "That's silly, if you are going to be positive at 11:30 why not be positive right now?" You — "O.K. You talked me into it." Silly — yes and even ludicrous, *but* it works because you are laughing at your problems instead of crying about them.

I believe this example will help you accept my statement that there are no hopeless situations. A famous painting shows the Devil across a chess board with a young man. The Devil has just made his move and the young man's king appears to be checkmate. Total defeat and despair are registered on the young man's face. One day the great chess genius, Paul Mercer, stood looking at that painting. He carefully studied the positions on the board and suddenly his face lighted up as he shouted to the young man in the painting, "Don't give up, you still have a move." You too will *always* have "one more move"

Let me emphasize a point. Attitude is catching. It's like the flu. If you wanted the flu, you would go to someone who has it and become exposed to it. Any time you want to "catch something," just go where it's prevalent. If you want to catch the right mental attitude, go where that attitude exists. Start by going to the people who have the right mental attitude. If the right people aren't always available, then go to the right book, or to the recording of a dynamic speaker.

In today's world, virtually everyone agrees on what I've been "selling" you. Teachers, coaches, doctors, sales managers, mothers, etc., *all* agree that the right mental attitude is important. The question, Coach, is: "How do we get — and then keep — the right mental attitude, regardless of "outside" conditions, people, weather, etc.?" Glad you asked. The answer is in the next two chapters.

NOTES AND IDEAS

CHAPTER TWO

INSURING YOUR ATTITUDE

YOUR MIND WORKS THIS WAY

Most successful, happy, well adjusted people I know, want to know the whys and hows of life. Give them reasons for doing things when you tell them what to do and they will feel they are part of the project and not just employees following orders. Results are definitely better. Since this chapter might be the most significant one in the book [it is definitely the one which will produce the fastest results.] I want to explain in lay language the way the mind works so that you will understand why we suggest taking certain steps and following the procedures we recommend. Then we get into a very specific procedure which will enable you to "insure" your attitude and build a foundation so solid that your attitude controls your circumstances instead of *your* circumstances controlling your attitude.

The mind works like a garden. Everyone knows if you plant beans you won't raise potatoes — you will raise beans. Obviously you don't plant a bean to raise *a* bean — you plant a bean to raise *lots* of beans. Between planting and harvest there is a tremendous increase in the number of beans. That's the way the mind works. Whatever you plant in the mind is going to come up — multiplied. Plant *a* negative or *a* positive and you reap in multiples because between planting and harvest, imagination enters the picture and multiplies the result.

In some ways the mind also works like a money bank, but in other ways, it is quite different. For example, anybody and anything [radio-T.V., etc.] can make either positive or negative deposits in your mind bank. Generally speaking, *you* are the only one who makes deposits in your bank account and *all* bank deposits are positive.

You are the *only* one who determines who will make withdrawals from either the bank or the mind. *All* withdrawals from the money bank reduce the account. Withdrawals from the mind increase its strength *if* you use the right "teller."

In your mind bank there are two tellers — both of whom are obedient to your every command. One teller is positive and handles positive deposits and positive withdrawals. The other teller is negative and will accept all negative deposits and provide you with negative feedback.

As the owner of your mind, you have complete control over *all* withdrawals and most deposits. The deposits represent your total experience in life. The withdrawals determine your success and happiness. Obviously, you can't withdraw anything that hasn't been deposited. [That's true in the cash bank too, isn't it?]

Each transaction involves a choice of which teller to use. Confront the negative teller with a problem and he will remind you of how poorly you performed in the past. He will predict failure with your current problem. Confront your positive teller and he will enthusiastically tell you how you successfully dealt with far more difficult problems in the past. He will give you examples of your skill and genius and assure you that you can easily solve this problem. Both tellers are right because: Whether you think you can or think you can't — you are right.

Obviously you know you *should* deal only with the positive teller, but can you and will you? The natural *tendency* is to make your withdrawals from the latest deposits in your mind *regardless* of whether it was powerful and positive or critical and negative. I emphasize that you have a tendency to withdraw the latest deposit. Obviously the *total* deposits in your mind will dominate the withdrawals.

Question please? Have the deposits been predominately honest — or dishonest? Moral or immoral? Conservative or liberal? God-directed or self-centered? Wasteful or saving? Bold or cautious? Lazy or industrious? Positive or negative? Free enterprise or socialism?

This I stress. Lots of negative garbage is and has been dumped into your mind *but* a lot of good, clean, powerful deposits and affirmations of "you can do it" have also been injected into your mind and more are on the way. Now we get into the specifics on how to bury the negative with even more positive deposits so that your positive teller is always armed with positive answers when you approach him for a withdrawal.

GARBAGE ON THE FLOOR
VS. GARBAGE IN THE MIND

If I were to come into your home with a pail of garbage and dump it on your living room floor, we would have problems — fast. One of three things would happen. You would either whip me physically, call the police to have me arrested or get your gun and say, "Now, Ziglar, I'll just bet you can clean that garbage off the floor." I'll just bet I could, too. As a matter of fact, I would probably do it so well there wouldn't be a trace of garbage left. Interestingly enough, however, you would probably continue to tell your friends and neighbors about the guy who came in and dumped garbage on your floor. For months you would probably say, "I started to shoot him and now I kinda wish I had." You'd make a big deal of the garbage on the floor.

What do you do to the people who dump garbage into your mind? How do you respond to those people who come along and tell you the things you can't do as they build ceilings over your capability? How do you respond to the people who say unkind things about your product, your community, your church, your country, your family, your boss or your school? What do you do to those people who dump their negative garbage into your mind? Perhaps you just grin and say, "That's right, this isn't really going to hurt me. It doesn't bother me to dump the garbage in." Let me tell you something, my friend, that's where you're just as wrong as you can be. If you dump garbage in, garbage will come out. The person who dumps garbage into your mind will do you considerably more harm than the one who dumps garbage on your floor.

Every thought that goes into your mind has an effect to some degree. For example, exhaustive research concerning the common cold has resulted in almost no reliable data on either the cause — or the cure for the cold. However, it has been conclusively established that you are far more likely to "catch" the cold when you are emotionally down or depressed. "Stinkin' thinkin' " does cause problems, doesn't it?

On the other side of the ledger, "positive thinking," like Dr. Norman Vincent Peale has been saying for years, produces positive results. In 1969 Charles Ritter of Sac City, Iowa had cancer and one kidney had to be removed. Three months later a malignancy was discovered in each of his lungs. Since Charley was physically unable to undergo surgery, the doctors at Mayo Clinic asked him if he would be willing to try an experimental drug. With nothing to lose and a life to gain, Charley Ritter agreed to give it a try. This particular drug apparently works only on people over sixty years of age and it only works in about 10% of the cases. It worked on Charley. He lived six more years and then died of a heart attack. The autopsy revealed no trace of his ever having had cancer. Incidentally, the doctors at Mayo Clinic have discovered that the cancer victims on whom the drug works have two things in common. They *all* have a tremendous *desire* to live and they *all believe* the drug will work on them.

THIS IS RIDICULOUS

I'm constantly amazed at the inconsistencies concerning our thinking about the relative value of what goes into our minds. It is the unanimous opinion of serious students of progress that education is important. They quote study after study that "proves" the value of an education and they present irrefutable evidence for their case. They "prove" that what you learn — what you put in your mind, does have an effect — a positive one. Ironically, many of these same people will vehemently argue that we shouldn't worry about pornographic filth being printed and circulated or shown on TV because this material which you put in your mind couldn't possibly have any effect on you. I hope you agree that thinking like this is a little inconsistent. Obviously, you can get information from the printed page, the spoken word, or the TV screen, that inspires you to greater heights — *or* negatively affects both motivation and morals.

I hasten to add this is not an opinion. In 1972, the Surgeon General of the United States, after a two-year study, declared that evidence showed a definite casual relationship between televised violence and antisocial behavior. Dr. Albert Bendura of Stanford and Dr. Leonard Berkowitz of the University of Wisconsin produced studies which show that people who see violence portrayed will behave nearly *twice* as violently as people who have not seen it. Presentations of violence can cause *anyone* to become more aggressive. Children, being more suggestible, are even more vulnerable. According to Dr. Berkowitz, "It's pretty certain that people who watch sex movies are going to be sexually active afterward." Since the average American youngster spends approximately 15,000 hours watching TV by the time he graduates from high schools, *what* he views will definitely affect his thoughts and, hence, his actions.

PLANT NEGATIVES — REAP NEGATIVES

Unfortunately, because of our negative environment, most people expect the worst and they're seldom disappointed. They plant the negative, so they reap the negative. Here's an example. Tomorrow morning when you report for work, imagine you see a note on your desk from the boss saying, "See me as soon as you arrive." You head for his office, but his secretary intercepts you and explains he is on long distance for a few minutes, and you'll have to wait. Now the thought process starts. "I wonder what he wants. Could he have seen me leave early yesterday? I wonder if he knows about Joe and me having that argument in front of the staff? Or is it . . .?" On and on the thoughts go. It's true, we plant a negative seed and all too often reap a negative harvest.

Let me give you another example. Little Johnny comes home from school with a note from his teacher suggesting a conference. Your first thought is, "I wonder what the problem is?" Perhaps you ask, "I wonder what he has done this time?" It's unfortunate that we put so many negatives into our minds, because **whatever we put into our minds is going to come out of them.** It's like the story of Teresa Jones, from Wilmington, Delaware. She had a serious kidney infection. An operation was scheduled to remove one of the kidneys. After they put her to sleep, they ran the final test, and discovered that the operation was not necessary. They didn't remove the kidney, but when she awoke, the first thing she said was, "Oh, my back. Oh, I hurt. Oh, I feel so bad. Oh, it hurts." When Teresa was told they had not performed the operation, she was slightly embarrassed. Obviously, she went to sleep expecting to wake up hurting, and that is exactly what she did. In her mind, her pains were just as real as if the operation had been performed.

Whatever you put into your mind becomes a part of the total you. For example, had you been born in China, spoken the Chinese language, and listened to Chinese ideology all of your life, you would in fact be Chinese because **you are the sum total of what goes into your mind.** The statement, if you do not live the life you believe — you will believe the life you live, is far more than just a cliche. Every action you take and every thought you put into your mind is going to have its effect.

THE WORLD'S MOST DEADLY DISEASE

When I was a child, polio was a dreaded disease that took a heavy toll each year as it reaped havoc in the form of crippled legs, twisted bodies and untimely deaths. Then Dr. Jonas Salk and his colleagues developed the Salk Vaccine and polio's devastation was largely curtailed. However, there is still an occasional incidence of polio when a parent or guardian, for whatever reason, does not get a youngster inoculated against the disease. When this happens, and thank God it is a rare occasion, many people shake their heads and wonder why anyone would neglect so simple a thing when the procedure is almost 100% safe and effective. Incredibly enough, however, there are approximately 20,000,000 youngsters today who have not taken the Salk Vaccine and some health officials believe there is a real danger of a new outburst of the disease.

To tell the truth, I can't understand why this condition exists, but let me tell you about another disease which is infinitely worse. It affects people of all ages and crosses all race, creed and color lines. It causes more physical and emotional problems than all other diseases combined. It sends more people to an early grave, breaks up more marriages, orphans more children, causes more unemployment, sends more people to the welfare rolls, creates more drug addicts and alcoholics and causes more crime than all other diseases combined. Additionally, it is the most contagious disease known to man.

This dread disease is "hardening of the attitude" and it's caused by "stinkin' thinkin'." Fortunately, there is a cure for the disease if you already have it, and the cure is effective for both mild and very severe cases. And that's not all. We have now developed a 'vaccine' procedure which reduces to almost zero the possibility of acquiring this dread disease if you don't already have it.

Now before we proceed, let me ask you a question. What would you think of a person who is in daily contact with polio but refuses to take the vaccine to protect himself against the disease? Remember now, the vaccine is free, painless and available, and the "boss" has promised him a raise if he will just take this simple step to protect himself and his fellow workers from this highly contagious disease.

Careful with your answer because I'm obviously setting you up and "leading" you. However, it's not "down the primrose path," it's up the stairway to the top.

Realistically, you'd probably be pretty critical of that person, wouldn't you? You might even say he was crude, thoughtless and not exactly a mental giant.

Now for the next obvious question. What would you think of the person who refused to vaccinate or protect himself against "hardening of the attitudes" despite the fact the inoculation was painless and fun, adding that it would not only protect his mental and physical health but would improve it? Furthermore, it would increase his job and guarantee a raise while improving his zest for living and his relationship with friends, family, associates and even strangers. Just what would you think of *anyone* who refused such a vaccine?

You probably smiled gently [if you are not already afflicted with hardening of the attitudes] and in essence said, "a person would be doubly foolish to refuse such a treatment." I hope that's what you said because you are now going to be given an opportunity to say *yes* to the vaccination which will eliminate the stinking thinking and help you avoid the hardening of the attitudes which we discussed on the dust jacket of this book. This treatment is really an insurance policy which is unique in every way imaginable. It costs no money, is guaranteed renewable, and benefits increase in direct proportion to the number of times you use it. It is a personal policy since the benefits are personal, but is also a "group" policy since you can extend the benefits to other people and increase your own benefits at the same time. If you're concerned about "what's involved" let me put your mind at ease by assuring you that time, effort and dollar cost are all less than zero. Every moment invested is returned many fold in increased effectiveness. The financial investment will be so small it could not possibly affect your standard of living while the results *will* change your way of life and bring substantial financial returns. Every ounce of energy you "spend" on this policy will be returned in greater energy, enthusiasm and zest for living. I will state without equivocation that if you will "buy" the policy and follow the formula for just 21 days that *all* the benefits I've discussed and promised you will be yours. Direct Question. Will you buy the policy and accept the benefits with no strings attached? If you answered "yes" then I'm certain you would be willing to sign the following policy. [Remember, from the beginning I assured you that this is an *action* course which requires *commitment* if you are going to get *results*.]

LIFETIME INSURANCE POLICY

ELIMINATING STINKING THINKING
TO AVOID
HARDENING OF THE ATTITUDES

Being of sound and ambitious mind and having an intense desire to live a long, happy, useful, productive, fun-filled, rewarding life, I hereby agree to accept all the joys and benefits of this Lifetime Insurance Policy which is designed to eliminate stinking thinking and avoid the deadliest of all diseases — Hardening of the Attitudes.

Because I am a mature and responsible person who wishes to live until I die, I understand that by accepting the benefits, I fully expect to "enjoy the premiums" by accepting the opportunities and responsibilities which are an integral part of the policy.

Since I know the skeptics and critics are neither secure, happy or even welcome in most places and since faith is the cornerstone of happiness, I hereby, in faith, affix my signature which guarantees that I will follow through on the procedures Zig Ziglar is going to outline so that I might enjoy *all* the benefits herein described.

IN FAITH, HOPE AND LOVE

Date_____   _____
                                        your signature

I guarantee the validity of this policy if you follow it exactly as we suggest. It *will* work regardless of your age, sex, creed, size, or color.

Zig Ziglar

Now that you have signed the policy, I must confess that along with all those promises there is one thing I "forgot" to tell you. [Now, dear reader, please slow down to about twenty words per minute for the rest of the paragraph.] After you read the preceding sentence and saw that I had "forgotten" to tell you something, what was your instant thought? If it was along the lines of "just as I figured, there's always a catch," then I'm going to really urge you to be especially careful in following through on every phase of the formula because *you* have a need which this formula can fill.

THE FORMULA — POLICY — VACCINE, ETC.

If you want to get enthusiastic about anything, whether it's life, a job, a sport, our country, etc., you dig in and get some information and knowledge about the matter. It's generally true that *people are down on the things they're not "up on."* Learn something about the new town, your neighbors, or the sport in which your son or daughter is interested. This is a starting point, but let's see how we can develop enthusiasm for all that life has to offer. Psychologists have long known you will be enthusiastic if you act enthusiastically. **Assume a trait or characteristic, and later you will possess it.** You grab it — and then it will grab you.

This formula will not only enable you to develop instant enthusiasm and the right mental attitude, but it will be "on call" 24 hours every day. It will result in your being so charged up, motivated, excited, and turned on you will be able to multiply your effectiveness. Now let me warn you about something I touched on in the last paragraph. Enthusiasm gets to be a way of life, and it's tough to be enthusiastic about just one thing. You're going to discover that as you generate enthusiasm, you are going to have so much fun, attract so many good things and accomplish so much more, that you might have some happy financial problems. Good things and good people will be attracted to you and you'll have more fun and achieve more total success.

Not only will you receive substantial benefits — some of which will start the first day — but your friends, associates, relatives, and even complete strangers will benefit. I realize I'm making some strong claims, but literally thousands of testimonials — all say the same thing. It works.

STEP ONE —
REVERSE THE WAY YOU GET OUT OF BED

If you want to develop enthusiasm and the right mental attitude about all life has to offer, you'll need to **reverse the way you get out of bed.** No, I'm not talking about getting out of bed backwards, I'm talking about reversing the way most people start their day, which is either in neutral or in reverse.

When the alarm sounds off, they moan a bit, slap their faces and say, "Oh no, don't tell me it's time to get up already — I feel like I just laid down." Many people start each day like it's going to be another yesterday — and they didn't like yesterday. With this kind of start, is it any wonder one "bad" day follows another bad day? There is a better way to start your day, and it will produce dramatically better results for you. Follow this procedure and you'll acquire enthusiasm as a permanent way of life.

Now I want to give you some bad news and some good news. Bad news first. By following this procedure you'll probably feel foolish and perhaps even childish. This will be somewhat diminished by the fact that your mate [if you have one] will be the only one who'll know about it. Now for the good news. First, you'll get more enjoyment out of life for yourself and for those with whom you work, live and associate. Then, you'll earn more money. You might not receive it immediately, but you will earn it, and that means very shortly you'll receive it. [Seriously now, you *would* be willing to feel slightly ridiculous five minutes each day if it meant more fun *and* more money, wouldn't you?]

Tomorrow morning when the alarm clock goes off, reach over and shut it off. [I think that's important.] Then, immediately sit straight up in bed, clap your hands and say, "Oh boy, it's a great day to get out and take advantage of the opportunities the world has to offer." Now, I want you to see the picture before you continue. You're sitting on the side of the bed, two-thirds asleep with hair in your face. Not only that, but you're slapping your hands like a 9-year-old child saying, "Oh boy, it's a great day to get out and face the world." If you live to be a hundred, you'll never tell a bigger one than that. But let me emphasize something important. You're up, and that's where you wanted to be when you set the alarm and you're taking control of your attitude.

I emphasize this with the full realization that this book will be read [already has been] by successful men and women of all ages and from every walk of life. I'm fully aware that some of you will think this is a little juvenile. If that is the way you feel then I especially urge you to give it an honest try, because *your* need is great. After all, you have nothing to lose — and a lot to gain.

Incidentally, it's super good if you have a big mirror, to see how totally ridiculous you look. It's a one-act comedy in full color and no normal human being can view this scene without breaking into hilarious laughter. It's ridiculous and absurd, and that's what makes it exciting. You're now laughing at yourself and as long as you're doing this, you have no real problems that can't be solved. It's the person who can't laugh at himself that can't tolerate someone else laughing at him. It's a sign of emotional maturity and stability to be able to laugh at yourself. It works even better if husband and wife "get up" together, because now you have a double comedy. As a couple you end up laughing *with* each other rather than *at* each other. This immediately makes life more fun.

When you start the day with a lot of excitement and enthusiasm you're on target according to the Bible. Psalm 118:24 says, **"This is the day which the Lord has made. I will rejoice and be glad in it."** I wish I had the space to share with you the number of phone calls and letters I've gotten from husbands and wives who say, "You know, because of this we did start laughing together again, and it turned our marriage around."

SING IN THE SHOWER

Now that you're up, take a shower and, if there are no small children asleep, sing a loud cheerful song. Now, don't give me this old jazz about, "Yeah, but I can't sing." Listen, I once got a letter from Mitch Miller asking me not to "sing along with," and my own children ask me not to sing in Church. Neither the tune nor your talent for singing is important. The *idea* is the thing. The concept of singing in the shower is simple.

You can't be negative at the top of your voice. William James said, "We do not sing because we are happy. We are happy because we sing." [Besides, it's your "bath right"]. Along the same

238

lines, "We do not stop working and playing because we grow old, we grow old because we stop working and playing."

For the man of the house there are some extra benefits if you take one more step. When you walk into the breakfast room, slap the table a couple of times and say, "Honey, I see you've cooked bacon, eggs and grits for breakfast. That's what I was hoping you were going to prepare." Even if you've had the same meal every day for the past 622 days, an interesting thing takes place. First of all, she looks at you in shocked surprise and the shock value alone is worth a great deal. Chances are, even if the breakfast isn't really that good, she'll be motivated to do better the next day. This means you can't lose.

Now let me explain what this procedure accomplishes. Since thought precedes action, you plan the action at night in order to execute it the next morning. This sets up a habit of planning positively, and it has far-reaching results because, **"When you sow an action, you reap a habit; when you sow a habit, you reap a character; and when you sow a character, you reap a destiny."** The reason is simple. Logic will not change an emotion [like being negative], but action will. Or as my good friend Bruce Norman, Principal of Magnet High School for Health Professions in Dallas, Texas, likes to say, "you can't 'feel' your way into a new way of acting, but you can 'act' your way into a new way of feeling."

The end results of these actions will be a greater — more vibrant enthusiasm, and history conclusively proves that your destiny is greater with the attitude of enthusiasm. When you get up with enthusiasm and go to breakfast with enthusiasm, you're beginning to set the stage for a good day. A day is a miniature lifetime, and with lots of good days — you have a good life. This also benefits family and friends because enthusiasm is more contagious than the measles. Once you have it, it will spread to your family and associates and everybody benefits.

These actions also have an additional benefit because they provide an effective frontal assault on one of man's greatest stumbling blocks in the climb to the top of the stairway, namely, procrastination. If procrastination is one of your problems, these simple procedures could well be the starting place for over-coming that problem. This will become even more evident when we get into the section on habits. For the moment, it should be obvious that before you can go anywhere you must first get started. It should be just as obvious that **how you get up in the morning will play a big part in how high you go up in life.**

At this point, I'll just observe that this getting up in the morning procedure is a "good" habit and every good habit has to be "grabbed" and held on to for dear life. An encouraging note, however, is the fact that from the beginning, maybe even from the first day you will receive some "interesting" benefits and in just 21 *consecutive* days the changes will be dramatic.

On the other hand, every "bad" habit is sneaky and will slip up on you so gradually that before you realize you have the habit — the habit has you. I devote two full chapters to habits at the end of this Segment, so let's get on with the formula.

STEP TWO — ESTABLISH SOME SYMBOLS

In America today, we live in an essentially negative society. For example, the tens of thousands of appliances that hang on street corners in every town, city and crossroad around the country are referred to as "red," "stop," or "traffic" lights. This is obviously negative, because in reality the lights are "go" lights. If you don't believe this, just watch what happens any time one of the lights is not working. Traffic will back up for several blocks. It isn't because a "red," "stop," or "traffic" light has been cut off, but because a "go" light is out of order. Why then do people call them "stop" lights? It's simple, they are SNIOPS. They hear others refer to the "red" lights, so they follow suit.

The unfortunate fact about this is, the average American spends something like 27 hours every year in front of these "go" lights waiting on the right color, so they can "go." How do most people spend the 27 hours? Generally speaking, they do three things. First, they get a firm grip on the steering wheel to make absolutely certain the car doesn't run off with them. Second, they firm their lips and tighten their mouth in such a way that they can talk to the "go" light if need be. Third, and most importantly, they sit in their automobiles pressing their foot on the accelerator. They apparently feel if they race their engines the light will change faster. Do you plead guilty to doing this?

Chances are strong that you are guilty, without realizing it. If you are — and if you thought it was silly to start the day by slapping your hands, what do you think about racing your car engine to change a light?

PERSONALIZE IT

Let's think this through together. Instead of using that procedure while waiting at the light, give it an entirely different treatment. Two things can be done constructively. First, as you sit there waiting on the right color, you want to personalize the light. Look at it and say, "That's mine. It was put there for me. It has my name on it. It was put there so I can go further, faster, easier and more safely to my destination. You see, in reality, it is a "go light." Second, when you're involved in such a way that you can talk about the "go" light. Here's where the fun begins. I challenge you, whoever you are, whatever you do, and wherever you might be, to use the word "go" light in a conversation and maintain a straight face. I just don't believe you can do it. The very instant you say "go" light, two things will happen. First of all, you will break out in a big smile and the person with you will also smile. Secondly, the instant you say the word "go" light, your attitude will start to change. You will come back to the pages of this book and recognize the practicality of what I'm saying. As you look at the positive aspects of life, one word or action will precipitate a series of positive thoughts, which are the forerunners of positive actions, which produce positive results.

GO LIGHTS, STRONG ENDS AND WARMS

I have a close friend in Winnipeg, Manitoba. Really, he's more like a brother than just a friend. His name is Bernie Lofchick and he is easily the most positive man I have ever met. He is so positive that not once has he ever had a cold, although he will admit he occasionally does have a "warm." He is so positive he never refers to the "weekend" because that's negative. He calls it the "strong end." As you read these words, you might well think, is all of that really necessary? I say, "No, you can be mediocre without those little things." But I hope I'm talking to the "you" who has already testified that you want to get more out of life. You do, don't you? [Say "Yes."] Again, I want to emphasize, it's not the big things that make the difference, it's the little things.

When you start adding things like "go lights," "warms" and "strong ends" to your conversation and your life, a dramatic change will occur. You'll enjoy life more and have more fun which means you will be healthier and live longer because this procedure will bring a smile to your face and laughter to your heart. This is verified in the book of Proverbs, **"a merry heart has a continual feast."** With this approach to life, the third step toward controlling your attitude becomes easy and simple.

STEP THREE —
SET YOUR GYROSCOPE FOR SUCCESS

Several years ago, an episode on "Candid Camera" made an indelible impression on my mind. A movie star was stationed in the corridor of an office building. She had a large, heavy suitcase with her and was looking for someone to carry it into an office a short distance down the corridor. Each time a man appeared, she would ask for help. In each instance, the response was favorable. As he would lift the suitcase and start down the corridor with the movie star, they would engage in small talk. The movie star would show him which office was hers, but when the man would attempt to carry the suitcase into the office he would find it a difficult task. He could go into the office himself but the gyroscope inside the suitcase was set to go straight ahead and it *strongly* resisted turning from its set direction.

Inside of every creature on the face of the earth there is a gyroscope which comes as standard equipment at birth. Take a young squirrel located a thousand miles from any other squirrel. When cold weather approaches he will store nuts for the winter, although he might never have lived through a winter. This is the law of self-preservation. It is his built-in gyroscope. Likewise, a young duck who has never lived through a winter will fly south even if he is totally isolated from all other ducks. The law of self-preservation demands it. That is his built-in gyroscope.

Man, too, has a gyroscope, but with a difference. The difference is, man can set his own gyroscope. Go to a lake or the seashore and look at the sailing boats. You'll notice they will be going in 360 directions, and you'll notice that the wind is blowing in only one direction. So, if the wind is only blowing in one direction, how can the boats be going in so many different directions? The answer is simple. There is a human being on the boat who has set the sail. It's the set of the sail that determines the direction of the boat. It's the way you set your sail [gyroscope] that's going to determine the direction you will go — and direction determines destiny.

MINOR ADJUSTMENT FOR MAJOR SUCCESS

Remember the cookware salesman I mentioned in an earlier chapter? Every day he set his gyroscope. As a matter of fact, he set the gyroscope several times during the course of each day. This was necessary for his success and it is for yours too. As I indicated earlier, there are going to be numerous diversions and occurrences over which you have no control. You can't predict with certainty what things stand between you and your destination. I would emphasize, however, when something throws you slightly off course, it isn't necessary for you to go all the way back to your original departure point. You simply make a slight adjustment and continue on toward your goal. Remember, **go as far as you can see, and when you get there you will always be able to see farther.**

How can you set your own gyroscope? The answer is simple, but first let me ask a question. When you're involved in a lengthy telephone conversation, are you guilty of doodling? Do you draw squares, rectangles and circles? If the conversation is quite lengthy, do you start the shading process and add designs within the shading? How do you rate yourself as a doodler? As you might know, some advanced doodlers leave the doodles around hoping they will "be discovered." What is the highest price you've ever received for a doodle?

During all my years of working with many, many people, I've never met anybody who has sold a doodle. With this in mind, I'm of the firm opinion that the doodle market is limited. Instead of doodling, which is non-profitable, take a clean sheet of paper and start writing, "I can, I can, I can . . ." Then spell out specifically what you can do. Write your objectives over and over on a sheet of paper and on your bathroom mirror. Then at the bottom of your sheet of paper or mirror, write I will — I will — I will. This process will "set your gyroscope" by burning your objectives indelibly into your subconscious mind.

For many people, *See You At The Top* has been the road map to greater accomplishment and this simple formula has been the catalyst that started them. It could well be the catalyst you seek but I must warn you, there is a certain danger involved in following the formula. When you buy the ideas, adopt the attitude and follow the procedures I recommend, you'll encounter some interesting reactions. Some will criticize you and say you're different, and of course they'll be right. You'll be so different you'll be one of the few people in the game of life who will be able to open life's vault of valuables and get what you want instead of having to want what you have. For what it's worth, I wouldn't be overly concerned about the critics. Since the beginning of recorded history, no one has erected a statue to a critic. So, they must not be held in too much esteem.

Some people will laugh at you, but let me emphasize a point. It will be the little world and the little people who are missing the good things in life who will be doing the laughing. It should be quite satisfying to know that the little world laughed, but the big world gathered on the banks of the Hudson River to watch Robert Fulton go steaming past. The little world laughed, but the big world was tuned in when Alexander Graham Bell made his historic telephone call. The little world laughed, but the big world was at Kitty Hawk when the Wright Brothers got off the ground that first time. The little world might well laugh as you start your journey, but I assure you the big world will be gathered at the finish line cheering you across. Best of all, **what you get by reaching your destination isn't nearly as important as what you become by reaching that destination.**

CHAPTER THREE
STEP FOUR — FEED YOUR MIND

The first three steps of the formula to control your attitude are extremely simple. To review the formula: Step 1 — Get up in the morning with the enthusiastic hand-clapping; Step 2 — Adopt the symbols, "Go Lights," "Warms," and "Strong Ends;" Step 3 — Set your gyroscope with positive "I Can's."

Step Four is more involved so I'm devoting this entire chapter to it. I assure you the subject matter deserves every line of space.

PHYSICALLY HUNGRY — EAT

Question, please! Did you eat anything last month? What about last week? Yesterday? Today? Chances are you are quite puzzled at these questions. Of course you ate last month, last week, yesterday and today. Do you plan to eat tomorrow? If you do, does that mean what you ate today was no good? Absolutely not. It simply means what you ate today is for today. The average person in America not only eats every day but, generally speaking, he eats his meals on schedule. I've observed if a person gets busy and misses a meal, he generally tells anyone who will listen, "You know what? I was so busy yesterday I didn't have time to eat lunch." Then he repeats it to make certain his listener got the message. To him, it's a big deal to miss a meal and he wants others to be aware of his "sacrifice." Suppose the same individual was asked about his mental appetites? "When is the last time you deliberately, on a pre-determined schedule, fed your own mind?" What do you think his answer would be? For that matter — what is *your* answer? Your answer is important because you have mental appetites just as you have physical appetites.

MENTALLY HUNGRY — WHAT DO YOU DO?

People are funny. I've never met an individual who was hungry and heard him say, "I'm about to starve. I wonder what I should do? Do you have any suggestions? Can you give me any idea how to solve this problem?" I probably never will be confronted with that particular situation. The hungry person knows if he's hungry, he can solve that problem by eating.

From the neck down, very few people are worth more than $100.00 a week. From the neck up, there is no limit to what an individual is worth. So what do we do? We feed our stomachs, the $100.00 part below our necks, every day. How often do we feed our minds, the part that has no limit to its value, earning and happiness potential? Most of us feed it accidentally and occasionally, if it's convenient or we don't have anything else to do. The excuse we often give is our lack of time. This is ridiculous. If you have "time" to feed the $100.00 part of you every day, doesn't it make sense you should *take* time to feed the part which has no ceiling to its potential?

On many occasions, I have encountered people who are despondent, negative, defeated, down on themselves, broke, unhappy and you name it. If it's on the negative side, it will fit them. The funny thing about these people is that they're the ones who resist to the bitter end any feeding of their minds or their attitudes. They badly need inspiration and information but they consistently refuse to attend seminars or get involved in reading good books or listening to motivational recordings. It's really funny to listen to some of these people talk — perhaps I should use the word "tragic?" When we refer to extremely successful people and mention how optimistic and positive they are, the failure will say, "No wonder they're positive and have good attitudes, they're earning $50,000 a year. If I were earning $50,000 a year, I would be positive too." The failure thinks successful people are positive because they earn $50,000 a year. This obviously is in reverse. Successful people earn $50,000 a year because they have the *right mental attitude*. Wouldn't it be marvelous if it had been arranged so that an empty head, like an empty stomach, wouldn't let its owner rest until its owner put something in it.

It's true in every field of endeavor, whether it's law, medicine, sales, teaching, coaching, science, or the arts; the top people — or those who are headed for the top — are the ones who regularly show up for seminars at their own expense. They read good books and regularly listen to motivational recordings. They deliberately seek information and inspiration and, as a result, they are constantly on the grow.

DO IT WELL — SUBCONSCIOUSLY

Why are successful men positive? To reverse it, why are positive men successful? They're positive because they deliberately feed their minds with good, clean, powerful, positive mental thoughts on a regular basis. They make them a part of their daily diets just as surely as they make food a part of their physical diets. They know that if they feed their bodies above their necks they'll never have to worry about feeding their bodies below the neck. They won't have to worry about the roof over their heads, or the financial problems often associated with old age. As we dig into the learning process and look at some real life examples it will become obvious why this is true.

Virtually everything we learn, we learn consciously. But it's only when we do it subconsciously that we do it well. You learned how to drive a car consciously. Remember? If your car had a clutch do you remember the instructions you gave to yourself? Push in the clutch. Press the accelerator — just a little. Careful now — push the gearshift lever. Now, let the clutch out — easy does it. Pull the gearshift lever. Do you remember? Do you also remember you would buck and jump and probably kill the engine?

You were a menace to society and a candidate for the morgue because you were learning to drive consciously. Some time later, you could press the accelerator, shift the gear, let out on the clutch, unwrap a piece of gum, roll down the window and talk about your neighbor all at the same time. You could do these things with complete safety because you moved the driving process from the conscious mind into the subconscious mind. You learned to drive consciously and later it became "unconscious" or automatic. It was almost a reflex action.

Every musician — regardless of the instrument — went through the slow and often painful process of learning to consciously play that instrument. During this learning process friends and relatives studiously avoided listening to the efforts of the aspiring Ignace Paderewski. The musician plays skillfully only when he plays instinctively or subconsciously. Then everyone wants to listen — free, of course.

Do you remember when you learned how to type? You had to concentrate on every stroke as you beat out about ten words per minute. You were typing consciously and you were doing a miserable job. Later, you no longer thought about the key you were going to hit, you just typed. You were then doing it subconsciously and doing it well.

Once you learn to do something consciously, you can move it into the subconscious and do it well. Everything you do well will be done subconsciously. This includes your attitude. You can move your attitude reactions into the subconscious. You can do this so completely you will instinctively react positively to negative situations as well as positive ones. That's a promise. It takes dedication, work and practice, but it can be done. A positive response to any stimulus can become something like a reflex-action or a conditioned response.

In the bonus chapter at the end of the Segment we give more insight on the subconscious mind and its instinctive or conditioned use.

NOW HERE'S AN OPTIMIST

By feeding your mind over a period of time with the good, clean, powerful information you can even develop an attitude like "This Old Boy Down Home." He was caught by a flash flood and ended up on his rooftop. One of his neighbors came floating by on his house. In this dire state of affairs he quipped. "John, this flood is just awful, isn't it?" John replied, "No, it's not so bad." The neighbor, somewhat surprised, retorted, "What do you mean, it's not so bad? Why, there goes your hen house floating downstream." John simply commented, "Yeah, I know, but six months ago I started raising ducks and there they are, everyone of them just swimming around. Everything is going to be all right." "But, John, this water is going to ruin your crops," the neighbor persisted. Still undaunted, John replied, "No, it's not. My crops were already ruined and just last week the county agent told me my land really needed more water, so this solved that problem." The pessimist tried one more time to get to his cheerful

248

friend. He added, "But look, John, the water is still rising. The first thing you know, it's going to be up to your windows." Grinning wider than ever, our optimistic friend replied, "Man, I hope so, they are powerful dirty and need washing."

O.K., it's a joke. But, as is often the case, there is much truth in humor. It's obvious our hero had decided to react to the situation in a positive manner. After all, the dictionary says that **attitude is a posture or position assumed to serve a purpose.** Over a period of time you can so condition your mind that you will instinctively and automatically react positively to the negative situations you encounter in life. In order to get — and stay — this way you have to feed your mind a lot of good-clean-powerful-motivational messages — and then you have to keep on feeding it. I mentioned early in *See You At The Top* you could completely bury the old garbage [remember the shopping center built on the garbage dump?] but you could then turn on the radio or TV, glance at the newspaper, talk to a negative person or even chance to overhear a passing conversation and boom-boom — somebody else has dumped some fresh garbage in your clean, positive mind. Now what do you do, Charlie Brown? Answer: Exactly what we have been talking about in these last two chapters. Pre-condition your mind with the "getting up," identifying the positive symbols like "go lights," etc., and "setting your gyroscope" [you do that while talking on the phone]. Then you follow the procedure in this chapter of feeding your mind — regularly. The reason is simple. There are:

THREE KINDS OF MOTIVATION

The first is "fear" motivation which says, "If you're not in by 11:00 p.m., this will be the last night this month you can go out." Or, "If you don't increase your sales, you will be fired." For some people, fear motivation works, but with most people it doesn't because it causes resentment which leads to rebellion.

Fear motivation might be like this Texas story. A rich Texan threw a mammoth party one night and invited dozens of people with special emphasis on young men of marriageable age. As the evening wore on and most of the guests were feeling no pain, the host invited everyone to join him around the pool which he had carefully stocked with water moccasins and alligators. He challenged his guests to swim the length of the pool and offered the choice of three substantial prizes, $1,000,000 in cash, a thousand acres of choice land, or his daughter's hand in marriage. The words were scarcely out of his mouth when there was a loud splash followed by a furious thrashing of water and the almost immediate emergence of a young man from the opposite side of the pool, who had just set a never to be broken world record.

The host enthusiastically congratulated the young man and then, true to his word, asked the dripping winner about his choice. Would it be the $1,000,000? The young man shook his head no. The 1,000 acres of land? Again, no. Then would it be the hand of his daughter in marriage? When the young man again said no, the host, somewhat exasperated asked, "then what do you want? The young man quickly responded, "I want to know the name of the man who pushed me in the pool."

The second is incentive or "carrot" motivation, which is simply reward for accomplishment. It says, "If you lead the company, you'll win a trip to Hawaii. If you raise your profit percentage three points, you'll get a raise in your department. If you perform adequately, you'll be given a permanent assignment." This motivation works for considerably more people in the free enterprise system.

You've probably seen the picture of the donkey pulling the cart. In this picture the carrot is dangling in front of the donkey. When the donkey walks toward the carrot, he pulls the cart. There are several factors which must be present in order for this kind of motivation to work. The cart has to be light enough, the stick holding the carrot must be short enough, and the carrot enticing enough to get the donkey to do the job. Experience teaches us that we must permit the donkey to take an occasional bite of the carrot in order to keep him from becoming discouraged. Otherwise, he's going to feel he is involved in an exercise in futility and will quit trying for the carrot. When the donkey does get a bite of the carrot, he satisfies his appetite. When he's no longer hungry, some adjustments must be made. For example, the stick must be shortened, the carrot sweetened, and the load lightened if the donkey is to be motivated into action.

Eventually, the process reaches a stage where it becomes impractical. The rewards or incentives are so high that the profit is removed from the picture and the program grinds to a halt. On occasion the participant reaches a "comfort zone" and doesn't need — or want more comfort — or carrots. What do you do now?

MAKE HIM THIRSTY

The answer is simple. Change the donkey into a race horse and make him want to run — implement the third kind of motivation — internal. That's what this book is helping you do. The old saying, "You can lead a horse to water, but you can't make him drink" is true, but if you let him lick the salt block long enough he will get thirsty and want to take the drink. My natural optimism leads me to believe this book will be *your* "salt block." A 25 year "hard line" study at Harvard University under the guidance of Psychologist David McClelland establishes precise scientific verification that you can change motivation by changing the way you think about yourself and your circumstances [Reader's Digest, May 1975, page 89]. That is exactly what this book is all about. I'm convinced — because of results already obtained — the information in this book combined with the follow-up procedures will enable you to change the way you see yourself and your circumstances [for the better, I might add] which means you will *improve* your performance.

My "intellectual associates" and I often discuss motivation in our "bull sessions." They are almost unanimous in their conviction that all motivation is "self" motivation, that no one can "motivate" any one else and they "prove" and theorize at length and in depth on the subject. My favorite answer is this analogy.

My favorite relaxation on Sunday afternoon is to build a fire in our den and watch it burn out of one eye and the Cowboys out of the other eye. Occasionally, when the Cowboys get way ahead, I drop off for a little snooze. Generally speaking, when I awaken the flames have died and the logs are smoldering. I get up and grab my "poker" and give the logs a few healthy pokes. Almost immediately the flames shoot up and I have a beautiful, flaming fire again. I added no more wood to the fire. All I did was "shake up" what was there and stir up a little activity which brought in some extra oxygen which started the blaze.

This information is designed to stir up that part of you which could be, like the fire, smoldering at the moment. You've heard most of it but chances are excellent that you have not *really* seen or heard it because you aren't utilizing the information for maximum results by *doing* something.

There is a difference in hearing, reading, and learning. I'm talking about learning it so completely that it is as much a part of you as your hands and arms. I'm talking about learning it so well you know it consciously and feel it subconsciously so that you instinctively and automatically react positively to the negative events of life. This is attitude control and these next three examples prove this objective is desirable, reachable and can be "stirred up" by an outside "poke" or stimulus.

YOU CAN CHANGE OR BE CHANGED

A number of years ago, Joost A. Meerloo, M.D., wrote a book entitled, *The Rape of the Mind.* In his book, the author explains why some of our prisoners-of-war during the Korean War became turncoats, rejected America and stayed in North Korea. Also, why countless others became so embittered and confused that their value to themselves and to the free enterprise system was largely negated.

Meerlo explains that the young G.I. prisoner would be subjected to a "brainwashing" procedure for ten or twelve hours from two skilled Communist brainwashers, followed by a second and often a third team. During this 24 to 36 hour ordeal, the young G.I. was fed the full measure of Communistic garbage. Everything he ever believed in was challenged. His mind was saturated with a mixture of truth, half truths and outrageous lies. After 24 to 36 hours of this treatment, without sleep and without anything to eat, the young G.I. would be physically, mentally, spiritually and emotionally exhausted. After a number of sessions like this the young G.I. would "throw in the towel" and exclaim, "All right, all right, I'll do it or I'll believe it, just let me get some sleep." Of course, his godless tormentors had no intention of letting him sleep at that point. They continued to pour the garbage in. These young men were helpless in the face of their captors. The only exceptions, as Meerlo pointed out, were those who had strong religious convictions and God's help in resisting the brainwashing.

Isaiah 40:31 explains why. **"But they that wait upon the Lord shall renew their strength; they shall mount up with wings as eagles; they shall run, and not be weary; and they shall walk, and not faint."** In Hebrew the word "renew" is Chalaph, which means to change — or to "exchange." When you serve God you change or exchange your strength for His. That's the best swap you'll ever make because there are many things you can't do, but there is nothing good you and God can't do.

Frankly, when I heard of these young men turning against their country, I was horrified. After reading Meerlo's book, I am convinced they were helpless at stopping the transformation of their thinking as they would have been in stopping a tank with their bare hands. I would like to stress that in most cases, these young men initially resisted the onslaught, but still fell victim to the ideology that was forced into their minds. Now think about this. They fell victim *against* their wills to a doctrine of lies and destruction. Does it make sense to you that if you regularly, by choice, fed your mind good, clean, powerful messages of information and inspiration, you would derive tremendous benefits from it?

The next story makes a strong case for this point of view.

GET THAT MUSIC OUT

Shinichi Suzuki is an unusual Japanese scientist who performs what many people consider to be one of the miracles of our time. He takes babies a few weeks old and starts playing beautiful, recorded music next to their beds. He plays the same tune many times and after about thirty days he repeats the procedure with another recording. He continues this process until the infant is about two years old. At that time, he starts about three months of music lessons for mother, with the two-year-old as an observer. Next he puts a miniature violin in the hands of the child who begins to get the feel of the instrument while learning bow movements. This first lesson lasts only two or three minutes. From there they gradually build up to an hour. By the time the child is old enough to learn that the violin is supposed to be difficult to play, he has already mastered it and is having fun in the process.

Recently Professor Suzuki conducted a concert with some 1,500 of these Japanese children performing. Average age of the children was about seven and they played the classics, Chopin, Beethoven, Vivaldi, etc. Significantly, Suzuki emphasizes that the vast majority of these children had no "natural" musical talent. However, he believes every child has talent which can be developed by following the same procedures we use in teaching children to speak. A baby is around older people who constantly talk, so the first step is **exposure**. Next, the baby tries to talk which is **imitation**. Friends and relatives brag on the baby which gives **encouragement** and motivates the baby to try again. This is the process of **repetition**. Then the baby starts adding words and tying them together into phrases or sentences. This procedure is **refinement**. At age three or four, the child has quite a vocabulary and still can't read a word.

Professor Suzuki maintains that virtually anything can be learned by the same method. Looks like he just eliminated another series of "Loser's Limps" for a lot of people, doesn't it?

From cover to cover of *See You At The Top* I've stressed that **your rewards in life are due more to your behavior than to your birth.** Also, your behavior was tremendously influenced by your associates and by what you put in or permit to be put in your mind. The next incident emphasizes this in an intriguing way.

WHAT — NO STUTTERERS?

Several years ago a scientist working with two tribes of American Indians noticed that not one of the full-blooded Indians stuttered. Being a scientist, he wondered if this was a coincidence or if it was characteristic of Indians. His interest and curiosity led him to study every Indian tribe in America. He didn't find a single Indian who stuttered, so he studied their languages and discovered why none of the Indians stuttered. They don't have a word, or even a substitute word, for "stutter." Obviously, if there isn't a word for stutter, it would be impossible for an Indian to stutter. You might grin and feel that information is interesting.

But, so what? Let's pursue it a step further. We know that words paint pictures in the mind and that the mind thinks in pictures. For example, if you read or hear the words fail, can't, liar, or dumb, your mind completes the pictures that have been painted by the word. Now, if there is no word for stutter, the mind can't visualize or paint a picture of a stutter. Result: no stuttering.

The International Paper Company has statistical evidence supporting their claim that the bigger a person's vocabulary, the bigger the income. I'm convinced you can build your income, your enjoyment, and *change* your life by changing your vocabulary. Take the word "hate" and remove it from your vocabulary. Don't see it, think it, or read it. Write, feel, see, and dream the word "love" in its place. Take the word "prejudice" out of your vocabulary. Don't see, think, or say the word "prejudice." In its place put "understand." Take the word "negative," and substitute the word "positive." Obviously, the list of words to be removed and replaced can be virtually endless — as will be the benefits that follow. **Your mind acts on what you feed it.** Change your mental diet and eliminate the negative input. You will first reduce, then virtually eliminate the negative output.

WHAT AND WHEN DO YOU EAT — MENTALLY?

By now you should be completely convinced that what you put in your mind is terribly important to you and your future. So the question is obviously, "How do I feed my mind — when do I find time to eat those mental meals when I'm already running just to stay even?" Let me answer by asking if you heard about the woodcutter whose production kept going down because he didn't *take* time to sharpen his axe?

Think about this: the average man spends over $200 per year, and more time than he'll admit, dressing up the "outside" of the head [shaves, haircuts, gook, etc.]. *Nobody* knows what the average woman spends doing the same thing. [Personally, I don't want to know what my redhead spends!] Question! Doesn't it make sense to spend at least that much time and money dressing up the "inside" of the head?

In my judgment, the greatest educational, motivational tool at our disposal today is the portable cassette player. I value cassette education and motivation so highly that if I could not replace my own cassette player, $5,000 would not buy the one I have. Strong statement, *yes* — but not nearly as strong and helpful as cassette education and motivation can be. I do not personally know a self-made millionaire who does not have and use one for motivation and education.

The range of material available is as endless as the times and places you can use them. A humorous, motivational, educational or religious message will speed up housework and remove much of the drudgery. You can get ideas and inspiration while shaving, dressing, or applying makeup. You can transform "dead" time you normally spend fighting traffic to "live" time getting the motivation and education that will give you the mental and emotional edge in today's competitive world.

For example, a University of California study reveals that a person living in the Los Angeles area could acquire the equivalent of two years of college in three years of normal driving time by listening to cassette recordings. Total usable time you invest, if you listen while driving, would be almost zero.

As a group, the people who regularly listen to the right cassette recordings are the happiest, best adjusted, most excited group I know. Now combine this with a sound reading program and you are really in business. The rule is — when you are moving — listen. When you are seated — read. This literally saturates your mind with the optimistic outlook on life. It also gives you an excellent overall education and a set of values and attitudes that will be tremendously helpful in your life.

Reading requires planning, so you might need a new set of reminders to acquire the habit of reading. The standard "explanation" most people give is, they don't have "time." Obviously, time availability varies, but to say you don't have "time" to feed your mind is just another "Loser's Limp." We do what we have to do and we do what we want to do. Now if we will make time for what we should do [read good literature], we will soon reduce the list of things we have to do.

Suggestions: Don't borrow or lend books. Buy them as often as possible and build a library you have personalized with markings for future reference. Keep good reading material in strategic spots around home. [1] By your bed. [2] In the bathroom. [3]

Standing up on top of the TV. [4] By your favorite chair. [5] In a quiet spot where you can isolate yourself.

HERE'S WHAT THE SUCCESSFUL PEOPLE DO

Alan Bean [U.S. Navy Captain and NASA Astronaut] is a man I'm privileged to know on a personal basis. He, too, listens to motivational recordings regularly. Captain Bean, one of the first men to walk on the moon, was the commander of the second sky lab space station mission. He was also involved with the Russian Cosmonauts in the joint U.S./Russian space effort.

Recognizing the critical importance of self-image, goal setting, proper mental attitude, etc., Captain Bean listened to motivational recordings in his car on his way to work at NASA for training for the 59 day extended flight in space. I'm naturally pleased that he selected some of my recordings as part of his program. These recordings covered much of the material you're reading in this book. I hope you don't consider it a bad pun when I say this proves that the material is "out of this world." To show you just how keenly Alan Bean feels about these concepts, he volunteered his rather limited time and offered some invaluable suggestions for this book so all of you might receive additional benefits in your life.

Let me point out that *all* astronauts, after every conceivable test known to man, were selected with more care than any group ever chosen for any purpose since the beginning of recorded history. Each one *had* to have a strong, healthy self-image. Each one *had* to be able to work with and get along with his fellowman under the most difficult circumstances imaginable. Each one *had* to be goal-oriented. Each one *had* to have the right mental attitude, including mental toughness, discipline, determination and a super positive mental attitude. Could you imagine a negative thinker aboard the platform wondering if they were going to get back to earth? Each one *had* to have *all* these qualities *before* he was selected for the space program. Obviously, they had to maintain those qualities in order to stay in the program. In addition to their lives being at stake, these men carry national pride and honor. The pressures on them are tremendous.

World Wide Distributors is the largest distributor of housewares in Canada. At their recent convention in Winnipeg, Manitoba, the General Manager told me that 17 of his top 19 sales people, including his top eleven, listened every day to motivational and sales training recordings. He emphasized they don't listen because they are the best, they are the best because they listen. As a matter of fact, sales managers and corporate executives everywhere assure me that their top people, almost without exception, listen and read on a regular basis.

The point I so badly want to make is this, men and women who need this kind of motivation less than anyone else on planet Earth are the ones who seek it, and use it the most. I'm convinced this is the reason they are where they are. For a long time they have been doing the things I'm now urging you to do. The reason is apparently a very simple one. The drive that takes men to the top is a drive that thrives on constant nourishment and reinforcement. Men who reach the pinnacle of success in their present professions invariably recognize the fact that there is plenty of room at the top, but not enough room to sit down. They also understand that the mind, like the body, must be constantly nourished. They know if it is important to regularly feed their bodies from the neck down, it makes even more sense to feed them from the neck up. They understand that nourishment must be physical, mental and spiritual.

THIS IS AN ILLUSION

Many people have the erroneous concept that they do not "need" to listen to cassette recordings or read inspirational books except when they are "down" or depressed. The "need" when you are "down" is more obvious and the benefits can be substantial but the total long-range benefits could be greater if you listen or read when you are emotionally "up." The reason is two-fold. When you are "down," you are more likely to either "grab at straws" and end up with the wrong straw or take the opposite approach and summarily reject many valuable ideas. When you are down in the dumps, you are more likely to be concentrating on the problem instead of the solution.

When you are emotionally up and riding high, your optimism

and ambition are working overtime. Your imagination is in high gear and you are considerably more responsive to positive suggestions of your capability. You are solution conscious instead of problem conscious so you are more responsive to good ideas, and you are far more likely to "act" on these new ideas. That's when you will raise your performance level considerably. Your attitude, enthusiasm, spirit of cooperation and value to your employer will pole vault upward. That, my friend, is when you get those raises and promotions.

Sandy Breighner, one of the most dynamic and completely motivated people I know, reinforces this thought and makes an additional contribution. Sandy, who sells sales training and motivational programs to many individuals and major corporations, points out that a person can often read a book or listen to a tape series and derive so much benefit they move to a higher level of understanding and awareness. From this new level — the person who reads or listens again to the same material will "hear" or "see" things they completely missed the first time. This "moves" them to a still higher level of understanding and accomplishment. This is the reason any success-minded person should build his own "success" library for ready reference which leads to constant growth.

This should not be construed to mean you should not seek motivational help when you are down. I just want to make certain you understand that motivational books and recordings can serve as a stepping stone to get you out of the dumps — as a step ladder to get you off mediocrity row or as an unencumbered escalator to help take you to the top. Initially, you might have to "force" yourself to read and listen on a daily basis, but after you have done it for a time, you'll discover three things: you'll enjoy it, you'll learn from it and you'll begin to instinctively and subconsciously take action on what you are reading and learning. Again, those who feed themselves motivational material regularly are the ones who benefit the most.

In the next two chapters, I go into considerable detail concerning both good and bad habits. I'm now discussing a good habit and, as you'll see, it's necessary to force yourself to take action on this good habit. Force yourself to associate with the right people. Force yourself to follow the "hand slapping," "go light" routine. Force yourself to listen to the recordings. Do this for 21 days and the habit you "grabbed" will grab you.

ONLY FOR THOSE SERIOUS ABOUT SUCCESS

Realistically the early morning hand slapping bit is not something you will continue as a way of life. Initially, however, it generates instant enthusiasm and produces dramatic results which provide the encouragement you need at the time you probably need it the most. It conditions and prepares your mind for an awakening experience which *will* give you a richer and more exciting way of life if you give it the full 21 day trial. Now let's take a look at the best way to *continue to grow* mentally, physically, and spiritually.

After arising [with or without hand slapping] and *before* any negative thoughts or input enters your mind [*no* newspapers, radio, or TV], go to a quiet "success" spot in your home for your first mental snack. Select an inspirational self-help book [I list 40 in this book] and read 10 to 15 minutes. Next, take a 15 minute walk or jog and make a mental note of the *good* things you observe. Then devote a few minutes to an exercise program *prescribed by your doctor* and designed to fill a time slot and *not* to challenge you to do "X" number of anything. *While* you are doing the exercises, listen to cassette recordings of an educational, motivational, nature. *Now.* Before you rush off with a full head and an empty stomach eat a nourishing breakfast, so you will have the energy to use the good stuff you just fed your mind. Starting your day — every day — with the right kind of mental, spiritual, and physical breakfast will guarantee you a full and rewarding day — and life.

Yes I'm fully aware that I am asking you to get up early to do these things. *Yes,* I know you are already busy and pushed for time, and *yes,* I know it takes money for books and cassette recordings. However, the time will be returned in the form of greater energy, enthusiasm, and stamina, and possibly several extra years of life. The investment in books and tapes will bring greater earnings plus an infinitely richer and more rewarding life. Actually I'm suggesting that you invest time and money to make certain you enjoy "the richer life" on a permanent basis.

CHAPTER FOUR

HABITS AND ATTITUDES

FIRST YOU GET THE HABIT

When you choose a habit, you also choose the end result of that habit. Good habits are difficult to acquire, but easy to live with. Bad habits are easy to acquire, but difficult to live with. Almost without exception, bad habits come slowly and pleasantly and, in most instances, the habit has you before you're aware you have it. As a rule, there's little or no pain involved, although we often find people who learn to smoke or drink or get hooked on drugs, despite the fact they suffered discomfort in the early stages of acquiring these habits.

Let's look at smoking, which psychologist Murray Banks, contends is a sure sign of an inferiority complex. You probably recall taking that first cigarette to be "one of the gang." Your entire body rebelled and said, "No, No." However, you "forced" your body to accept the cigarette. You were determined to show your peer group you could be a "big" boy or girl and smoke like they did. Remember how proud you were the first time you blew a smoke ring and then blew a smoke ring through a smoke ring? How thrilled you were the first time you inhaled without choking. How "sophisticated" you felt when you learned to talk with smoke coming out of your mouth at the same time. And weren't you excited when you could "casually" do all of these things without revealing you were a newcomer to the "coffin tack" club? Wouldn't it be nice if you could put cigarettes away as easily as you picked them up? Incidentally, if you are even casually concerned about the effects of smoking you will be pleased to know we have a clinic in Dallas which has tested over 27,000 people for 11 years on a new type cigarette which is half filter and half tobacco. There has not been a single case of cancer. Unfortunatey there have been an awful lot of hernias. [Yes, Cindy, that's a joke.]

To show you the maturity, or lack of it, behind the thinking that goes with smoking, some authorities estimate that less than five percent of the smokers in America acquired the habit after age 22. This indicates that thinking, mature people who observe smokers for any length of time won't take up the habit. It's also significant that 21,000,000 adults and over 100,000 doctors have quit smoking since the link was established between cigarette smoking and lung cancer.

But, let's return to the story of how you acquire the habit of smoking. Even though your body bravely, and in some cases strongly resisted smoking, you continued to force cigarettes upon your system. Your body then made some adjustments. In effect, it said, "Okay, I'll do it, but I won't like it." You then said, "That doesn't matter, you're going to do it anyway." Later on, your body made further concessions and said, "I don't know why I objected, actually, it's not that bad." Still later, your body adjusted until you actually enjoyed smoking. At that point you told your friends you smoked because you enjoyed it. After all, you assured them, a person needed to do some things he enjoyed. You even told them you could quit any time you wanted to because you had already quit a dozen times so it wasn't really a "habit." Finally, your body made its final adjustment when it acquired the total habit and demanded that cigarette.

THEN — THE HABIT GETS YOU

This is evidenced by the number of people who have nicotine "fits" from the time they run out of cigarettes until they can buy, beg, borrow or steal another. I've seen an otherwise healthy 200-pound man reduced to a quivering mass by a craving for a cigarette that weighed less than 1/10th ounce. It almost makes me wish we were creatures of logic instead of creatues of emotion, doesn't it you?

Yes, habits are funny things. What's funny, or rather tragic, is that bad habits are so predictable and avoidable. Despite this, there are people by the millions who insist on acquiring habits that are bad, expensive and create problems. In the case of tobacco, the user discovers **the chains of habit are too weak to be felt until they are too strong to be broken.** The habit they weren't going to get, got them.

Morality or immorality are habits. Both are "caught" more

than taught. A completely moral person can become immoral in a gradual process that is almost completely predictable. The "good" boy or girl is accidentally or inadvertently exposed to a situation they abhor and find distasteful. At a party, banquet or social function he might be drawn into a group that believes in free love, trial marriage, drug experimentation, wife swapping, drunkenness, etc. Although there is intitial objection and complete disapproval of the actions, if some member of the group appeals in some way to this individual, look out. A relationship could be in the formative stage. If further contact is made, the natural turn of events will lead the person who was originally quite offended into more and more associations with the individuals they have met as well as others of the same persuasion [birds of a feather do flock together].

The mind is a marvelously, flexible mechanism that can do a remarkable amount of adjusting and rationalizing. The sins, or immoral acts that were so abhorred originally, become less objectionable after a few additional exposures where "tolerance" is advocated as "the" most desirable virtue. Tolerance gradually changes to acceptance, particularly if a genuine attachment is formed with the individuals involved. Acceptance moves to one of tacit approval which changes into approval and then involvement. Throughout the process, the rationalization procedure has been going full speed ahead.

The same procedure pertains to pornography. The affect of pornography was hit hard by Professor Alexander M. Bickel of Yale University Law School. In commenting on the affect of pornography he stated, "What it does produce is a moral atmosphere, and *the moral atmosphere is the ultimate regulator of conduct.* If something can be said, if it can be shown, if it is obviously permitted by society, then that society begins to think it is do-able."

ONE BITE AT A TIME

Eating too much is a habit, and for many people it has become so deeply ingrained they are unaware of the amount of food they consume. This might have been started by well-meaning but misinformed parents who thought that loving a child meant giving him whatever he wanted at the moment. My age group produced a number of "fatty's," because the parents of my generation had a hard struggle getting enough to eat, and food represented security. They also felt it was sinful to waste food. As a result, numerous parents admonished their children to "clean the plate." This extra food on a regular basis resulted in a weight gain of a few ounces each week. Gain one ounce per day and you'll gain nearly 23 pounds for the year. An ounce isn't much, but 23 pounds is a lot. If you have a weight problem, you didn't acquire it by overeating yesterday, and you're not going to solve it by starving tomorrow. You added your excess weight one bite at a time until obesity became a fact. With rare exception, you simply ate too much too often. You'll solve the problem the way you created it — one bite at a time.

For many, it's a slightly different problem. Some people are so taste and pleasure oriented, they often acquire destructive eating habits with a high concentration of starches and sweets. Combine this with a "no exercise" way of life, and weight piles on even faster than an ounce a day.

If too much weight is a problem for you, let me urge you to turn back to Chapter Four in the Segment on Goals and review what you need to do to get rid of the weight.

THE WISEST — AND THE STRONGEST FELL

We're kidding ourselves if we think we won't be influenced by associating with the wrong crowd. Solomon, the wisest man who ever lived, married Philistine wives who worshipped idols. Guess what? It wasn't long before his mind and judgment were no match for the evil which surrounded him. He too began to worship idols. Samson was the strongest man who ever lived, but under constant sexual pressure from Delilah, he succumbed to her wishes and told the secret which reduced him to blindness and slavery. Proverbs 22:24-27 is crystal clear about what the wrong association does; so is the Apostle Paul, when he writes, "Be not deceived; bad campanions corrupt good morals." (1 Cor. 15:33 A.S.V.)

The best example I can give is that of the "accent" in speech. I'm certain you have observed that when a Southern boy or girl moves North, in a matter of months, he or she will acquire an accent. If a Northern boy or girl moves South in a matter of months we will have him or her talking normally. You adjust to, are influenced by and become part of what you associate with. Recently, my 12-year-old son was asking for lunch money. I tried to "sell" him on the idea of skipping a high carbohydrate lunch and eating a nutritious protein bar. He was pretty firm in his refusal, so I pointed out that I was doing what I was trying to get him to do. His reply pretty well said it all, "Yeah, Dad, but you're not around a bunch of kids eating hamburgers." That same "peer group pressure" plays a dramatic role in influencing youngsters on drugs, dress, sex, violence, etc.

Not only do **we acquire the characteristics of the people we associate with** on a steady basis, but we also become immune and desensitized to the noise and odors of our environment. People who live in paper mill towns, or close to fertilizer plants grow so accustomed to the odors they never notice them until someone else points them out. As a teenager during World War II, our house was just 10 miles from the oil field and trains came by in an endless stream 24 hours a day. We grew so accustomed to the noise and the shaking of the house that we were completely unaware of their passing — unless one stopped. Then the silence woke us up.

These examples emphasize that when you are around or with a negative, evil, or destructive situation or environment long enough you will go from objection to tolerance, from tolerance to acceptance, and from acceptance to participation and even enjoyment. It makes no difference how little it was to start with, it will grow.

MY AMBITION — TO BE A HEROIN ADDICT

Drugs, including alcohol, represent the greatest single threat our youth have ever faced. It has been my lot to be involved in the war on drugs these past few years. During my involvement, I've never talked with a drug addict who admitted he or she started out to become an addict. Nor have I ever talked to a youngster on "pot" who told me that "pot" was just his starting point for moving to the "hard stuff." I've never had anyone lay out a schedule of how he was going to move first to "hashish," then to "speed" and finally to "heroin." I've never had anyone ridicule "pot" as "kid stuff" or just a phase he was going through. Never once have I had a youngster say he was ambitious to move from the "soft stuff" to "H," the real kicker, like the cool cats. In every single case the kids stress they are "too smart" for that kind of stuff. They know what it will do to them, and they vow they will never, never get hooked. These are famous last words, because just as the dying flicker of a match can start a forest fire, the all-consuming craving for "another fix" — or one more drink — is generally started by the lighting of that first "reefer" of marijuana, or taking that first drink, many months earlier. **Habit is a cable; we weave a thread of it each day until it becomes too strong to break.** *Then the strength of that habit cable takes us to the top — or ties us to the bottom, depending on whether it is a good habit or a bad one.*

YOU ARE THE DOCTOR

In working with people with problems, there are judgments to be made which sometimes belie the facts. Take, for example, a woman pregnant with her fifth child. She comes to your office seeking advice about whether or not she should have an abortion. Here are the facts. She has tuberculosis and her husband has a veneral disease. Of her four children, one was born dead, one was mentally retarded, one was deaf and the other blind. Naturally, with this kind of history, she is terribly concerned about what to do. She wants you to make the final decision for her. What about it? Chances are you would decide in favor of an abortion. If you had been the doctor in this actual case, you would have denied the world the music of Ludwig Von Beethoven. With *all* the facts you probably would have made the wrong decision. A decision, I might add, which could not be reversed.

There are many facts we don't have about drugs, and especially marijuana. However, as the evidence is gathered, it becomes more and more obvious that its use is fraught with peril. Evidence is solid that it affects judgment, multiplies the incidence of birth, reduces self awareness and creates the *illusion* of greater insight and emotional maturity. Many times the users thought they were getting "smarter" but no one else did. Pot also diminishes sex drive, distorts distance and actually destroys cells, while creating apathy among habitual users.

Occasionally, a youngster might be warned by a real friend who understands the risk involved in using marijuana, but the changes brought about by its use are so subtle the user sees no danger and detects no change. They believe that smoking pot is harmless. But as Neil Soloman, M.D. points out, this belief is as wide spread as it is wrong. It's true that pot is harmless by comparison with, say heroin, but by the same logic, it's also all right to cut off your foot compared to slitting your throat. Many users go to great lengths to point that out. It's "his life" and if it hurts anyone, it will be no one but him. Besides, it's fun and he is now accepted as "one of the gang." Even if this were entirely true it is still sad to watch young people cripple and sometimes destroy their lives. From a tragic personal experience, however, I can tell you that pot smokers, like drinkers, often hurt and destroy people other than themselves. An older brother and his wife lost their youngest son, who was an outstanding young man of 25, when he was hit by a car driven by a youngster high on pot who misjudged his speed and the distance involved. The grief of the parents and loved ones is indescribable and the recurring guilt feelings of the boy responsible for the tragedy will undoubtedly have a sobering affect on anyone familiar with the family. I pray that those who contend that pot is harmless will never have to deal with just one grief stricken member of an innocent victim's family. Many, many times the individual involved with pot grows bolder and indulges more frequently. Finally, he is "hooked" and progressing on the road to the big "H." That is the route most hard core addicts take, according to the world's foremost authorities — the hard core addicts themselves.

TIME TO MOVE UP

There's a funny thing about the use of marijuana. After a time, one member of the group suggests smoking "pot" is kid stuff. What they should do is try "hashish," "speed," or something with a bigger kick. They point out, "If you think pot is fun, you should try . . .!" They easily "sell the idea" because the group is already involved. Once they've justified the habit in their own minds, it's easy to move from that first step and you can bet your last nickel the source of supply for pot will have access to the hard stuff.

You can also bet if your friends or loved ones are involved, they weren't originally involved by a sinister, underworld character. They were "sold" by someone they knew and trusted. When a person gets involved in an illegal activity, he figures it will lessen his own guilt if he can persuade others to join him. With the exception of alcohol, marijuana is the most dangerous of all the drugs. Without exception, every hard core addict I ever met told me he started on "pot." My associates in the drug war make the same observation.

Authorities are in near-unanimous agreement that marijuana is not physically addictive. However, in Chairman Claude Pepper's Congressional Investigation of marijuana, he was confronted with an uneducated youngster who asked, "If marijuana is not habit forming, how come I can't quit?" The committee never answered him. Psychologists say pot is not habit forming physiologically but it is psychologically. It's sad to play this word game with kids because it is tougher, much tougher, to shake a mental habit than a physical one. Arrested heroin addicts [there is no such thing as a "former" addict any more than there is a "former" alcoholic], fight the mental addiction to heroin many years after all their physical needs have passed. Some never get over a craving for a "fix."

UNFORTUNATELY — IT'S PLEASANT

There is no hangover or physical discomfort that follows a marijuana "high." Since the smoker had a good feeling, was relaxed and at peace, he can see no reason "why not," and he's on the way — down. The changes pot makes are so gradual the user is almost never aware of them. The changes are so slight you waste your breath mentioning them because the user couldn't and wouldn't believe you. The people who see him every day aren't even aware of the change. Generally speaking, it's the friend or relative who hasn't seen him for a few weeks who first notices the change.

Originally, when a youngster starts on this "habit," the cost is small and can be managed out of the regular allowance. When users get into the drug scene on a more regular basis, however, more money is required. At that point, money starts disappearing from the top of the dresser, Mom's change purse or Dad's wallet. As the habit grows, the need for money and the skill for acquiring it grows. Now the prospective addict starts taking more money and selling items from the house that are not likely to be missed. As the habit grows, the addict moves his petty thievery to the local stores. He sells these stolen items through a "fence" at a price roughly ten to twenty-percent of the true market value. At this price, some ingenuity is required to support even a small habit.

The deeper and more involved the habit becomes, the greater the thievery. The move into the hard drugs, involving the regular use of things like "speed," "LSD," "heroin," cocaine, and others increases the thievery at an alarming rate. The greater the habit, the greater the cost, until eventually the addict has to steal on virtually a full time basis. Eventually this reaches the limit. Girls frequently turn to prostitution and the boys to procuring. The next step comes when involvement is so heavy the addict can't raise enough money to support it. At that point the nice boy or girl across the street, who started out "just smoking pot," becomes a pusher. None of these kids would have believed it was possible or that it could happen to them.

KILLED — WHILE ON A TRIP

There are two things we need to understand about drugs. First, there is no way to predict what the addict will do while under the influence of drugs. Second, there is no way to predict what he will do to satisfy the craving once he has the habit. There are cases where addicts have done everything from selling their own sisters and wives into prostitution to killing their own relatives to acquire money to support the habit. One boy literally killed his friend and ate his heart while on an hallucinogenic trip.

When an addict becomes a pusher, he is in a unique position. In most cases, he can't sell his product to established users so he has to "create" a new market. The new "pusher" would literally get his throat cut if he attempted to sell another pusher's "customers," so he carves out his own territory. This creates a vicious cycle because the new pusher must get more people started on the same habit he himself took up so casually. Oh, what a price to pay just to be "one of the gang."

JUST WHO IS RESPONSIBLE?

This way of life had led my generation to be highly critical of the younger generation. We've said some pretty hard things about immoral, irresponsible kids and accused them of being the "worst" generation in history. There's a good chance we were right, but unfortunately we made the mistake of focusing on the problem while largely ignoring the *cause* of the problem. However, as I did my research for this book, it became increasingly evident that youthful behavior was often the result of following adult examples and falling victim to the temptations made possible by an older generation.

By now you have a clear picture of what I believe, so I won't do any re-hashing other than to remind you that, "as ye sow, so also shall ye reap." Ideas and suggestions are planted by the television screen [which has surpassed both the home and the church as the greatest influence in America today], theatres, radios, books, magazines, and the conduct of people in general. Obviously, most T.V. stations, newspapers, massage parlors, movie houses, drug import businesses, drinking and gambling establishments, etc. are not owned by teenagers. However, the victims are often youthful and the results are as devastating as the profit to the owners is enormous. Today, when I look at a younger generation *in* trouble, I am forced to admit that my peer group, my generation, stands guilty *with* the youth.

This is not a "cop-out" of the premise that each individal who reaches the age of accountability *must* accept his responsibility to mankind and *will* stand in front of the judgment seat of Almighty God. I'm simply acknowledging the responsibility my generation must accept because of what we *did* to promote these builders of destructive habits, or *did not do* through economic and legislative pressure to prevent their spread. The greatest of all mistakes is to do nothing because you think you can do only a little.

HE DIDN'T MEAN IT

Profanity is another bad habit. It's disappointing to hear anyone use profanity of any kind, because we have no way of knowing where or when it's going to stop. I often hear people burst out in some "colorful expressions." In many cases an associate or subordinate will explain that "John doesn't mean a thing by it [cursing] — that's just the way he is." My problem is similar to yours. I can't tell when a person means something or when he doesn't. I consider it rude to interrupt such a person after every statement to inquire if it is part of what he "means" or part of what he "does not mean."

I find it difficult to believe anyone has ever favorably influenced another for their mutual benefit by using profanity, but I know of many instances where sales were lost, friendships disrupted, opportunities missed or courtships terminated because of it. Profanity is another of those bad habits which creeps in so gradually most are unaware they're acquiring it.

Even rape is generally the end result of an escalating bad habit. According to Dorothy Hicks, M.D., reporting on the results of studies done in Florida, most rapists started in the same way. Dr. Hicks points out that rape on the part of the *habitual* rapist is an act of violence and not an act of sex. At that moment, the rapist hates women and could care less about her age or appearance and often can't recall anything about her. She then points out that rapists start as peeping toms, next they begin silently entering bedrooms where they watch women sleeping. They then move to non-violent rape which progresses to violent rape.

The habitual liar, the person who is chronically late, the promiscuous individual, the one who "didn't hear the alarm" and sleeps on, all got their start in the same manner. A slight concession initially, which led to more and bigger concessions until eventually these bad habits become a way of life.

SLOW AND EASY

All bad habits, trends, cancers, etc., start slowly, quietly, and apparently harmlessly. This is true on a personal, national and international level. Initially, it seems so foolish to make an issue out of "such a little thing." No one knew this better than Nikita Khrushchev, the butcher of Budapest, who ruthlessly slew tens of millions. He clearly stated the Communist position in the Congressional Record of the United States. "We cannot expect the Americans to jump from Capitalism to Communism, but we can assist their elected leaders in giving Americans small doses of Socialism until they suddenly awake to find they have Communism."

The "small doses" Khrushchev spoke of started during the depression years when the relief programs got a foothold. It was during this period that Americans started electing their Senators and Congressmen because of their "promises" to vote more aid for their section of the country and not for their ability, integrity and patriotism. When Americans started looking for a "handout" instead of a hand, we were laying the first foundation stones for a national policy built on fear and greed instead of strength and dignity.

The first "small doses" in the bad habit of establishing a "no win" policy took place when Truman stopped Patton and his tanks on the outskirts of Berlin, denying the Allies the victory Almighty God had given us over a godless enemy. This set the stage for the "no win" policy that has dominated our national thinking ever since. He did it for our "friend" and ally, Joe Stalin, who rates second only to Mao Tse-Tung in the number of millions slaughtered. Later, despite the eloquent pleas of Churchill, we refused to attack the soft underbelly of Europe and lost those countries to Communism. The trend continued when we invited Russia to enter the war against an already defeated Japan and lost North Korea to Communism as a result. Later — still on our giant surrender program, we listened to George Marshall when he assured us that Mao and his buddies were a bunch of harmless agrarian reformers. We withdrew our aid and abandoned our long time friend and ally, Chiang Kai Shek to the Communist hordes and lost China to Communism.

By now it should have been obvious to every politician and voter in America that we were on a collision course with disaster but we still had some lessons to learn. In Communism we found a willing teacher. We had victory in our grasp in Korea, but liberal thinking and our "no win" policy forced us into a stalemate which exists today. Next came Cuba when — despite some alarming intelligence reports — we aided Fidel Castro in his takeover. More recently we've experienced the tragedy of our "no win" policy in Viet-Nam. Most knowledgeable military men say we could have won that war quickly by shutting down the Ho Chi Minh Trail and closing Haiphong Harbor in the early days.

Let me also remind you that Khrushchev did say they were going to "bury" us and that the Communists have broken *every* treaty signed with a Western nation when it was to their advantage to do so. Cambodia and South Viet-Nam have fallen to the Communists despite the Paris Cease-Fire Agreement signed by the United States and South Viet-Nam with North Viet-Nam and the Viet Cong.

Communists are simply not bound by the same moral laws that govern us. They label themselves as the "People's" party and liberators, but surely you have noticed what happens in *every* instance when they "liberate" a country. Have you noticed a flood of refugees going from West Germany to East Germany, from Hong Kong to Red China, from Miami to Havana or from Western Europe into Hungary and Russia? More recently, have you seen any refugees fleeing north to Hanoi to embrace their "liberators?" [Two reasons you never see refugees running to their Communist "liberators" are; historically they always lose their freedom and they want to eat and no communist country on earth can feed itself.]

Again, *all* trends and habits — both personal and national — start weak and slow but ultimately get fast and strong. I'm convinced there is time to reverse the trend but we must make our stand personally — and as a nation — now. If everyone — starting with you — keeps himself morally sound and strong, we have nothing to fear from an outside or inside foe. The hour is late — but it's not too late to reverse the trend. I'll have more to say about the solution to this problem as we close the book.

BAD HABITS COME SLOW AND EASY

I emphasize that every bad habit you have was acquired slowly and easily. The analogy on marijuana applies equally as well to drinking. There are still those parents who condemn drugs but defend their own drinking. Many will say, "How, where and why did our boy or our girl ever acquire such a habit? How could they turn to drugs when they have everything?" The kids might ask you parents the same question. After all, alcohol is a drug too. Some parents, in self-righteous indignation, say, "How could they do this to us?" Let me emphasize one point. Many parents will start the day with a "pep pill." Later, to settle their nerves, they take a "tranquilizer." To curb their appetites, they take a "diet pill." Before dinner they have a "cocktail" and they finish the day with a "nightcap." During the day they smoke a pack or two of "cigarettes" and throw in a couple of "aspirin" for good measure. Then, the parents indignantly say, "Where do the kids come up with the drug habit?"

Many years ago, while driving with my mother from Columbia, South Carolina to Charleston, South Carolina, I asked about a former classmate of mine in my hometown of Yazoo City, Mississippi. My mother lowered her voice and whispered, "Why, Son, he has turned into the 'worst kind of drinker'." I half jokingly asked, "Mother, what is the 'worst kind of drinker'?" She explained to me that my classmate would buy a bottle and in the quietness of his home, take a drink. She stressed that he never denied his family anything, never became abusive and never got drunk. She stressed that his drinking did not affect his job, that he was a "respected" member of the community and had recently been elected to a political post.

Somewhat started, I facetiously asked, "Mother, is that really the 'worst kind of drinker'?" She assured me in no uncertain terms it was and her reasoning was simple. He set a "good" example of drinking and his children saw nothing wrong with Dad, who worked so hard to support them, relaxing and taking a drink. They identified drinking with a kind, considerate devoted husband and father. As Mother pointed out, no one wants to emulate the drunk. Had this man been inclined to abuse his family and deny them the necessities of life, the children would have been disgusted with drinking. Had he been an occupant of skid row or a sot who was inclined to roll in the gutter, no one would have wanted to "be like him." [Could this be the reason the liquor industry piously urges you to drink in "moderation?"]

To reinforce what my mother is saying, France has the

highest per capita wine consumption of any country in the world. They also have the highest rate of alcoholism of any country in the world. For fear you might think this is a "coincidence," let me add that Chile has the second highest per capita consumption of wine and the second highest rate of alcoholism in the world.

One more "coincidence" needs to be spotlighted. It's too early to obtain a definite figure but there has been a *dramatic* increase in teenage alcoholism which coincides directly with the sudden splurge of TV advertising of sweet wines. The added tragedy is that these commercials, along with the ones on beer, concentrate on the major athletic events with their high percentage of youthful audiences. The hypocrisy is incredible. Athletics to build life and health, being sponsored by alcohol which destroys life and health.

The drinking habit starts with the consumption of a small amount of alcohol in the wine. Over a period of time, the body increases its desires and tolerances for more of the alcohol and the results have been disastrous. When I see parents giving a toddler a sip of their beer, I can't help but wonder if I'm observing the making of another alcoholic. It's bad enough when a person stumbles on his own into the alcoholic jungle. For a parent to lead a youngster into that jungle has to be one of the most despicable and/or foolish acts of our time.

Obviously, it is a misguided act carried out in ignorance, but until we spread the truth to enough people, alcoholism will continue to grow. It is important that we continue to learn about alcoholism and take every conceivable action to restore alcoholics to productive lives. These steps, however, without education toward prevention, make as much sense as putting an ice cube on a thermometer after it registers your temperature at 103 degrees in the mistaken belief you are "curing" the fever.

Surely as a civilized nation, we can learn from the sad experience of France and Chile — as well as from the estimated 9,000,000 alcoholic Americans. [Some authorities place that figure closer to 25,000,000.] As of this moment, liquor is the number one "drug problem" in America, and it's growing by leaps and bounds — particularly among the youth. In New York City, for example, a recent survey revealed that 12% of the pupils have a drinking problem and nearly 60% of the high school students in America get drunk at least once each month. The same survey recommended that prevention be initiated in the elementary grades. They are partially right. It should be *reinforced* in the elementary grades. It should be *started* by Mother and Dad by example and teaching while the children are still on Mama's knee.

Despite this fact, there are some parents who proudly state that their kids don't fool with dope — they only drink. They even boast that they are teaching the kids "how" to drink properly. Is this possible?

Authorities now know that approximately one person in sixteen who takes a social drink, will become an alcoholic. To repeat myself, alcoholics, like other drug addicts, never start out to become alcoholics but **all bad habits start slowly and gradually and before you know you have the habit, the habit has you.**

The Surgeon General of the United States requires that cigarette manufacturers place a mild warning on a pack of cigarettes — and well he should. The mystery is, why he doesn't demand a much stronger warning on every bottle containing alcohol. To compare the dangers of cigarette smoking with the dangers of drinking is like comparing the killing power of a pea shooter with a 50-caliber machine gun. If there is any doubt in your mind that alcohol is our biggest killer, let me point out that according to Time Magazine, our twenty-year involvement in Viet-Nam cost us approximately 141 billion dollars and 56,000 dead. In the same twenty years the drinking driver took approximately 500,000 people to a premature death and cost us nearly half a *trillion dollars.* If the same people who demonstrated so violently against our involvement in Viet-Nam would demonstrate just half that much against our involvement in the liquor industry and its infinitely heavier toll in human suffering, they would render a *real* service to America.

The Supreme Court of public opinion is still the highest law in the land. Question: Why don't you put this book down, pick up your pen and write your Senator and Congressman a letter suggesting that he can become a national hero — and perhaps get your vote in the next election — by introducing legislation to properly identify what alcohol does. Our laws require that we identify what's *in* the bottle, but it makes more sense to tell the public what the contents do.

BUT THEY WERE SO LITTLE

On the western slopes of the Rocky Mountains, a giant Sequoia lies rotting. It was a growing sapling when Christ walked the shores of the Sea of Galilee. When Columbus discovered America, it was reaching maturity and it looked down from lofty heights during the American Civil War. It withstood the ravages of fires, floods, storms and droughts. It seemed destined to live many more centuries. Then, a few years ago, a tiny beetle started to burrow into its bark and lay the eggs that would produce other beetles. It seemed like an unequal battle at first, but the few beetles multiplied into hundreds, then into thousands and finally into millions. First they attacked the bark, then they worked deeper and deeper into the trunk, and finally, they were eating at the very heart and strength of that magnificent forest giant. Then one day, after withstanding the elements for centuries, the rains came, the winds blew, the lightening flashed and the giant Sequoia fell. Not because of the elements. It fell because of the weakening effect of those tiny beetles. Bad habits do the same to people. They slowly take a toll until the day comes when the man, like the tree, falls.

Gone With The Wind was the first family movie to use a profane word and did it ever get a reaction! As a 7th grader in a predominantly Southern Baptist environment, I shall never forget the reaction of the community. They were dumbstruck and horrified. The liberals scoffed and said it was ridiculous for us to worry. What harm could one little word do? The next year saw another word added to the acceptable list for the family theatre and we were on our way — down.

Over ten years ago, Jack Parr was "panned" unmercifully because he referred to a "water closet" on his program. Then, as one TV writer expressed it, "We started to grow up." Hard-core pornography began to move from "adult" book stores to the magazine racks of the family drugstore. Other programs and discussions on TV used more and more "blue" material until it became an "anything goes" format for the viewer.

Today, you can view movies like *Last Tango in Paris* and *Deep Throat* in "family" theatres. You can tune in on talk shows and listen to the open endorsements of free love, trial marriage, homosexuality, etc. It all started with a tiny crack in the dike. The breakdown of morals for the individual begins with a slight concession. First one and then another. Promiscuity begins when a boy or girl "surrenders" that priceless virginity, and morality is thrown to the winds as the confused passion of the moment usurps the place of genuine love.

Tragically, once the barrier has been lowered, it is much easier to lower it the second and subsequent times. Yes, bad habits start slowly and easily, and before you are aware you have the habit — the habit has you — and the results are disastrous. One thing we know, however, is that bad habits are the results of bad learning, and if it can be learned it can be unlearned.

Now that we've identified some of the bad habits, let's go to the next chapter and learn how to eliminate or unlearn those bad habits — and acquire the good ones.

NOTES AND IDEAS

CHAPTER FIVE
STOP BAD HABITS — START GOOD HABITS

AVOIDING THE HABIT

Obviously, it's better to never acquire the habit of smoking, drinking, drugs, law breaking, promiscuity, cheating, cursing, finger nail biting, overeating, etc. Since concerned parents and responsible citizens all over America are vitally concerned about these matters let's look at a few guidelines which should be helpful in avoiding the destructive habits.

Sam Maglitto, curriculum director at Bay City Independent School District, Bay City, Texas, makes the observation that if the philosophy of "See You At The Top" were taught at the fifth and sixth grade level, it would eliminate the need for sex education, drug education, and career education. That's a pretty strong statement but I might point out that Mr. Maglitto speaks from personal experience as a parent whose daughter has studied the philosophy and as a school administrator where the course is being taught. He feels that the first step is to sell our youngsters on the advantages of keeping clear minds, healthy bodies and sound morals and thus head off the problems and eliminate destructive habits before they start. Naturally, I agree.

The second step to avoiding bad habits, drugs in particular, according to Dr. Forest Tenant of U.C.L.A. is to "spank the kids and take them to church." I am certain that many of the civil libertarians will scream it's archaic to lay your hands on the kids. Psychologists, however, generally agree that when a child understands he is going to be held responsible for his deeds he is far more likely to be concerned with those deeds. Dr. Tenant did a comprehensive study of the drug problem among the GIs in Germany where America had a drug problem second only to the one in Vietnam. He discovered there were only two things that served as a definite deterrent as far as the use of drugs was concerned. The first was to take the kids to church fifty or more times by the time they were fifteen years old. The second was to regularly spank them moderately when the occasion demanded it. The Bible very clearly states that this is the procedure to follow if you love your child.

Psychologist James Dobson strongly feels it is most destructive to permit a child to go through life without the loving assurance expressed in discipline. Discipline assures the child he is worthwhile and that you love him enough to discipline him for conduct which is not in his own best interest.

Step number three is to set an example. When I was a young father, my mother repeatedly said to me, "Son, your children more attention pay to what you do than what you say." Parents who are sincerely concerned about their children not drinking, smoking, using drugs, or living in an immoral way should set the proper example. Evidence is conclusive that if parents smoke and drink, the children are far more likely to follow that example. As I previously stated, some parents start the day with a pep pill, followed by a tranquilizer to steady their nerves. During the course of the day they might take a couple of aspirins, have a cocktail before dinner, and a nightcap before retiring. Along the way they smoke a couple of packs of cigarettes and then they express amazement when their kids get involved in "drugs." They wonder out loud as to why, and how the kids — who had everything — could do such a thing.

Step number four is fight false advertising. The tobacco and liquor industries are undoubtedly the best financed and the most imaginative in their advertising campaigns. The beer people sell their beer with some of the most persuasive commercials on television. They are particularly adept at using athletic figures to peddle their beer, knowing full well that youngsters identify with athletes. And after all those guys sure made it big and if they think it is alright and fun, then obviously it is! The liquor industry sells gracious living and the "man of distinction" approach while piously adjusting their halos and suggesting that you drink in "moderation."

The cigarette ads sell the idea of "manhood" and "feminity" while emphasizing that you are a part of the "in" crowd and "sophisticated" if you smoke. This false advertising is so persuasive and repeated so many times that most kids *decide* to try smoking by the time they are seven years old. As mentioned earlier, thanks to the same advertising techniques, teenage alcoholism has dramatically increased the last five years.

TRUTH IN ADVERTISING

In my judgment we should fight this false advertising with truth in a dramatic way. For example, have you ever looked at an old lady with a cigarette dangling between her lips until she has to remove it to cough a few times? Or have you seen an old man with nicotine-stained fingers put a cigarette to his mouth, forget about it, and watch the ashes drop off on his clothes? Think about this phrase, "Kissing a girl who has smoked a cigarette is like licking an ashtray"? Now that you've thought about it, does smoking add to your sexuality and sophistication or does it take away from it? Additionally, girls, there is irrefutable evidence that cigarette smoking causes your skin to be dry and wrinkled before your time.

To add insult to injury [I believe we are safe in referring to lung cancer and heart disease as injury], Uncle Sam contributes millions of dollars to support the tobacco farmers with crop subsidies, then after spending millions of dollars proving that smoking causes cancer and heart disease he spends hundreds of millions of dollars supporting the treatment of the cancer which he contributed to the cause of in the first place! So surely Uncle Sam, with enough pressure, would be willing to spend additional funds fighting the sale of the product which he encourages with the subsidy. Obviously I say this with tongue in cheek but it is interesting to listen to someone explain why we should support the raising of tobacco — then restrict the advertising because it is injurious to health — then contribute to the cancer research and treatment to fight the cancer caused by smoking cigarettes which our tax-supported dollars had already proved caused cancer. [You might want to re-read this paragraph.]

LET THE KIDS SEE FOR THEMSELVES

Step number five in avoiding bad habits is to take your children on field trips and let them see the result of smoking, drinking, and drugs. I suggest you visit someone who has emphysema or lung cancer caused by smoking and take your child with you. Give him an opportunity to talk with a person [preferably someone you know] who is afflicted with emphysema or lung cancer and let him listen to their labored efforts at breathing. Admittedly, this is drastic but remember the victim started with one cigarette. In all fairness to your youngster, this gives him the opportunity to see the other side which the cigarette ads leave out. There's not much "glamour," "sophistication," "sexuality," "taste," or "relaxation" in a cancer — as any victim who has "bought" the cigarette commercials will tell you. Strong! Perhaps. But sometimes we need to let the kids know that in the case of bad habits you do *pay* the price.

You can reinforce these fields trips with casual inquiries among smokers in the presence of your youngsters. Ask the smokers if they would — knowing what they now know — start smoking again. The vast majority will emphatically state that they would not repeat the mistake.

A couple of thoughts are most important. The decision to smoke, drink, use drugs, overeat, engage in pre-marital sex, etc., are emotional and not logical decisions. In most cases the youngers had an emotional need for acceptance which they felt these acts or habits would provide. That's the reason demonstrated love and open communication are so important between parent and child. That's also the reason I would urge you to embrace the philosophy of See You At The Top as well as the two books by Dr. James Dobson which I list at the beginning of Segment Two. When your child [you, too] has accepted and approves of himself [healthy self image] he does not require the acceptance and approval of others. Additionally, when our goals are well defined, we clearly understand that destructive habits greatly reduce our chances of reaching those goals and we give considerably more thought to gambling with the future which we have carefully planned.

If either you or your children are young and involved in social drinking, let me suggest you go to skid row, look in the gutters and remember what you see. Decide if you're willing to risk even sixteen-to-one odds that it couldn't happen to you. It could. Next, go to a couple of A.A. meetings. You'll be shocked to see brilliant and talented people from all walks of life who thought it could never happen to them. As you listen to their stories, you'll get a different look at the alcohol that appears to be as harmless, as sophisticated and being as much "fun" as advertisements depict. As you listen to alcoholics tell their stories, remember, every single case started with one drink. Remember that over 25,000 people will be killed on our highways this year by drunks who originally started with only one drink. There's no "distinction" in that statistic and there's no distinction in drinking.

Let your youngsters ask the victims how many of them had *planned* on becoming alcoholics. I believe it would have a sobering impact. Any youngster who hears the scream of a drug addict fighting withdrawal symptoms, and hears a simple explanation of the birth place of those screams, would have a large part of his curiosity satisfied. I believe taking our kids to the courtroom where the judge is sentencing an outstanding fourteen year old boy or girl to reform school because of thefts they committed to feed the drug or drinking habit or to receive a thrill while "proving" they weren't chicken would have a rather sobering effect. Admittedly, some of these steps are severe but the future of someone you love could be at stake. That's serious.

BREAKING DESTRUCTIVE HABITS

Let's now look at what you can do to eliminate a destructive habit, whether it is obesity, habitually being late, profanity, smoking, having a short temper, homosexuality, alcoholism, promiscuity, etc. The first and most important thing you must do is to decide that you want to eliminate the habit. That is a decision you and only you can make. Without this motivation on your part, no person or procedure will have any significant impact. If someone else "talks you into it" the chances are strong you will perhaps start but the effort will be short lived. [Remember, you generally don't reach someone else's goal.] Many times you end up further behind than you would have been had you not attempted to quit a habit which you were not ready to give up [weight lost and regained is a classic example]. So first, and most important-ly, decide you no longer are going to be a slave to any destructive habit. Decide you want to have control of your life, that you want to be free, that you want to do things with your life instead of having things done to your life.

LISTEN TO THE QUITTERS

It's tougher — much tougher — to quit a bad habit, but unfortunately the results are fun and much more rewarding. Former smokers, alcoholics, fat folks, etc., unanimously — and in glowing terms — give me a tremendous number of details concerning the joy and excitement of shedding those pounds, giving up the weed, and getting off the bottle. The ex-smoker talks about the exciting taste of food — the clean smell of the air, clothes, furniture, etc. They talk about a new-found self-respect and satisfaction from whipping a habit that would have taken from two to ten years off their lives — and a lot of living out of their lives. [According to a June 1, 1977 Associate Press story, the Royal College of Physicians in co-operation with all of Britain's Medical Colleges conducted a study which revealed that each cigarette cuts $5\frac{1}{2}$ minutes from a smoker's life span, that roughly one in three smokers die because of smoking and roughly 50 million working days are lost in Britain each year through illness caused by smoking. They also found that a smoker who quits gains immediate benefits and in 10-15 years the extra risk of dying early disappears. Incidentally, a $5\frac{1}{2}$ minute loss of life per cigarette translates into 28 days per year of smoking if you smoke just one pack per day.] As you decide that you are going to seek the richer life, listen to the ex-smokers explain why they are exuberant with the realization that they will be here those extra years and that they are using their money for worthwhile rather than destructive purposes.

If you're obese I urge you to go to several of the Weight Watchers or Overeaters Anonymous meetings and listen to people who have lost from 50 to 350 pounds. *Listen* to them talk of the struggles they had but of the rewards that are now theirs. *Listen* to the sheer joy of being able to buy a suit or dress off the rack at a reasonable price. *Listen* to them talk about a new found romance in their life and the thrill of being able to tie their shoes without grunting and walk up a flight of stairs instead of having to wait for the elevator. *Listen* to them talk about the accolades that are pinned on them for their new svelte figure rather than the ridicule, laughter, and contempt that was often heaped upon them and by the unspoken words that were often on the minds of their associates. *Listen* to those quitters who quit eating so much and it will help you quit eating too much.

The arrested alcoholics talk about all their new friends and how they got their old ones back. They, frequently with tears in their eyes, tell of regained families — the resumption of long interrupted careers — new self-respect — new social life and a feeling of tremendous accomplishments from paying their own way — and then some.

YOU WIN — BY BEING A QUITTER

Interestingly enough, many of these people quit their bad habits in exactly the same way they acquired them — by association with the right people with positive goals in life. This has long been known in the case of alcoholics through Alcoholics Anonymous and more recently compulsive gamblers through Gamblers Anonymous and for the obese person, Weight Watchers, T.O.P.S. [Take Off Pounds Sensibly] and others. The reasons these organizations work when everything else has failed are numerous. The alcoholic, compulsive gambler or the obese person, is suddenly thrust into a group of people who are succeeding in whipping the problem that has been whipping them. They are with and around concerned, caring people who know the bitterness of defeat and the sweetness of victory. Countless stories of "I did it and so can you," give the victims of these habits the confidence and the support he or she needs. Surrounded by the optimism, enthusiasm and encouragement of a right thinking environment, the results are dramatic. Again, again, and even again, will I say that your associates do influence your habits and you don't pay a price for success, health, happiness, etc., you enjoy a price.

Two other factors with considerable impact are involved in the case of A.A. First of all, the alcoholic is brought to the complete realization that there is absolutely nothing that he or she can do about their alcoholism themselves. They are helpless and it is not because they do not want to quit drinking. No sane person would want to be an alcoholic and bring about the suffering to themselves and their families. When the alcoholic admits that he must have the help of a higher power then he is on his way to solving the problem. They identify God by saying, "God as you understand Him." Since I am not bound by any of the restrictions they are bound by, I simply say God, period. I refer you back to Isaiah 40:31 and remind you that in that verse to "renew" means to "change" or "exchange." It's true you can't — but God can. It is stressed that the alcoholics' only hope is a power source greater than their own. [John 15:5-7 is quite clear on this.]

Until the alcoholic reaches that conclusion, his chance of "arresting" the disease is remote. Ditto for the hard-core drug addict. Nor does A.A. and its members permit the alcoholic to get hung up on a lot of "cop-outs." [My mother was scared by a runaway horse before I was born, I was rejected by my classmates, my mother took me off the potty too soon, etc.] Alcoholics are forced to admit they are alcoholics *because* they drink too much booze, period. Psychologically when an individual is brought face to face with the fact that regardless of the excuse he used to start a destructive habit he is the only one who is going to suffer the consequences. When he understands and accepts full responsibility for his behavior, a giant step has been taken to break that habit.

Many times the individual can be brought face to face with the reality that his reason for starting a habit no longer exists. For example, he might have started smoking, cursing, gambling, drinking, using drugs, etc. because of insecurity and the need to be accepted by his peer group. With this realization and the building of that healthy self image the individual is freed of the reason for these destructive habits and his chances of quitting are enhanced.

An active youngster — perhaps an athlete — burns an enormous amount of energy and needs a large amount of food. However, when the physical activity declines the need for much of the food no longer exists but the habit of eating the larger amount has been established. Complete awareness of his current needs and best interests are very helpful in converting the habit of filling former needs with the advantages of dealing with the current problem to solve present needs.

Step number three is substitute. There is really no such thing as eliminating a habit. You simply subsititute a good one for a bad one. The alcoholic substitutes optimistic, dedicated, caring friends in a positive atmosphere of hope and encouragement for the booze, bars, boredom, bums, and bellyaches that are frequently the alcoholic's constant mental and physical companions. Psychologically, it's important to have a new activity or habit to fill the void when you start eliminating any bad habit or habits. When the alcoholic sees the result of stopping the bad habit of drinking and the changes taking place in the lives of the other alcoholics as well as their own they set new goals of their own and for the first time they "see the reaching".

Since bad habits are in your mind [the physical need or desire for tobacco, alcohol and drugs is comparatively short] I refer you back to Chapter Three of this Segment. Keep your mind busy as you fill it with good, clean, inspirational, confidence building, "you can do it" messages from the printed page and the spoken word. You cannot concentrate on two things at the same time. By occupying the mind positively, you are substituting the craving for a "bad habit" by building your character with desire for long-lasting success and happiness. In other words, don't be unwise in your habits but rather aspire to maturity and wisdom and keep your mind well and emotions focused on positive ideas.

Breaking the smoking habit can even be simple — I didn't say easy — according to my good friend Bill Schmelzer, M.D., who offers this suggestion for breaking the smoking habit. In the spot you now have your cigarettes, place a pocket sized New Testament. When the urge to smoke — or far more likely, the habit-formed movement of automatically reaching for your cigarettes — hits you, you will reach for your cigarettes but you will fill your hands with God's lifesaving Word instead of shortening your life expectancy. As you reach for the Testament, simply pray, "Lord, help me." Then read two passages of scripture: John 15:5-7 and Philippians 4:13. By taking these steps you will be fulfilling the muscular habit while at the same time substituting the physical habit of smoking for the habit of drinking from God's lifesaving Word. After a few days this will become automatic and one more bad habit will bite the dust. This will add years to your life. Now turn to Ephesians 2:8-9 and learn how to really extend your life span — like forever. Not only will this get the smoke out of your eyes now but more importantly it will help keep the heat off you later.

I ALREADY KNEW THAT

To eliminate or whip the bad habit, I also urge you to regularly review the Self Image Segment so you will be constantly reminded that you are a deserving person. You also deserve the rewards that go with whipping the bad habit. Get back in the Segment on Goals. Learn to "see the reaching." Visualize yourself as "free" of that destructive habit. See yourself as winning — and you will take a giant step toward winning.

As I have said, the best way to "stop" a bad habit is to never start it. If you don't smoke that first cigarette, take that first drink, tell the first little white lie, have that "harmless" cup of coffee at lunch or after work with that "nice" man or woman at the office, smoke that first joint, read that pornographic or homosexual literature the first time, play bingo or buy a lottery ticket, or cheat in school that first time, then we would have no problems with any of the final habits that result from those initial actions.

If you have any devastating habits, then you neither need nor want me or anyone else telling you, you shouldn't have started those habits. What you do want to know is how to stop them. Again the best, simplest and surest way is to ask God for help.

Evangelist David Wilkerson, author of *The Cross and the Switchblade*, reports that their organization uses no "crutches," no medication of any kind in their dealing with hard-core drug addicts. They use only the healing grace of Jesus Christ and they are successful in over 80% of the cases. I have visited with numbers of the residents at D.A.R.E. [Drug Addicts Rehabilitation Enterprises] in Albuquerque, New Mexico. They ranged in scope from petty thieves and prostitutes to counterfeiters and murderers. About the only thing they have in common is an addiction to drugs and a desire to be free of the habit. At D.A.R.E. the only cure they use are Biblical principals. If the addict stays on campus 48 hours, the recovery rate is over 85%. In most instances the addict suffers none of the familiar withdrawal pains or symptoms and they use no drugs or medication of any kind. By contrast, the federal government operated the most modern facility in the country in Lexington, Kentucky with the latest technological methods and medicines. The facility cost millions to build and the per patient cost ran into thousands of dollars. However, less than 2% of the addicts were helped to permanently kick their habit. The results were so disappointing the facility was closed.

As a practical matter, let me ask you a question. If you were faced with a serious operation and only two surgeons were available, which one would you choose? One assures you that 2% of his patients recover and the other one points out that over 80% of his patients recover. We both know which one you would choose, don't we? Drug addiction and alcoholism are bigger than the individual, so it takes something bigger than the individual to whip these self-induced diseases.

GRAB GOOD HABITS

In Chapter Two of this Segment, I described in considerable detail the procedure for getting up in the morning. In my judgment, this is a good habit. I emphasize that when you start a procedure like my getting-up routine, it's going to be tough in some ways. It is a habit you will have to force yourself to "grab." Then you'll need to hold onto it for all you are worth. After a few days, an interesting thing will begin to happen. It will get easier and even become fun. Do it for 21 days and you'll have a "good" habit. The results will be so great that you'll start living in a different world. You'll become a happy, more motivated, excited and enthusiastic person. Take a careful look at any good habit and try to acquire it. You'll get much more out of life if you do.

In Segment Four of See You At The Top, I have described goal setting in minute detail. I point out that when I started my exercise program of running, it was a tremendously tough habit to acquire. I literally had to force myself to run that first day . . . and the second . . . and the third. However, as the days turned into weeks and the weeks into months, it became easier and easier to get out and run. It became easier because I started experiencing the joy of accomplishment. Now, I'm unhappy when circumstances beyond my control make it difficult and sometimes impossible for me to run. The habit of running and exercising, like all good habits, was tough to acquire. However, when we acquire the "tough" habits, they become "fun" habits, especially when we remember that doing the tough things today will prepare us for the big things tomorrow.

YOU OWE IT TO YOU

Saving money is another good habit. Initially, you have to force yourself to pay yourself before you start paying your other bills. But, let me suggest that, regardless of what your income might be, your first responsibility is to save a portion of every dollar you earn for you and your future. The excitement of saving grows with every dollar you add to your account. Soon this "good" habit is ingrained and becomes a part of you. It is permanently ingrained in you when, as the Chinese say, your children [dollars] have children and then those children have children.

Yes, saving money is a good habit, but initially you must "grab" it and hold on for dear life. Early in the game, there will be many times [would you believe with every pay check] when you will be tempted not to pay yourself this time because . . . Let me state this with all the persuasiveness at my disposal: "Regardless of how good the reason for not saving might be, it's not as good as the reason for firmly establishing the habit of saving." Many years ago my first employer, in Yazoo City, Mississippi, pointed out that if I could live on a certain number of dollars per week, I wouldn't starve on 10% fewer dollars each week. Obviously, he was right.

He was also right when he stated that the ability to save money was a strong indication of character and that **if you didn't save something on your current income — you wouldn't save anything on your future income.**

One thing all "success philosophers" agree on is the absolute necessity of saving money regularly if you expect dame fortune to smile on you. The money itself can be critical when busines opportunities, or reverses enter your life. The benefits you derive from disciplining yourself to forego the pleasures of the moment to accomplish your objective are even more important.

Courtesy, happiness and enthusiasm are all good habits. You can literally force yourself to be courteous, happy and enthusiastic with every person you meet. After you have forced yourself to be so for a short period of time, the habit takes over.

Smiling is a habit. Occasionally someone will say they dislike an insincere smile. Personally, I'd rather see an insincere smile than a sincere grouch — wouldn't you? Fortunately, once you've smiled a few smiles of any kind and have gotten into the habit, the smiles will cease to be insincere. Remember what William James said about singing? The same thing is true about smiling. We don't smile because we're happy, we're happy because we smile. Another significant reason you should smile is people "react" to you according to the way you "act" towards them. Smile at them and they'll smile back at you. Scowl at them and they'll scowl in return. As you discover the benefits of smiling you'll have acquired a good habit. In the process, that smile of yours will become quite natural because it will be an outward expression of an inner feeling. As a fringe benefit you will also discover that a smile is one little curve that sets a lot of things straight.

Being optimistic, attentive to your wife or husband, or attending church are also good habits. One exciting fact about a good habit is, every good habit has a friend and companion. Acquire *any* good habit and you get an automatic bonus in the form of an additional "good" habit. Example: Saving money increases your security, which gives you added confidence, making it easy to be relaxed and *friendly.*

Initially, you might have to work at all of these good habits, but their affect on you and the people you're around will be so dramatic that soon you'll no longer have to work on them. Those "good habits" will be working for you, and that's the stuff of which success and happiness are made

Yes, habits will either make or break us. Good habits are hard to acquire but easy to live with. Bad habits are easy to acquire but hard to live with. In reality, as in all the good things in life, it boils down to the choices we make. We can choose to be happy, healthy, pleasant, courteous, successful, etc. We make the choice when we choose our habits. After we make the habits, they make us. It has truly been said that **we build our character from the bricks of habit we pile up day by day.** Each one might seem like a little thing but before we're aware of it, we've shaped the house in which we live.

Someone observed that success and happiness are not destinations — they are the entire trip. Life is exciting and this trip to the top will get even more exciting to you with each step. It's universally true that the closer we get to the objective, the more likely we are to "smell the finish line" and increase our tempo. I hope and believe that you're feeling much of this excitement as you look at the stairway to the top and see yourself on Step Number Four.

So here we are at Step Number Four and those glass doors on the executive suites of tomorrow, with all the rewards they hold for us, are getting closer and closer. I'm proud of you and how far you've come. I'm even prouder of the fact that you're continuing your climb to the top. Let me remind you, however, keep using the Trigger Pages as I urge you to commit yourself more and more to excellence.

Now, I think it's time to display a little exuberance. So, on the Stairway to the Top page, with the little man representing you, why don't you write "WHOOPEE!" in big bold letters. Aw, go on, it's your book.

NOTES AND IDEAS

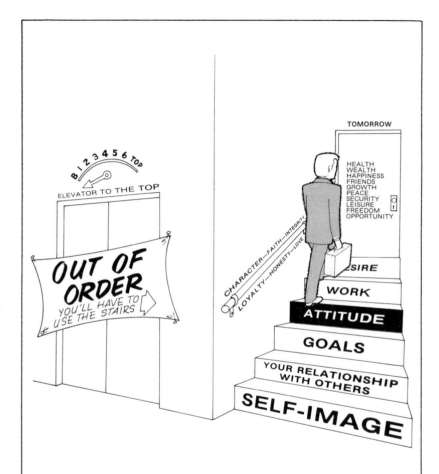

It's your attitude and not your aptitude that determines your altitude.

BONUS CHAPTER
THE SUBCONSCIOUS MIND

THE "DREAM" EMPLOYEE

Suppose — just suppose — you were an employer with a work force of one. What kind of employee would you want? If you were given the choice of ordering this employee out of a catalogue, what characteristics would you like for him or her to have? Would you like for him to be completely dependable, totally honest, always on the job, completely willing to follow instructions, extremely brilliant and capable, very pleasant and agreeable and more than willing to work for room and board on a lifetime contract? Sounds like the ideal employee, doesn't it? If you had such an employee, how would you treat him? The answer to that question is terribly important because this "ideal" employee's performance is entirely dependent on his treatment. If you are courteous and thoughtful, he will work long and hard. If you are rude and inconsiderate, he grows stubborn and rebellious. Brag on him; tell him how bright he is and he will perform brilliantly. Call him lazy, stupid or irresponsible and he will rebel and get so upset he would foul up a two-car parade. Tell him you love and respect him and he will stay up all night solving your problems. Fuss at him and tell him you don't love him and he becomes so frustrated he can't give you the time of day.

Considering everything, if such a prospective employee showed up at your door looking for a job, would you hire him? Silly question, isn't it? After you hired him, how would you treat him? We both know the answer to that one, don't we?

Oh, I almost forgot — this "dream" employee is easily influenced by the people around him. If he's around negative "garbage dump" thinkers, he too will become a negative "garbage dump" thinker and he won't be much fun nor will he be very productive. Surround him with a bunch of positive thinkers, positive talkers and positive doers, and it's positively amazing how much he can produce — and how pleasant he is to be around.

I'll bet you just decided to carefully surround this dream employee of yours with positive people and a positive environment. I'll bet you plan to be extremely nice, pleasant and make it a point to carefully notice all the good things he does, so you can "brag" on him, so he'll do even more. There's no doubt that you would think, work, plan, and maybe even scheme a little bit to get maximum production. You have everything to gain and absolutely nothing to lose by being super nice to this super employee. You'd play that one smart, wouldn't you?

The answer to that last question is probably yes — and I'm certain you would "plan" to do exactly that. However, the chances are enormous that you would probably abuse and misuse this dream employee. I say this because based on the misery and poverty that exists in millions of lives, most people do abuse and misuse this fantastic employee or servant *which is your subconscious mind*. This incredible employee or "servant" will perform *exactly* like the "dream" employee I described. Honestly, now how have you been treating this prized employee, your subconscious mind, who will do exactly as commanded *regardless* of whether the instruction is positive or negative? It will bring you what you want, or what you don't want, according to the instructions you give it.

Now let's take a look into this subconscious mind of ours — see what happens as we use it — and learn more about how to regularly and deliberately make it a better, more productive employee or servant. I'll set the stage by using some examples and analogies selected at random from three different areas to give you a fast peek at the strength and versatility of this fantastic servant.

THE SUBCONSCIOUS MIND

Charles Dennis Jones, a husky black man was actually about six feet tall, but those who saw the incident I'm about to describe say he was a giant. A truck had run off the road and crashed into a tree with enormous impact. The engine was forced back into the cab and the driver's body was twisted under the roof. His feet were caught between the clutch and brake pedals. The doors were crushed and bent out of shape. Wreckers were called and a supreme effort was made to open the cab and free the driver. However, the wreckage was such that despite the best efforts of skilled men, the doors refused to budge. To make matters worse, a fire had started in the cab. Concern turned to panic because it was obvious that before the fire engines could arrive, the driver would be burned to death.

Despite the fact that the power of the wreckers had been unable to open the door, Charles Dennis Jones decided to see what he could do. Bracing himself against the door, he started to pull. Slowly, grudgingly, the door began to give way. The force of Jones' effort was so great that the muscles in his arm expanded until they literally burst the sleeves of his shirt. Finally, the door was open, Jones reached inside and bare-handedly bent the brake and clutch pedals out of the way. He freed the man's legs, snuffed out the fire with his hands and crawled inside the cab with the badly injured driver. Bracing himself in a crouching position with his feet on the floor and his back against the top of the cab, he lifted the roof by his enormous strength. This freed the driver and spectators were able to pull him to safety. Then Charles Dennis Jones quietly and quickly disappeared.

Later, when he was found, someone asked him why and how he was able to accomplish such a Herculean feat. His reply was a very simple one. He merely said, "I hate fire." He had a reason. A few months earlier he had been forced to stand by and watch helplessly while his small daughter burned to death.

On another occasion, a 37-year-old woman lifted a car weighing over 3600 pounds, enabling her small son to be pulled to safety. She did that without thought or hesitation. She had a reason.

Surely you've experienced an occasion when you've been driving down the street, not thinking about anything in particular. Then, suddenly, a thought comes to you and you exclaim, "That's it! That's the answer. Boy, oh boy, why didn't I think of it before?" You've just gotten the answer to a problem that you've been wrestling with for days and you're so excited you can scarcely contain yourself.

Interestingly enough, Charles Dennis Jones, the 37-year-old woman and you were all doing the same thing. You were using the knowledge, strength and power of your subconscious mind.

For years, man has dreamed of unlocking the enormous potential of his subconscious mind so it could be put to work on a regular basis. Through the centuries, man has been able to use this enormous power only occasionally and accidentally. Until recently, little has been known about this mysterious force or intellect we call the subconscious mind.

Let's explore it from a layman's point of view and see how it works and how it relates to the conscious mind. Then, I'll give you some steps that will enable you to unlock much of this enormous power within you.

The conscious mind is the calculating, thinking, reasoning portion of your mind. It has the capacity to accept or reject whatever it is presented. Generally speaking, whatever you learn is learned consciously. However, if you are going to do anything well, you must move it from the conscious to the subconscious.

The subconscious mind has a perfect memory. Everything you have ever seen, heard, smelled, tasted, touched or even thought about has become a permanent part of the subconscious mind. Twenty-four hours a day, seven days a week, 365 days a year, the subconscious mind is awake and responsive. It accepts, without question, what it is told and doesn't analyze or reject any information. It accepts a command or instruction and fills orders just as surely as a typewriter will type the key that is punched. The subconscious mind has both unlimited power potential and storage capacity for all the information we feed into it.

WHAT ABOUT HYPNOSIS AND THE SUBCONSCIOUS?

Hypnosis, which deals primarily with the subconscious mind, is a mystery to most people. It's either accepted or rejected according to the extent of the information or misinformation people have about it, but most people don't really understand it.

Actually, we hypnotize ourselves from one interest to another all through our lives. It is indeed unfortunate that most people hypnotize themselves into getting the things they don't want instead of into getting the things they do want. The objective of a hypnotist is to help you to relax, concentrate and use your own subconscious mind.

Hypnosis is not a game you play with a friend or someone who has taken a mail-order course in it. It isn't necessarily true that you won't do anything dishonest or immoral under hypnosis. That is one reason you should be very careful and permit only a highly-trained professional to hypnotize you. It's a fairly simple process to hypnotize someone, but it's not quite so simple to bring that person out of a hypnotic trance. If an untrained or unskilled amateur hypnotist should panic while you are "under," the results could be quite serious.

The power of post-hypnotic suggestion is well known. An amateur hypnotist who promises to "cure" or "solve" your weight, smoking, drinking sex, etc., problems might do exactly that — and leave you with some other problems that could be even more serious. Simply stated, hypnosis, when properly used by an expert, is good. In the hands of an amateur it could be dangerous. For example, some dentists use hypnosis quite successfully. Doctors also use it for minor surgery. Hypnosis definitely has a place, but not in the game room and not by the amateur.

HYPNOSIS FOR STRENGTH AND CONFIDENCE

A college student was given a newspaper with three paragraphs encircled which he was instructed to memorize. He concentrated on the assignment until he felt he knew it. He quoted the three paragraphs almost verbatim, missing only one or two words. The psychologist then asked how much of the rest of the paper he had memorized. The student smiled and said, "I didn't memorize anything else, because I was concentrating on the three paragraphs."

The psychologist hypnotized the young man and an amazing thing happened. Not only did he quote the three paragraphs, he also quoted much of the rest of the page. The information picked up from the newspaper was fed directly into the subconscious mind, which has a perfect memory. This should not be too surprising if your vision is normal, because you can see objects on the right and left as well as directly in front of you. If this were not true, you would be a menace to society and to yourself while driving, walking or riding a bicycle.

As we stated earlier, most people "hypnotize themselves into negative images and into getting the things they don't want."

Fortunately, you aren't "most people," and with the aid of this information — combined with the books and cassette recordings available on the market today, you will be able to "hypnotize" yourself into things that are good, clean, positive and powerful. In short you will "hypnotize" yourself into using the strength, talent and information you already have. This will enable you to get what you want.

Like everything else, it will require considerable effort on your part but I repeat what I said earlier. The reward for accomplishment is so great you will truly accept my contention that you don't "pay the price," you "enjoy the price."

THE CLEAN DESK

There probably isn't a person who will read these pages who hasn't gone into a business office and seen a desk buried with work. It is covered with everything from yesterday's newspaper and today's emergencies to last year's tax returns and next month's budget projections. You and the owner of the desk both make the same comment, "You can always tell a busy man . . ."

You can also tell something about the earned income of the person behind the desk. Almost, without exception, if the desk is piled high and cluttered, we have a person who has an earned income of less than $20,000 a year. Some notable exceptions would be, authors, salesmen, sales managers and entrepreneurs, who do their thinking and planning away from their desk. Now, a clean desk does not necessarily mean a big income, but the overwhelming majority of the people who earn in excess of $50,000 a year will have a clean desk.

Here's why. Many times you've been at your cluttered desk with several things to do. You're busy on one project when, for no apparent reason, you pick up another project and start working on it. Your *vision* had "picked up" the other paper and you inadvertently reached for it. Instead of focusing your full powers on the problem at hand, you dissipate your concentration into several areas. You are dealing with a dozen different problems — and not *really* concentrating on any of them.

Now, hypnosis is really your capacity to center or concentrate on a specific subject. So, you take everything off the desk and get it out of sight. Since it's impossible to do more than one thing at a time, place your projects on the desk — *one* at a time. Three things will immediately happen. First, the instant the desk is clean, you feel better psychologically. Second, not only will you be able to do a better job, but you'll be able to work considerably faster. Third, you'll be able to find what you need, when you need it, which means a tremendous savings in time for you.

When you leave a clean desk in the evening, you leave a completed day's work. Psychologically you feel you've accomplished something — you *finished* a project instead of feeling you *left* a project. There is a difference. When you start the next day you feel you have a fresh start instead of going back to the same old thing. When you finish and file your work instead of picking it up and putting it down and picking it up and putting it down again, you can turn out more and better work. The sense of relief of staying "caught up" is fun. To know you're doing more and being more is also fun. It has a built-in positive reward.

WARNING

Since the subconscious mind without question accepts what we "feed it" and has a perfect memory, many things can be detrimental to us when we leave our minds open to *everything*. For example, some of the music being played on radio stations today advocates the use of drugs, free love, trial marriages and "doing your own thing," regardless of how it might affect others. When this kind of garbage is "dumped" with a rhythm beat into an open mind the results can be disastrous. The Manson case is a tragic example. Charles Manson's motivation for the sadistic murders of Sharon Tate and other innocent people was planted in his mind by the message in a Beatle recording. This is one of the major reasons *no one* should go to sleep with the radio playing. You can't sleep as well, and you literally leave your mind open as a catch-all for every wild idea that is broadcast. This could account, in part, for some of the unpredictable behavior of some people, and explains why some "open" minds should be "closed for repairs." Much of what I'm saying about hypnosis, sleeping with the radio on, etc., is just common sense. Common sense tells us it isn't wise to turn our minds over to anyone other than a trained and trusted professional who guides us in psychological counseling or personal growth.

USE THE SUBCONSCIOUS

Since the subconscious mind never sleeps, we have extra learning and motivation time while our conscious minds are asleep. Let me give you a simple, personal experience that illustrates this use of the subsconscious mind. One of our daughters had a bed-wetting problem which concerned us, so we were thrilled to learn about "sleep teaching" and the sub-conscious mind. We decided to try an experiment. After she fell asleep, either her mother or I would kneel by her side and say, "You are a pretty little girl and we love you very much. Everybody loves you because you are so pleasant, cheerful and happy. We love you because you only sleep in a warm, dry bed. You always sleep in a warm, dry bed. If you should need to use the bathroom, you'll wake up in plenty of time." We were careful to never say, "Don't wet the bed." You *must* not give a negative instruction in such a situation. Always talk in terms of the positive. We reinforced this during the day when our daughter was in listening range. We would casually say how pleased and happy we were that she was getting to be such a big girl. How proud we were of her, etc. This was positive reinforcement to the conscious mind for the positive instruction she was taking directly into the subconscious mind. Results were dramatic. In just ten days she stopped wetting the bed and only had one or two "accidents" the rest of her childhood.

THE STEPS ARE EASY

The deliberate use of the subconscious mind is an exciting possibility for you, and the benefits are almost unlimited. There are six steps or prerequisites necessary to deliberately use the subconscious mind on a daily basis. First, you should know that everything you've ever seen, heard, smelled, tasted, touched, or thought about has become a permanent part of you. It's in the computer, stored and waiting for you to use. This computer of yours can take isolated facts acquired over a period of many years and tie them together in a marvelous manner. You can have solutions to problems and answers to questions that will astound you, especially the first few times it happens.

Second, you should know that the subconscious mind responds to stimuli, not pressure. You can't "demand" an answer by a specific time. That won't work. You can stimulate the subconscious into further activity by listening to recorded educational and motivational material. The more forcefully and enthusiastically the new material is injected into the mind, the more usable it is. Best of all, the more new material you add, the more usable the information you already have will become.

Third, you should remember you can fool or mislead the subconscious mind. If you put the wrong thoughts or information in, the subconscious mind will respond. That's why it's so important to be careful about the books you select and read, the company you keep, as well as the TV programs and movies you watch. If you put negative stuff in, you'll get a negative feedback. Computer people call it "Gi-Go:" garbage in — garbage out. That's one of the major reasons I object to much of the TV programming. When we see a hero or heroine in difficulty, we tend to identify with them. We often acquire the same problems we observe day after day, just as others do. Did you know, for example, that nearly two-thirds of the medical students acquire the symptoms of the disease they are studying? This is called "identification" in psychology.

Fourth, "Don't take your problems to bed with you," is erroneous advice because that's the place to *solve* many of your problems. Here's how. When you lie down at night, relax and get perfectly still. Then relive the happy experiences of the day and put all disagreeable experiences aside. As you lie there, be still and know that it's this quietness that produces power. For those of us who have the extra benefit of believing in Almighty God, we can redirect this step and simply say, "Lord, I know You have the answer, so I'm going to turn the question over to You. Now that it's in Your hands, I'll patiently await your solution." That's called faith, and it's your reaction to God's ability. During such a quiet moment at Valley Forge, George Washington found the strength to lead this country to freedom. During another quiet moment at Gethsemane, Christ found the strength for His awful ordeal. As you lie there, listen and reflect on all of the blessings that are yours. A quiet confidence will come over you as you listen for words and seek strength that will enable you to succeed and be happy in the game of life. This procedure will enable you to go into your deepest level of sleep. Your security is almost total. Negativisms don't exist so your creative or subconscious mind is free to "do its thing." And as Dr. Schuller says, this tranquitility produces creativity.

Sixth, you should have a pen and pad, or better yet, a cassette recorder at your bedside. Many times your subconscious mind will work so swiftly and effectively that you will wake up in the middle of the night with a fabulous idea or a solution to a problem. Regardless of how wide awake you might be when the idea or solution comes to you, odds are you won't remember it the next day. By recording the thought or idea, you assure yourself of returning to a deep and restful sleep because you know when you awaken, the idea or solution will be instantly available to you. For this reason, it is IMPERATIVE that you have a pen and pad or cassette recorder next to your bedside for immediate use. After all, you woke up for a reason; don't blow it by trying to get five more minutes of sleep. Incidentally, if you experience any difficulty going back to sleep you should quietly and confidently close your eyes and say, "thank you, thank you, thank you for health, wealth, happiness and peace." Then repeat over and over, health, wealth, happiness and peace.

As you follow these steps, you'll be amazed at how fast you get answers to questions. Just as significant is the fact that as you get results, your confidence will grow. This will give you more results, which gives more confidence *ad infinitum.*

SEGMENT SIX

WORK

PURPOSE: I. TO SELL THE IDEA "THERE AIN'T NO FREE LUNCH."

II. TO CLARIFY THE DIFFERENCE BETWEEN "PAYING A PRICE" AND "ENJOYING A PRICE."

III. TO INTRODUCE YOU TO A NEW ATTITUDE AS IT RELATES TO YOUR JOB OR PROFESSION.

IV. TO EXPLAIN WHY YOU MUST PUT SOMETHING IN LIFE BEFORE YOU CAN GET ANYTHING OUT.

ADDITIONAL READING MATERIAL

Bob Richards — *THE HEART OF A CHAMPION*

Glass, Kinder and Ward— *POSITIVE POWER FOR SUCCESSFUL SALESMEN*

Alex Osborne — *APPLIED IMAGINATION*

CHAPTER ONE
WORKERS ARE WINNERS

FREE LUNCH

Many years ago, a wise old king called his wise men together and gave them a commission. "I want you to compile for me the 'wisdom of the ages'. Put it in book form so we might leave it to posterity." The wise men left their king and worked for a long period of time. They finally returned with twelve volumes and proudly proclaimed that this truly was the "wisdom of the ages." The king looked at the twelve volumes and said, "Gentlemen, I'm certain this is the wisdom of the ages and contains the knowledge we should leave to mankind. However, it is so long, I fear the people won't read it. Condense it." Again, the wise men worked long and hard before they returned with only one volume. The king, however, knew that it was still too lengthy so he commanded them to further condense their work. The wise men reduced the volume to a chapter, then to a page, next to a paragraph and finally to a sentence. When the wise old king saw the sentence, he was absolutely elated. "Gentlemen," he said, "this is truly the wisdom of the ages, and as soon as all men everywhere learn this truth, then most of our problems will be solved." The sentence simply said, "There ain't no free lunch" — and there "ain't."

It's ironic, [or is it hypocritical], that responsible people agree with the "No Free Lunch," and "You Can't Get Something for Nothing" philosophy, but often vote for legalized gambling, horse racing, dog racing and state lotteries. No wonder the young people are confused about what mother and dad really do believe. A wise man observed that the Success Family has Work as the father and Integrity as the mother. If you can get along with the "parents" you won't have any trouble with the rest of the family.

Work is the foundation of all business, the source of all prosperity and the parent of genius.

Work can do more to advance youth than his own parents, be they ever so wealthy.

It is represented in the humblest savings and has laid the foundation of every fortune.

It is the salt that gives life its savour but it must be loved before it can bestow its greatest blessing and achieve its greatest ends.

When loved, work makes life sweet, purposeful, and fruitful.

[*Anonymous*]

THE CONCRETE MIND

Let me urge you to keep an open mind as we explore the importance of work. As you probably know, some people's minds are like concrete — all mixed up and permanently set. Yet we know the mind is like a parachute, functional only when it is open. We also know you can send a message 24,000 miles around the world in less than a second, but it often takes years to penetrate that last ¼ inch of skull surrounding the mind.

Many times I've seen people sincerely motivated and enthused about a philosophy that promises them more in the ball game of life. They listen attentively to the beauty, happiness, joys and benefits that go with having the right mental attitude, a healthy self-image, setting goals and all the positive aspects of the philosophy. Unfortunately, many times the practical application of the philosophy goes in one ear and out the other. I would like to stress the fact that **the most practical, beautiful, workable philosophy in the world won't work — if you won't.** A wise man expressed it well, "Education covers a lot of ground, but it won't cultivate any of it."

Unfortunately, too many people quit looking for work as soon as they find a job. They're like this old boy down home. When asked how long he had been working for his company, his reply was a classic, "Ever since they threatened to fire me." Someone asked an employer how many people he had working for him and he said, "About half of them." Isn't it amazing the number of people who show up for work and then avoid it like the plague!

WORK — ALMOST A CURE-ALL

The wise old king hit the nail on the head. When men learn that if they want to occupy their places in the sun, they'll have to expect some blisters; much will have been accomplished. Work is the price we enjoy to travel the highways of success. We can best guard against losing our shirts by keeping our sleeves rolled up. Many people believe success is dependent upon the glands, and they're right if they're referring to "sweat glands." America was built by people who worked, and pulled on the oars, not by those who rested on the oars.

It doesn't matter how smooth and easy the going might be, there are some who'll lag behind. By the same token, no matter how tough the going might be, there are those who will forge ahead. To quote the oldie, **"When the going gets tough, the tough get going."** The chairman of the board of one of America's major rubber companies stated that work should be fun. Will Rogers made the observation that, "In order to succeed, you must know what you are doing, like what you are doing and believe in what you are doing." According to H. M. Greenberg's psychological evaluation of over 180,000 people, nearly 80% reluctantly go to work every day. They simply don't like what they do. That is tragic. It's a small wonder we have second-rate performances and often third-rate merchandise.

I'm often astonished at the number of people who respond to questions about their work in a completely negative vein. Ask someone how he is doing and he will probably say, "Considering it's Monday, I don't guess it's too bad," or "Fine since it's Friday." It's an unfortunate fact that nearly 80% of the timepieces are used to tell people when to *quit* work. Small wonder that more workers are known as "eager leavers" than "eager beavers."

Recently, while speaking in Las Vegas, I was told on good authority that one of the casinos is large enough to enclose two full size football fields. Hundreds of devices exist in this mammoth room to separate a patron from his money. In this casino, as in all the other gambling establishments in Las Vegas, you can't find a single clock. No, not one. The reason is obvious. People gamble for a variety of reasons, but it's safe to say they enjoy gambling. They become so engrossed in gambling they are totally oblivious to time. Obviously, the owners of the casinos don't want clocks to remind the gamblers of time. As a result, many people gamble for hours. In some cases, they gamble until they've lost everything they have or until they literally go to sleep at the tables. I'm convinced that if gamblers became that engrossed in their careers, they could acquire the material goods *and* satisfy their psychological needs which they never can satisfy at the gambling table.

WORK IS AN ATTITUDE

When I entered the business world, I often heard speakers elaborate on the enormous sacrifices involved in climbing to the top. Later, after I became a speaker, I frequently repeated these sentiments. However, as the years passed, I realized that most of the men and women who were moving to the top were not "paying a price." They worked hard because they truly enjoyed their careers and the work involved. The top people in any field get involved in what they are doing, become engrossed, dig in, and their success comes because they love what they're doing. They choose to spend those hours at their work. They have a job, but more importantly, the job has them. In short, they have a tremendous attitude which often changes a job from drudgery to pure joy. That is one reason I've emphasized the importance of having the right mental attitude.

Several years ago, when I was on a speaking tour of Australia, I met a young man named John Nevin who had that right mental attitude about what he was doing. He was in love with life, his family, and with his job. He not only had a "job" selling the World Book Encyclopedia, but the job had him, which meant that his progress was fast and inevitable. He moved from a "part timer" [his regular job was delivering milk], just fourteen years ago to Managing Director of Field Enterprises for Australia. Recently John became the second non-American to be elected to the board of Field Enterprises, USA. He is financially secure and grateful for the fact that he is living and working in a country that believes in the free enterprise system.

This little story Charles Getts tells in *Guideposts* emphasizes the attitude of "enjoying" the price.

> *In old age*, Pierre Auguste Renoir, the great French painter, suffered from arthritis, which twisted and cramped his hand. Henri Matisse, his artist friend, watched sadly while Renoir, grasping a brush with only his fingertips, continued to paint, even though each movement caused stabbling pain.
>
> One day, Matisse asked Renoir why he persisted in painting at the expense of such torture.
>
> Renoir replied, "The pain passes, but the beauty remains."

THIS WAY — TO A RAISE

In your present situation or job, when you show up for work on time, give an honest day's effort, are loyal to your employer, and accept an agreed-upon sum of money for your work — you and your employer are exactly even. You are doing enough to keep your job, [unless there is a recession], but not enough to get the raise your employer would like to give you. My observation is that your employer is almost always anxious to pay you more money, *but* he runs a business — not a charitable institution. In order for him to pay you more, you must make yourself more valuable to him. You do this with extra effort — extra loyalty — extra enthusiasm — extra hours, and by assuming extra responsibilities. In a nutshell, you go the extra mile which is one stretch of highway where there are never any traffic jams. These steps guarantee your job in hard times and earn you raises and promotions in good times.

Your present employer will probably be the one to give you the raise, but the law is clear, "as ye sow, so also shall ye reap." So if you don't get the raise on your present job, you *will* get it from somewhere else. As a youngster in the grocery store I did a lot of running to the other stores to borrow and return items. My opposite number in the store across the street was a boy named Charles Scott. Charles "hustled" like nobody I've ever seen. He *never* walked while on an errand for his boss. One day I asked Mr.

Anderson, my boss, why Charles Scott was always in such a hurry. Mr. Anderson explained that Charles was working for a raise which he was certain to get because if his present employer didn't give it to him he [Mr. Anderson] would. Like the man said while talking to an employee seeking a raise, "I give you the raise you seek. It is to become effective, when you do."

That loud "Amen" you just heard came from Lou Scott, Vice President of Management Recruiters International, who has over 300 offices nationally and is the largest executive placement organization in the country. Their experiences show that over 95% of the people their offices place, excluding trainees on their first job, come to them employed. They also found that the "above average" worker who goes the extra mile and does *more* than he is paid to do has tremendous job security. To quote Lou, "The good ones just "ain't laid off."

Yes, it's the extras that produce dramatic results. We seldom, if ever, hear of the person who makes it big only by doing what he is paid to do. The reason is competition. Virtually everyone is willing to "show up" for forty hours. Beyond that point, however, most aren't interested, so competition drops tremendously. As a practical matter, it's fairly easy to win a race or a promotion when competition either quits or quits trying.

I'll concede that perhaps I feel the way I do about work because I was raised during the depression. As a small boy, I saw grown men leave home day after day seeking any kind of work doing anything, requiring only that it be honest. Their joy was so total when they found a job, it made quite an impression on me. I consider work a privilege because it gives us more than a living; it is preparation for life, as this story indicates.

A farmer had several boys and he worked them extremely hard around the farm. One day, one of the neighbors pointed out that it wasn't necessary to work the boys that hard to raise a crop. The farmer, quietly but firmly responded, "I'm not just raising crops, I'm raising boys."

SURRENDER A "LITTLE" — LOSE A LOT

I love the story of the old man in the Smoky Mountains. A number of years ago, some hogs escaped in a remote area of the mountains. Over a period of several generations, these hogs became wilder and wilder, until they were a menace to anyone who crossed their paths. A number of skilled hunters tried to locate and kill them, but the hogs were able to elude the efforts of the best hunters in the area.

One day an old man, leading a small donkey pulling a cart, came into the village closest to the habitat of these wild hogs. The cart was loaded with lumber and grain. The local citizens were curious about where the man was going and what he was going to do. He told them he had "come to catch them wild hogs." They scoffed, because no one believed the old man could accomplish what the local hunters were unable to do. But, two months later, the old man returned to the village and told the citizens the hogs were trapped in a pen near the top of the mountain.

Then he explained how he caught them. "First thing I done was find the spot where the hogs came to eat. Then I baited me a trap by puttin a little grain right in the middle of the clearin. Them hogs was scared off at first but curiosity finally got to 'em and the old boar that led them started sniffin' around. When he took the first bite the others joined in and I knew right then I had 'em. Next day I put some more grain out there and laid one plank a few feet away. That plank kinda spooked 'em for awhile, but that "free lunch" was a powerful appeal so it wasn't long fore they were back eatin. Them hogs didn't know it but they was mine already. All I had to do was add a coupla boards each day by the grain they wanted until I had ever'thing I needed for my trap. Then I dug a hole and put up my first corner post. Ever'time I added something they'd stay away a spell but finally they'd come back to git "somethin for nothing." When the pen was built and the trap door was ready, the habit of gittin' what they wanted without working for it drove 'em right into the pen and I sprung the trap. It was real easy after I got 'em coming for the "free lunch."

The story is true and its point quite simple. When you make an animal dependent upon man for his food, you take away his resourcefulness and he's in trouble. The same is true of man. If you want to create a cripple, just give a man a pair of crutches for a few months — or give him a "free lunch" long enough for him to get in the habit of getting something for nothing.

START ME — AND I'LL GO

There are three things that are hard to do. One is to climb a fence that is leaning toward you. Another is to kiss a girl who is leaning away from you. The third is to help someone who doesn't really want to be helped. Now, I have to be honest and admit to you that I've never tried to climb the fence. [You might need to think on that one for a moment.] Many times I've had people say, "If someone would give me a stake so I could 'get current' one time, pay all my bills and have $1000 in the bank, I could go the rest of the way on my own." The unfortunate thing is, many people believe this, and they "wait" for someone to come along and give them that start. I advocate helping people, but as I indicated in an earlier chapter, I believe **if you give a man a fish, you feed him for a day, but if you teach him how to fish, you feed him for life.** I believe in giving "fishing" lessons. Just helping someone get current and giving him a cash reserve is generally the wrong way to help. Invariably the individual takes the "bonanza" and spends it either to "catch up" or to get something he's been wanting but couldn't get. This simply continues and even reinforces the habit of spending which put him behind the financial 8 ball to start with.. Once you get the habit [whether it's a good one or a bad one] the habit gets you.

For example, several years ago during the 60's, there were a number of gigantic quiz shows. Many of you will recall that on these shows the winnings were $75,000, $100,000 and more. Seven years later a survey was conducted among "the big winners" on the shows. Interestingly enough, there wasn't a single person who had won $75,000 or more who had any more money than he had before he won that large sum of money. Each winner apparently took the bonanza and spent it instead of investing the money in blue chip securities or placing it at interest which would have meant a *permanent* raise in living standards. More recently the huge winners on the state lotteries of as much as $1,000,000 have had an overwhelmingly negative result. Lives have been disrupted, families upended, careers wrecked, old friends lost and attitudes and images have been severely damaged. Free lunches do not put you on easy street. More often, you lose more than you win.

312

WORK WEEK OR WEAK WORK

The tragic story of the American Indian will emphasize what happens when someone else "takes care of you." Around the turn of the century, the U. S. Government made a long series of treaties with the Indian tribes, particularly in the western portion of the country. The treaties involved many things, but the prime requirement was for the Indians to lay down their arms, go to reservations and let the Government "take care" of them. Today, all you need to do is to visit a reservation and observe the plight of the Indian to see what happens when man is forced to turn his self-respect over to someone else. **When you give a man a dole, you deny him his dignity and when you deny him his dignity, you rob him of his destiny.** I recognize that Washington is passing out a lot of apparently free lunches today, but those lunches are on consignment. Sooner or later you and I, as well as the people who receive them, will pay full price with interest.

We hear considerable talk about changing the work week nowadays. Many people feel we should only work 30 hours instead of 40 per week. They prefer a four-day week to a five-day one. I believe more would be accomplished if we concentrated on changing the "weak work" and let the "work week" alone.

Fewer people are bent from hard work than are crooked from avoiding it. Actually, life is like a grindstone. The "stuff" you're made of will determine whether it grinds you *down* or polishes you *up*.

WORK FOR YOUR LIFE

In my talks with companies and individuals around the country, I frequently ask people what they would put at the top of their list of desires for the tomorrows of their lives. One thing frequently mentioned is security. When I discuss the dignity of work and the security it affords, there is an example that intrigues, but doesn't surprise me. It pertains to what's happened in Sweden the last few years. The Swedish Government assures every individual that he will "be taken care of" from birth to death. Despite the fact that the Bible clearly teaches that those who don't work shouldn't eat, many Swedes believe the government owes them a living, that it should "take care of them." To a large degree it does exactly that. When a citizen goes to the doctor, dentist, or hospital, there are no bills to pay — the government pays them. When a baby is born, the government pays the bills and contributes to the support of mother and child. If the income is not adequate to maintain a minimum standard of living, the government steps in and makes up the difference.

To the casual observer, it would appear the Swedes should be the happiest people in existence, because of such a magnificent arrangement. They have got it made — or have they? In addition to having one of the highest tax structures of any Western nation, Sweden also has the fastest growing rate of juvenile delinquency. It boasts the fastest growing drug problem, the highest rate of divorce and the greatest decline in church attendance. All this adds up to problems now and still more problems in the future. This data tells us a considerable amount about the young and the middle-aged, but what about the old folks in Sweden? This "land of security" has the highest rate of suicide among the retired of any Western nation. It's obvious that there's a vast difference between building your own security and retirement as opposed to having someone else take care of you. Yes, **real security is truly an inside job.** It can't be given or provided — it must be earned.

Security is accurately spelled out by using each letter as the first letter of another word. (S)ecurity (E)arned (C)arefully (U)sually (R)esults (I)n (T)reasure filled (Y)ears.

GET BUSY — AND DO YOUR BEST

In America, leisure time has increased tremendously during the three decades since World War II. In this same time period, social problems and maladies have also increased. Frustrations, nervous breakdowns, broken marriages, alcoholism, drug problems and crime rates are directly related to too much time with nothing to do. Combine this with the permissiveness that has permeated our culture and the attitude of doing just enough to get by, and the problems are multiplied.

Workers often lose pride in their workmanship and their performance begins to go down. When performance goes down, shoddy merchandise is produced, and shoddy merchandise doesn't find a ready market because American consumers demand quality. They turn to foreign imports and the American producer is caught in the squeeze by lowered sales volume.

As a nation, we must resell the idea of performance and honest effort for an honest day's pay. Surely the world owes us a living, but we have to work for it. We have to reverse the philosophy of doing little and collecting much or we'll be caught in the pinch of pricing ourselves out of quality products and services. The only plan that is going to work over the long haul is an internal change in our philosophy. We must produce the quality merchandise people demand, at the right price or the American consumer will turn more and more to imported products.

Fortunately, we can do this. We say this without any mental reservation, because the American worker, under controlled tests, has consistently out-produced his Japanese or European counterpart on project after project. Better quality — better price. When we do as much as we can, American know-how and productivity is *still* the best in the world. Unfortunately, our recent efforts have not been the best. A 1974 survey of the 12 most highly industrialized nations in the world revealed that the American worker actually rated 11th in production. The net result is lower quality and higher price which means more foreign imports. Honest effort — not higher tariffs — is the solution to this problem. We don't "pay a price" for best effort, we "enjoy" it.

This Warner and Swasey ad says it quite well.

Order of the White Jacket. At the annual Homecoming of William and Mary College in Virginia, you might see a famous governor, or a college president, or any number of prominent business and professional people, proudly wearing a white jacket. The jackets signify that these men earned all or most of their way through college, waiting on tables.

They weren't ashamed of menial labor, they didn't hold out for the job they liked, they didn't ask for government help — they *waited on tables*, and it helped them earn the education they have since put to such splendid use.

The Order of the White Jacket has a roster of which any group in the land could well be proud. Perhaps there ought to be a chapter on every college campus in America.

That last A-Men came from the author's corner.

The dictionary indicates that security is freedom from risk or danger, to be free from doubt or fear, not anxious or unsure, etc. Personally, I think General Douglas MacArthur had a better definition. He said, "Security is the ability to produce." I agree. The person who gains his own self-respect and self-confidence by producing for his own needs is infinitely more secure than the one who leaves the solution to his problems or needs in the hands of someone else. As I've said earlier, **"Work gives us more than our living, it gives us our life."** A man or woman is seldom really happy unless he or she is sustaining himself and making a contribution to others.

FIRST — GET STARTED

Employers agree that an employed person is far more likely to get a better job than the unemployed one. This is especially true if the unemployed person has been out of work very long. Employment is the first rung on the ladder, and it's the toughest one to reach. If you have what it takes to get a job, it's easy to move up — after you move in.

One major problem that most people have is they place too many qualifications on a job. They seek the "perfect" job or employer without recognizing they might not be perfect employees. Many have been overly sold on the fact that a job should offer fulfillment, vacations, sick leave and retirement. For the successful, already employed individual who seeks a change, those factors are all obtainable in a job. For the unsuccessful and the unemployed, they might be overly ambitious objectives to seek at the starting point. Remember, grave diggers are about the only people who start on top — and they always end up in the hole.

You get to the top of any business by getting started, and a sense of urgency about getting started is necessary. Once you've started, it isn't so hard to keep going. If a job is difficult or unpleasant, do it immediately. The longer you wait, the more difficult and frightening it will become. It's something like standing on the high board of the swimming pool for the first time. As you try to decide whether or not you're going to dive in, the longer you wait, the less chance you have of making the dive.

NOTES AND IDEAS

CHAPTER TWO
BE READY

PATIENCE, PERSISTENCE AND PERSPIRATION

It's impossible to discuss work without weaving attitude into the subject. Thomas Edison is a classic example of how attitude relates to work. While being questioned by a young reporter about an invention he had been working on for a long time, he revealed one of the secrets of his greatness. The young reporter asked, "Mr. Edison, how does it feel to have failed 10,000 times in your present venture?" Edison replied, "Young man, since you are just getting started in life, I will give you a thought that should benefit you in the future. I have not failed anything 10,000 times. I have successfully found 10,000 ways that will not work."

Edison estimated that he actually performed over 14,000 experiments in the process of inventing and perfecting the incandescent light. He successfully found a lot of ways that wouldn't work, but he kept at it until he found one way that would. He proved that **the only difference between the big shot and the little shot is the big shot is simply a little shot who kept shooting.**

YOU ONLY FAIL BY GIVING UP

You aren't licked until you quit. To put it another way, when you put a little hump in "u," you change a "chump" to a "champ." Let's consider some other examples. Jerry West, one of basketball's all-time greats, was so bad as a youngster the neighborhood kids wouldn't let him play recreational basketball with them. Work and practice made the difference in his career.

Words like persistence, dedication, extra effort, and the blood, sweat and tears Churchill so eloquently described as he aroused England for Her finest hour might not sound glamorous, but they work — and are prime ingredients in the recipe for greatness. Realistically, these words describe the only characteristics that will overcome certain obstacles.

Demosthenes, the famous Greek orator, had such a speech impediment that he was shy and retiring. His father left him an estate that made him a wealthy man, but according to Greek law he had to establish his right to ownership in public debate before he could claim his estate. His impediment, combined with shyness rendered him helpless and he lost his estate. *Then*, he went to work and by sheer dogged effort scaled oratorical heights never before reached by mortal man. History neglected to record the man's name who took his inheritance, but school children around the world have learned the story of Demosthenes for centuries. It's true: Regardless of how many times you are "down," you are not whipped if you get up one more time than you are knocked down.

DON'T LET FAILURE MAKE YOU A COWARD

When you know in your own mind that you've given something your very best effort and you didn't succeed, don't quit. Simply start another project. A close friend involved me in a business transaction involving a gadget which didn't sell. Fortunately, I got out before the roof caved in. My friend, however, lost several thousand dollars. When it was all over, he philosophically stated, "You know, Zig, I hate to lose the money, but the thing that really concerns me is the fear that this will make me overly cautious and a financial coward regarding other business opportunities. If that happens, then my loss will be multiplied many times over." How true, how true.

One young man didn't let this happen to him. He was involved in an oil venture and ran out of money, so he sold his interest to his partners who stuck with it. After much time and effort, they got their break and hit a gusher. The company later became Cities Service, and we know it today as CITGO. The young man who withdrew, later got involved in the clothing business and fared even worse than he had in the oil business. As a matter of fact, he went broke. Still, he wasn't discouraged. Later on he got into politics. Historians are already saying kind things about Harry S. Truman, the two-time failure who kept getting back up until he became President of the United States.

Failure has been correctly identified as the line of least persistence, whereas success is often a question of simply sticking to the job and working and believing while you are sticking. If your particular job is harder than you might wish, just remember you can't sharpen a razor on a piece of velvet and you can't sharpen a man by spoon-feeding him.

Success occurs when opportunity meets preparation. Many times it is just over the hill or around the corner. Sometimes it takes that extra push to climb that hill or round that curve. The wit was right when he said, "If you have enough push you don't have to worry about pull."

President Calvin Coolidge wrote, "Nothing in the world can take the place of persistence. Talent will not. Nothing is more common than unsuccessful men with talent. Genius will not. Unrewarded genius is almost a proverb. Education will not. The world is full of educated derelicts. Persistence, determination and hard work makes the difference."

PERSISTENCE OVERCOMES RESISTANCE

As you continue your journey to the top, you must remember that each rung of the ladder was placed there for the purpose of holding your foot just long enough to step higher. It wasn't put there for you to rest on. We all get tired and discouraged, but as heavyweight champion James J. Corbett frequently said, "You become the champion by fighting one more round. When things are tough, you fight one more round." William James pointed out that not only do we have the second wind, but we have the third, fourth, fifth, sixth and even the seventh wind. There is an enormous amount of reserve inside each individual, but it's worthless unless you know it's there and persist in using it. World famous cellist Pablo Casals, long after he had achieved international recognition as an artist, still practiced six hours every day. Someone asked him why the continued effort. His reply was simply, "I think I'm making progress."

The opportunity for greatness doesn't knock; it's inside every one of us. However, we must work to get it out. We are often told to strike while the iron is hot, which is good advice. Better advice, however, is to make the iron hot by striking. Yes, persistence and effort are vitally important. Any sales manager will tell you that every "no" brings you that much closer to a "yes." It's not just a cliche' that it's often the darkest just before the dawn. When you work and develop your skills and talents your day will come. I might also point out that if your day never came, you would still be the big winner. Inside you, will be the knowledge that you're doing your best with what you have. With this approach to life, and the desire and determnation to stick to it, the odds are greater that you're going to make it and make it big.

Vince Lombardi, the legendary coaching genius who was the only man to ever coach three consecutive world championship football teams once said, "I've never known a man worth his salt who, in the long run, deep down in his heart, did not appreciate the grind and the discipline. There is something in good men that truly yearns for and needs discipline."

NO LAZY PERSON

Throughout this Segment, I've been talking about work and "selling" you on the idea. Therefore, it might surprise you now when I say **there's no such thing as a lazy person; he's either sick or uninspired.** If a person is sick, he should go to his doctor. If he's uninspired, there are several things he should do. He should read and re-read this book, listen to motivational speakers and associate with inspirational people. Bob Richards, former Olympic champion and one of the truly great speakers in America, makes a strong case for inspiration by association. He points out that the Olympics repeatedly produce record-breaking performances from the athletes because they are caught up in an atmosphere of greatness.

When a young man or woman sees other athletes from all over the world beating their former best efforts time after time, each one is inspired to "beat his best." Mankind at his best is capable of some awesome accomplishments and Richards points out that the association with champions brings out championship performances.

At the risk of oversimplification, I believe many "lazy" people have an image attitude problem. They are reluctant to give their job or profession a total effort. Feeling that if they give their all and don't make it, they'll be failures. They rationalize that if they give a half-hearted effort and don't make it, they have a built-in excuse. In their own minds, they don't feel like failure because they did not really try. They often shrug their shoulders and say, "It doesn't make any difference to me." It's the same way with many workers. Many times the unwillingness to work stems from other and deeper problems.

With this in mind, let me urge you to take another look at yourself. If, at this point, you are harboring any feelings of a poor image attitude go back to the second Segment and dig in until you have gotten your self-image where it belongs.

NOTES AND IDEAS

322

1. Start with a total effort.

2. Prime the pump (put *you* in whatever you do).

3. Persistence with perspiration before production.

4. Life returns so many rewards *after* you do your part.

CHAPTER THREE
PRIMING, PUMPING AND PRODUCING

PRIMING THE PUMP

One of the props I use in my talks around the country is an old-fashioned chrome-plated water pump. I personally love the story of the pump, because to me it represents the story of America, the story of the free enterprise system and the story of life. For your benefit, I hope you've had the opportunity of using one of these old-fashioned water pumps on at least one occasion. That experience will help you to appreciate the significance of this series of thoughts.

Several years ago, two friends of mine, Bernard Haygood and Jimmy Glenn, were driving in the South Alabama foothills on a hot August day. They were thirsty, so Bernard pulled behind an old abandoned farmhouse with a water pump in the yard. He hopped out of the car, ran over to the pump, grabbed the handle and started pumping. After a moment or two of pumping, Bernard pointed to an old bucket and suggested to Jimmy that he get the bucket and dip some water out of a nearby stream in order to "prime" the pump. As all pumpers know, you must put a little water *in* the top of the pump to "prime" the pump and get the flow of water started.

In the game of life, before you can get anything *out*, you must put something *in*. Unfortunately, there are many people who stand in front of the stove of life and say, "Stove, give me some heat and then I'll put some wood in you."

Many times the secretary comes to the boss and says, "Give me a raise and then I'll start doing better work and being more conscientious." Often the salesman goes to the boss and says, "Make me the sales manager and I'll really show you what I can do. It's true I haven't done much until now, but I need to be in charge in order to do my best work. So just make me the boss and then watch me go." Many times the student says to the teacher, if I take a bad grade home for this semester my folks will really lay it on me. So teacher, if you will just give me a good grade this quarter I promise I'll study real hard next quarter. My experience has been that it doesn't work that way. If it did, I could easily imagine a farmer praying, "Lord, if you will just give me a crop *this* year, I promise to plant the seed and work hard *next* year. What they are really saying is, "Reward me and then I'll produce." But life doesn't work that way. **You must first put something into life before you can expect to get anything out of it**. Now, if you'll just transfer this knowledge to the rest of your life, you can solve many of your problems.

The farmer must plant his seed in the spring or summer before he reaps the harvest in the fall. He also "puts in" lots of work before the crop reaches the harvest stage. The student puts in hundreds of hours of work before he acquires the knowledge and the graduation certificate. The secretary of today who is the office manager of tomorrow puts a considerable amount of extra into her job. The athlete of today who becomes a champion of tomorrow "puts in" a great deal of himself in the form of sweat and effort before he reaps the champion's reward. The junior executive of today who becomes the corporate president of tomorrow is that individual who puts himself into the job. The salesman today who becomes the sales manager of tomorrow is the person who understands the principle of priming the pump. When you put something "in," the law of compensation says you'll get something "out."

DON'T STOP NOW

Well, let's get back to my friends in South Alabama. South Alabama is hot in August and after a few minutes of pumping, Bernard worked up a considerable sweat. At that point he started asking himself just how much work he was willing to do for that water. He was concerned about the amount of reward he would receive for the amount of effort expended. After a time he said, "Jimmy, I don't believe there's any water in this well." Jimmy replied, "Yes, there is, Bernard; in South Alabama the wells are deep and that's good, because the deep well produces the good, clean, sweet, pure, best tasting water of all." Jimmy is also talking about life, isn't he? The things we have to work for are the things we appreciate the most.

By now, Bernard was getting hot and tired, so he threw up his hands and said, "Jimmy, there just isn't any water in this well." Jimmy quickly grabbed the pump handle and kept pumping as he said, "Don't stop now, Bernard; if you do, the water will go all the way back down and then you'll have to start all over again." That, too, is the story of life. There isn't a human being in existence, regardless of age, sex, or occupation, who doesn't occasionally feel he might as well "stop pumping" because there isn't any water down there. So if you occasionally feel that way, it should be comforting to know that you've got *lots* of company.

JUST ONE MORE TIME

Now let's look at something intriguing and obvious. There's no way you can look at the outside of a pump and determine whether it will take two more strokes or two hundred more to bring forth the water. There's often no way you can look into the game of life and determine whether or not you'll get the big break tomorrow or whether it will take another week, month, year or even longer.

This I do know beyond any reasonable doubt. Regardless of what you are doing, **if you will pump long enough, hard enough and enthusiastically enough, sooner or later the effort will bring forth the reward.** I also know that just as you add nothing to the score if you stop on third base you can't quench your thirst with the water that almost comes out of the pump. Fortunately once the water starts to flow, all you have to do is keep some steady pressure on the pump and you'll get more water than you can use. This is the story of success and happiness in life.

The message is clear. Whatever you're doing, work at it with the right attitude and the right habits, but above all, keep at it with bulldog tenacity and persistence. Just as the flow of water is often one stroke away, the sweet taste of success and victory is often just over the hill or around the corner. Whether you're a doctor, lawyer, student, housewife, laborer or salesperson, once you get the water flowing, it's easy to keep it flowing with a little steady effort.

I believe the story of the pump is the story of life and the free enterprise system. I say this because it has nothing to do with age or education, whether you are black or white, male or female, overweight or underweight, extrovert or introvert or whether you are Catholic, Jew or Protestant. It has everything to do with your God-given rights as a free person to work as long as you wish, as hard as you wish and as enthusiastically as you wish to get everything in life you really want.

As you move to the top, remember the story of the pump. If you start pumping casually or half-heartedly, you will pump forever before anything happens. Pump hard to begin with and keep it up until you get that water flowing. Then a great deal will happen. Once the flow of water starts, just maintain that steady pressure, and the time will come when the rewards will be so enormous that you'll be getting what you want instead of having to want what you have.

The analogy I used earlier of starting the locomotive is certainly appropriate here. It's often difficult to get the train started, but once it's moving, it requires considerably less fuel to keep it on its way.

Now as you look at the symbolic you on the stairway to the top, you find yourself on the "work" step. You are now ready to take the last or "desire" step which will put you squarely in front of the glass doors of tomorrow which are ready to be opened *by you.* At this point it is obvious that with a little extra "push," you have no need for "pull." So "push on" friend; you're just one exciting step from the banquet hall of life.

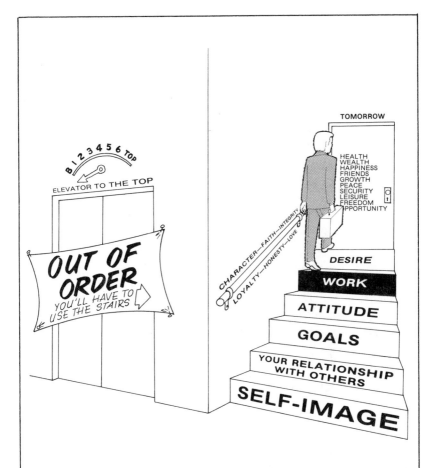

Success is not a destination — it's a journey. In your case you are well on your way and you're enjoying every step of it.

SEGMENT SEVEN

DESIRE

PURPOSE: I. TO FAN YOUR MOTIVATIONAL FLAME TO SUCH AN INTENSITY THAT THE HOT WATER OF MEDIOCRITY IS CONVERTED TO THE STEAM OF OVERWHELMING DESIRE.

        II. TO INTRODUCE YOU TO INTELLIGENT IGNORANCE AND TEACH YOU HOW TO TAKE LIFE'S LEMONS AND CONVERT THEM TO LEMONADE.

      III. TO LEARN HOW TO USE OBSTACLES AS STEPPING STONES TO THE RICHER LIFE.

      IV. TO SELL YOU ON FREE ENTERPRISE AND TO POINT OUT THE POSITIVE ASPECTS OF THE AMERICA I LOVE, TO EMPHASIZE ITS STRENGTH, COMPASSION AND GOODNESS WITH SPECIAL ATTENTION RESERVED FOR THE UNIQUE OPPORTUNITIES AMERICA OFFERS YOU.

       V. TO CLEARLY IDENTIFY THE STEPS **YOU** CAN TAKE TO PRESERVE — AND MAKE AMERICA EVEN STRONGER.

SPECIAL RECOMMENDATION

I believe every freedom loving American should read: *ONE NATION UNDER GOD*, Rus Walton.

        P. O. Box 2467
        Capitol Station
        Washington, D.C. 20013

CHAPTER ONE
FROM MEDIOCRITY TO METEORITY

THE "EQUALIZER"

In the old west, there was an equalizer; they called it the "six-shooter." It enabled a small man to chop a big man down to size. In today's world, the six-shooter is out but there is an equalizer — it's called "desire." **Desire is the ingredient that changes the hot water of mediocrity to the steam of outstanding success.** It's the ingredient that enables a person with average ability to successfully compete with those who have far more. Desire is the "extra" that makes the little differences and it's the little differences that make the big difference in life.

Desire is the extra. It's the part of the blanket that hangs over the bed that keeps you warm; it's the little extra that turns water into steam. At 211° water is hot enough for you to use to shave or to make a cup of coffee. Add one more degree and that hot water changes into steam which will power a locomotive around this country or propel a steamship around the world. That little extra is what will send you to the top of the ladder. It has done it for others. Ty Cobb, for example, had an enormous amount of desire. Grantland Rice relates this desire to us as he says, "I recall a day when Cobb played with each leg a mass of raw flesh. He had a temperature of 103° and the doctors ordered him to bed for several days. His team was playing that day, however, and as far as Ty Cobb was concerned that meant he would play. He did play and got three hits, stole three bases, won the game — and then collapsed on the bench."

When I think of desire, I think of another baseball player. For my money, Pete Gray is an immortal who belongs in baseball's Hall of Fame in Cooperstown, New York. As a young man, his overwhelming desire was to play major league baseball. "I'm going to make it all the way to the top," he repeated over and over again. His crowning ambition was to play a game in Yankee Stadium. In 1945, Gray made it to the major leagues with the St.

Louis Browns. He only played one year in the majors, was not a regular and never hit a single home run. Nevertheless, I insist that Pete Gray is an immortal who belongs in the Hall of Fame. I say this because he made it to the top despite the fact he had no right arm. He didn't look down at what he lacked. Instead, he looked up with what he had. Success in life is not detemined by having been dealt the good hand. **Success is determined by taking the hand you were dealt and utilizing it to the very best of your ability.** As Ty Boyd, an outstanding speaker and TV personality from Charlotte, N.C., says, "Play the hand you were dealt and play it for all it's worth."

Desire enables an individual to take whatever ability he has in whatever he's doing and utilize it to the maximum. Desire forces an individual to pull out all the stops and give everything he's got. It enables him to go full speed ahead with nothing held back. On a day-to-day basis the winning touchdown is generally scored by the individual or team who has pulled out all the stops. In my judgment each thing we do should be done to the best of our capabilities, whether we're taking an examination, reporting for work or getting involved in an athletic event. We should give it our best and then some, because **our yearning power is more important than our earning power.**

When we give it our all we can live with ourselves — regardless of the results. Less than our best effort has us saying, "If only" — and that's sad.

Knute Rockne pointed out that a lot of people thought they had to be either good losers or bad winners. He felt this was a lousy choice. He also pointed out that he had no desire to get enough experience at losing to be a good one. "Show me a good loser," he said, "and I'll show you a loser. Give me eleven lousy losers and I'll give you a national championship football team." I concur. The way a man wins, shows much of his character and the way he loses shows all of it. However, I'm speaking about the will, determination and desire to win. We simply don't have to make the choice between being good losers and bad winners. We can be good winners, and the more experience we have at winning, the better we become at acquiring the characteristics of being good winners. It works for teams, it works for individuals and it will work for you, guarantee it.

CALL OUT THE RESERVES

The desire to win enables many people to win, who at least theoretically couldn't, against overwhelming odds. Billy Miske was such a man. He was a fighter from the old school, and a good one at that. He fought men like Tommy Gibbons, Harry Greb and Battling Levinsky. He also fought Jack Dempsey for the heavyweight championship of the world. At 25, when he should have been at his peak and headed for even greater heights, he was hospitalized with a serious illness. The doctors told him to quit the ring. He should have, but fighting was the only thing he could do. By the time he was 29, his kidneys were shot. He knew he was dying of Bright's disease and he had only one fight that year. Too weak to go to the gym to train, and too sick to seek any other job, he stayed at home with his family and watched his family's finances reach desperate straits.

Christmas was around the corner and his love for his family cried out to him to provide that "Merry Christmas" for them. In November, Miske went into Minneapolis to see his friend and manager Jack Reddy to persuade him to arrange a fight. At first Reddy was adamant in his refusal. He knew of Miske's condition and he would have no part in such a fight. Miske pleaded his case well, explained he was broke and that he knew he wouldn't be around much longer. He had to have just one more fight because Christmas was on its way and his family was in need. Finally, Reddy agreed under the condition that Miske train and get in shape. Miske knew he was too weak to get into shape, but promised he would make a good fight.

Against his better judgment, Reddy finally gave in and matched his old friend with Bill Brennan. The fight was slated to take place in Omaha, Nebraska. Brennan was a tough, hard fighter who had gone twelve rounds with Dempsey. He was past his prime, but he was still a formidable opponent for a dying man.

Since Miske didn't have the stamina to train, he stayed at home to conserve his strength. He went to Omaha just in time for the fight. In those days, boxing commissions were considerably more lenient than they are today, so they passed Miske. The fight drew well and when it was over Billy Miske picked up his $2,400 purse and went home to his family and Christmas. He spent it all on the things the family wanted and had been doing without. It was truly a happy occasion, the biggest Christmas the Miske family ever had. On December 26th, Miske called Jack Reddy to take him to the Saint Paul Hospital where he died on New Year's day. The last fight on his record had been just six weeks before and his friends couldn't believe it. Billy was weak and dying and it would have been easy for him to have taken a dive. However, his pride and desire to be at his best for the family he loved, drove him to unbelievable efforts. Bill Brennan was knocked out in four rounds. Miske tapped his reserve resources because of his desire to win. Your reserves are available too — when you have the desire to use them.

When we give anything our total effort, we win regardless of the outcome, because the personal satisfaction of total effort makes us winners. Randy Martin, whom I mentioned earlier, entered the Boston Marathon for the first time in 1972. This race is in excess of 26 miles and is over an extremely difficult uphill-downhill course. Dr. Martin tells me that every finisher is given an award. Most of the runners don't enter the race with the belief that they can win, but anyone who finishes the race is a winner because the true reward of a thing well done is to have done it. This is a most important consideration, because in reality you are in competition with yourself. There is nothing as satisfying as knowing you have done your best, that you have driven yourself to use what you have to the very best of your ability. Total effort gives you a special kind of victory — victory over yourself because as one champion gymnast says, "Doing your best is more important than being the best."

THE WINNER — AND STILL CHAMPION

When I think of desire, I believe Ben Hogan rates close to the top of the list. Considering everything, Hogan could well be the greatest golfer who ever lived. He didn't have as much physical ability as many of his fellow golfers, but what he might have lacked in ability, he more than made up for in pesistence, determination and desire.

Ben Hogan really had two careers, because at the very peak of his game he was involved in a near fatal accident. One foggy morning as he and his wife, Valerie, were driving down the highway, they rounded a curve and saw the lights of a Greyhound bus immediately in front of them. Ben only had an instant to throw his body in front of his wife to protect her. This move undoubtedly saved his own life, because the steering wheel was pushed deeply into the driver's seat where Ben had been sitting. For days his life hung in the balance before he was pronounced out of danger. However, the doctors unanimously agreed that his career as a professional golfer was over and he would be fortunate to ever walk again.

But they didn't reckon with the will and desire of Ben Hogan. As soon as he could take those first few painful steps, he revived his dream of golfing greatness. He exercised and strengthened his hands constantly. He kept a golf club with him wherever he was and practiced his putting stroke at home on legs so shaky he could scarcely stand. At the first opportunity, he was back on the putting green staggering around. Still later, as he worked and walked and strengthened those scarred legs, he went to the practice tee. Initially, he only hit a few balls, but every session he would hit a few more. Finally, the day came when he was able to get back on the golf course. When he re-entered competition, his move back to the top was rapid. The reason is simple. Ben Hogan saw himself as a winner. He had such an overwhelming desire to win, he knew he would make it back to the top. Yes, **desire is the ingredient that makes the difference between an average performer and a champion.**

CHAPTER TWO
INTELLIGENT IGNORANCE

THE BUMBLEBEE CAN'T FLY

Desire creates intelligent ignorance. Intelligent ignorance is the characteristic or capability of not knowing what you can't do, and doing it anyway. Many times this enables a person to accomplish the near impossible. For example, a new salesman joins an organization. With no sales experience, he doesn't really know anything about selling. Fortunately, he doesn't know he doesn't know and somebody motivates him. The result is, he is so enthusiastic he leads the entire organization in sales. Not knowing he can't do it, he does it. Maybe that's why a "green" salesman is better than a "blue" one or a "yellow" one.

It's a well-known fact that the bumblebee can't fly. Scientific evidence about it is overwhelming — the bumblebee can't fly. His body is too heavy and his wings are too light. Aerodynamically, it is an impossibility for the bumblebee to fly, but the bumblebee doesn't read — he does fly.

BUILD ME A V-8

Henry Ford was a most unusual man. He was not a financial success until after he was forty years old. He had very little formal education. After he built his empire, he conceived the idea of the V-8 engine. Calling his engineers together, he said, "Gentlemen, I want you to build a V-8 engine." These brilliantly educated men knew the principles of mathematics, physics and engineering. They knew what could and couldn't be done. They looked at Ford with a condescending attitude of "Let's humor the old man because after all he is the boss." They very patiently explained to him that the V-8 engine was economically unfeasible, and they even explained "why" it couldn't be built economically. Ford wasn't listening, however, and simply said, "Gentlemen, I must have a V-8 engine — build me one."

They half-heartedly worked for a period of time, and reported back to him, "We are more convinced than ever that a V-8 engine is an engineering impossibility." Mr. Ford, however, wasn't easily persuaded. "Gentlemen, I must have a V-8 engine — so let's go full speed ahead." Again, they went out, and this time they worked a little harder, spent a little more time, and a lot more money. They came back with the same report, "Mr. Ford, the V-8 engine is an absolute impossibility."

The word "impossible" was not included in the vocabulary of the man, who had already revolutionized the industry with assembly line production, $5.00-a-day wages, the model T and the model A. With fire in his eyes, Henry Ford said, "Gentlemen, you don't understand; I must have a V-8 engine and you're going to build it for me. Now go do it." Guess what? They built the V-8 engine. They did it because one man was intelligently ignorant enough not to know that something couldn't be done — so he did it. We see this every day, don't we? One says he can't — and doesn't. One says he can — and does.

The "I CAN" concept is so important that Mamie McCullough, who teaches at Central High School in Thomasville, Ga., conceived the idea of using an "eye can" in her class [she teaches, among other things, the "I CAN" course with this book as the text]. Mrs. McCullough has the students bring a tin can to class and she attaches a picture of an "eye" to it so the can literally becomes an "eye can." If a student goofs and says "I can't" everybody reminds him or her that this is an "I CAN" class. *Positive* results have been *dramatic*.

With so many negatives being taught, isn't it refreshing and exciting to see what a little creative imagination and positive thinking can do? Can't you just image what 10,000 Mamie McCulloughs teaching this philosophy in schoolrooms all over America could accomplish?

INTELLIGENT IGNORANCE PLUS LEMON EQUALS LEMONADE

At one point, during World War II, General Creighton Abrams and his command were totally surrounded. The enemy was north, east, south and west. His reaction to this news [lemon]:

"Gentlemen, for the first time in the history of this campaign, we are now in a position to attack the enemy in any direction." General Abrams not only had the desire to live, he had the desire to win. **It's not the situation [lemon], but the way we react to it [use we make of it] that's important.**

What is intelligent ignorance? Intelligent ignorance is essentially the way you react to the unpromising or negative situations in life. It's that quality that enables you to take a lemon and make lemonade. It's shown in the attitude of two men who had polio. One became a beggar on the streets of Washington. The other was Franklin Delano Roosevelt. Intelligent ignorance is the seed of hope, the promise of good in everything that happens to us. Regardless of what happens, something positive can come from it, and we can make something good out of it. In short, we can take whatever lemon life hands us and convert it to a lemonade.

Charles Kettering had a rather unusual lemon. It was a broken arm. Many years ago he was in his front yard cranking his car and it "kicked" him. For the younger generation, that means the crank didn't disengage, jerked sharply as a cylinder began firing and turned the crank rather than the crank turning the engine. The sudden lurch broke Kettering's arm. What did he do? First, he grasped his arm in pain. Almost immediately, however, he thought, "This is a terrible thing to happen while you're cranking a car. An easier, better, safer way to crank cars must be developed or the masses won't have any desire to own an automobile." As a result, he invented the "self-starter." His lemon, a broken arm, is our lemonade.

Jacob Schick's lemon was a temperature that fell to 40 degrees below zero while he was prospecting for gold. He couldn't shave with a blade — so he invented the first electric razor which turned into a big enough gold mine to buy lots of lemonade.

Neal Jeffrey, third string freshman quarterback at Baylor, University, had a giant-sized lemon. He stuttered. He told Coach Teaff that his goal was to play first string quarterback for the Varsity. Neal's burning desire enabled him to realize his dream and in 1974 he led Baylor to its first Southwest Conference championship in 50 years. Neal made all Southwest Conference, and was voted most valuable player in the conference.

Eugene O'Neill was a drifter until his lemon, in the form of an illness, placed him in the hospital. He converted that lemon to lemonade because while flat on his back he started to write his plays. Hundreds of similar stories explain why — and "how" you can take virtually any lemon, apply enough desire, which creates intelligent ignorance and come out — with lemonade.

MIKE WELDON HAS A "SACK" OF LEMONS

At age one, Mike was taken sick and confined to a hospital where he contracted polio. At age two, he was an expert in walking with braces and crutches. By age sixteen, the deteriorating effects of the disease made him a paraplegic and he was confined to a wheelchair.

In August, 1971, at age twenty-one, Mike was laid off from his $2.99 per hour job as an engineering clerk. As you probably suspect, twenty-one-year-old paraplegics are not in heavy demand in the labor market. However, there is *always* a demand for dedicated, enthusiastic workers. So in just one month Mike was hired as a placement counselor with an employment agency in Rockford, Illinois, which was part of Management Recruiters International, Inc., which employs over 1,300 people.

In March, 1975, at the Sonesta Beach Hotel, Mike Weldon was honored as his company's Counselor of the Year. Believing **you can get everything in life you want if you help enough other people get what they want,** Mike is devoting his life to helping others, and as a result he earned over $60,000 in 1974 — a "recession" year. He doesn't believe he has a disability and everyone agrees he doesn't have a "Loser's Limp." Mike figures since life gave him a "sack" full of lemons, he might as well make a "tub" full of lemonade.

ERRONEOUS ASSUMPTION

Let's go back to World War II for a moment. Most of us know the war began when the Japanese bombed Pearl Harbor. What many people have forgotten is that many loyal Japanese-American citizens were just as upset over Pearl Harbor as any fifth-generation American citizen could have been. Many of these Japanese-Americans were treated shamefully, and placed in detention camps in the interior. The United States government assumed, erroneously as history has proven, that these Japanese-Americans were or might be disloyal. Finally, after much persuasion and soul-searching, many of these Japanese were given an opportunity to enter the war and prove their loyalty by fighting for America.

The 442nd Combat Regimental Team was formed. It was made up of Japanese-Americans. Interestingly enough, this regiment won more Congressional Medals of Honor and decorations than any regiment in the history of the U.S. Since the war, this group of Japanese-Americans has had the highest percentage of college graduates of any first-generation American people. They reacted positively to a situation that was both negative and highly emotional. They took a lemon and made lemonade.

Charles Goodyear's lemon was a prison sentence, resulting from a contempt of court citation. While in prison, Goodyear, didn't groan and complain. Instead, he became an assistant in the kitchen. While there, he continued to work on an idea. In the process, he discovered a method for vulcanizing rubber. His lemon, a prison sentence, became our lemonade. We have better tires, which means better travel and a better way of life.

Martin Luther's lemon was his stay at Wartburg Castle. His lemonade was the German translation of the Bible. Pilgrim's Progress was John Bunyon's lemonade. It was concocted while serving a jail sentence.

THE WINNER AND NEW CHAMPION

Many people who read the sports pages are aware that Gene Tunney became the Heavyweight boxing champion of the world because he whipped Jack Dempsey. They don't know that Tunney was able to take a lemon and convert it into a lemonade. When he first started his fistic career, he was a tremendously hard puncher with a knockout punch in either hand. While fighting exhibition bouts in France, as a member of the American Expeditionary Forces during World War I, he broke both his hands. The doctor and his manager told him he would never be able to realize his dream to become the heavyweight boxing champion of the world because of his brittle hands. Tunney was not disturbed and said, "If I can't become the champion as a puncher, I will make it as a boxer." History will tell that Gene Tunney was a student of the art of self-defense. He became one of the most scientific and skillful boxers to step into the squared circle. This skill as a boxer enabled Tunney to outbox and defeat Jack Dempsey for the heavyweight championship of the world.

Fistic experts are in general agreement that Tunney never would have become the heavyweight champion had he not broken his hands. They contend that Tunney could never have stood up to Jack Dempsey in a toe-to-toe slugging contest and survived. Since Tunney couldn't slug it out, he used his skill and technique as a boxer and became the heavyweight champion. His lemon, two broken hands, became his lemonade, the heavyweight championship of the world.

By now I hope the lesson is clear. If life should hand you a lemon, you'll have the main ingredient for your own lemonade. What happens *to us* is not the most important thing. With discipline, dedication, determination and desire, we can react positively, which greatly enhances our chances for victory. **Intelligent ignorance, a lemon and a lot of desire will help you get what you want out of life.**

FAILURE ROAD

Failure Road is cluttered with the creeping figures of countless people carefully explaining to anyone who will listen why something "can't be done." In the meantime, they are being passed by thousands with far less ability who haven't learned what "can't be done," so they, in their intelligent ignorance, are taking life's lemons and doing it. These residents of Failure Road often have more ability and fewer "problems" but they limp along on an assortment of Loser's Limps.

In the business community one of the most popular Loser's Limps is the traditional "these people are different," or "this is a depressed area." These are excuses, that Elroy Croston, who is in the construction business in Winner, S.D., could legitimately make — if he knew about them. Fortunately, Elroy, who is a dealer for Simpson Structures, is "intelligently ignorant" and doesn't "know" about his "limitations."

Croston's territory encompasses two Indian reservations and is bordered by three other reservations. This area has been described as "depressed" by the Government ever since Croston and Simpson joined forces in 1970. Each year during this period he has received an "Outstanding Dealer Award" — and has been No. 1 in volume or No. 1 in units for the past three years.

Even though Elroy Croston lacks the formal education normally associated with the business, Croston does not let "what he is not" keep him from capitalizing on "what he is." His "success" arsenal contains the positive qualities of patience, humility, dependability, confidence, understanding and belief. Chalk up another victory for the old-fashioned virtues and take your hat off to a good guy — with intelligent ignorance.

NOTES AND IDEAS

CHAPTER THREE
DAVID AND GOLIATH

I'LL BUY IT

In many ways the story of David Lofchick tells virtually everything I want to say in this book. In 1965, I was speaking at a seminar in Kansas City with six of America's top speakers. When the seminar ended on Saturday evening, I prepared for a solitaire dinner. However, as I stepped off the elevator into the lobby of the Muhlbach Hotel, I heard the booming voice of Bernie Lofchick from Winnipeg, Manitoba: "Where ya going, Zig?" Standing impeccably dressed, he called out across the lobby and flashed his ever-present grin. "I'm going to dinner, Bernie," was my reply. Then, with a sparkle in his eye, he said, "I'll tell you what I'll do, Zig. If you'll go to dinner with me, I'll buy."

Well, I have a standing policy. When anyone offers to buy my dinner, I let him. As we sat down to dinner, Bernie and I established a rapport that has grown until we are more like brothers than friends. In fact, I call him Brother Bern. We asked the usual questions that night. What are you doing here? What business are you in? How much family do you have? This kind of thing. After a few minutes, I commented to Bernie that he had certainly come a long way to attend a sales rally. "Yes, he replied, "but it was worth it because I got a lot of good ideas that will help our business grow." I persisted by pointing out it was a long way from Winnipeg to Kansas City and it costs a lot of money to travel that far. Bernie smiled and said, "Yes, but thanks to my son, David, I don't have to worry about the money." "That sounds like a story," I said, "Would you tell it?" With this invitation, Bernie opened his heart and poured out one of the most thrilling stories I've ever heard.

"When our son was born, our joy literally knew no bounds. We already had two daughters and when David was born our family was complete. However, it wasn't long before we realized something was wrong. His head hung too limply to the right side of his body and he drooled too much for a normally healthy child. The family doctor assured us nothing was wrong and David would outgrow this problem. Deep in our hearts, however, we knew better. We took him to a specialist who diagnosed the problem as a reverse of club feet. They proceeded to treat him for this condition for several weeks.

YOUR SON IS A SPASTIC

We knew that the problem was still more serious, so we took David to one of Canada's top specialists. After a very thorough examination, he said to us, "This little boy is spastic. He has cerebral palsy and will never be able to walk, talk or count to ten." He then, in effect, suggested we put our son in an institution 'for his own good' and for the good of the 'normal' members of the family." With his eyes spitting fire, Bernie said, "You know, Zig, I'm not a buyer, I'm a seller and I couldn't see my son as a vegetable. I saw him as a strong, happy, healthy baby who was going to grow into manhood and live a full and productive life. With this in mind I asked the doctor if he knew some place we could go for help. The doctor rather adamantly said he had given us the best advice available and stood up to indicate the interview had ended."

As Brother Bern related the story to me he made a significant statement. "The only thing the specialist had done was to convince us to find a doctor who was interested in solutions and who wasn't overwhelmed with problems."

SOLUTION CONSCIOUS — NOT PROBLEM CONSCIOUS

Before the Lofchick's search had ended, they had taken David to well over twenty specialists. Each one told them essentially the same story and gave them the same advice. Finally, they heard of a Dr. Pearlstein in Chicago. He was reputed to be the world's foremost authority on cerebral palsy. Patients came to him from all over the world and he was booked solid for well over a year. Since Dr. Pearlstein worked only through other doctors, Bernie enlisted the aid of his family physician. All the tests that had been

343

made on David were sent to Dr. Pearlstein and contact was made for an appointment. Unfortunately, Dr. Pearlstein was so heavily booked he advised the physician to contact him again at a later date. When the doctor gave Bernie this information and said there was nothing more to be done, Bernie took matters in his own hands. He decided to see if he could get an appointment with Dr. Pearlstein for David. After much effort, Bernie finally reached him by telephone one evening. He persuaded him to place David on standby for the next cancelled appointment. A break came just eleven days later and David had that appointment with Dr. Pearlstein and with destiny. Hope at long last had reared its beautiful but elusive head. It was a welcome sight and the Lofchick's embraced it warmly.

The disease, Goliath, didn't know it but he had a brand new opponent. After several hours of examinaton, the diagnosis was the same: David was a spastic. He had cerebral palsy. But there was hope, provided Bernie was willing to undertake the enormous and never-ending battle. The Lofchicks felt that no price could be too high to give their son his chance in life. So, they eagerly inquired what must be done.

Dr. Pearlstein and his therapist spelled out their instructions in minute detail. They were told that they were going to have to work David until he dropped and then they would have to work him some more. They would have to push him beyond all human endurance and then push him some more. He made Bernie and Elaine completely aware that it was going to be a long, difficult and sometimes an apparently hopeless struggle. He stressed that once they started this course of action they would have to continue indefinitely. He emphasized that if they gave up or slacked off, David would go backwards and all the work they had done would have been in vain. Yes, the battle for David against his Goliath affliction had really begun. The Lofchicks now had hope and the hope had believability. They headed for home with a lighter step, a lighter heart and prepared for the battle ahead.

A physical therapist and a body builder were hired and a small gym was built in the basement. Physical effort and mental toughness became the order of the day.

After months of excruciating and dedicated effort, small rays of hope began to appear. David acquired the ability to move.

Even though it took him a long time, he was able to move the length of his own body. A giant milestone had been reached.

HE'S READY

Still another one was reached with a phone call from the therapist who excitedly told Bernie he should leave his office and come home. When Bernie reached home, the stage was set and David was ready to prepare for a supreme effort. He was going to attempt a pushup. With an effort seldom equalled by an adult, much less by a six-year-old-boy, David called on all his reserves. As his body started to rise above the mat, the emotional and physical exertion was so great there was not a dry inch of skin on his little body. The mat looked as if water had been poured on it. When that one pushup was completed, David, the therapist, Mother and Dad all freely shed the sweet tears that clearly prove, **happiness is not pleasure, it is victory.**

The story is even more remarkable when you understand that one of America's leading universities had examined David and found that he had no "motor connections" to the right side of his body. That his sense of balance was such he would have serious difficulty learning to walk and he would never be able to swim, skate, or ride a bicycle. Yes, the disease, Goliath, was taking a licking. More importantly, while whipping his Goliath, David was learning from experience and teaching by example, some of the truly great lessons in life. His progress was steady and according to the medical experts even spectacular. David is truly a remarkable boy who has made enormous progress, which is not surprising because his parents saw David as a vibrant growing boy who was going all the way to good health.

Today, this "little boy" has virtually discarded his fourth bicycle except for those occasions when it's either too warm for him to ice skate or when he's not driving his car. Learning to ice skate was painful. Even though it took nearly a year just to learn to stand on those skates with the aid of a hockey stick, he went at it day after day. He did what was necessary to overcome his obstacles and succeeded so well he played left wing on the local hockey team. Even after these successes, the doctor still said it would probably take him two years to float, but he was floating in two weeks and swimming before the first summer was over. David has done as many as 1,000 pushups in a single day and once ran six miles without a break. At age eleven, he took up golf and applied the same enthusiasm and determination to it that he applied to everything he has tackled. Result: he has already broken ninety.

It's exciting to watch David grow and to know that *all* of the characteristics he is developing and principles he is applying to succeed physically and academically, will take him just as far in his chosen field of endeavor. It's also exciting to know *you* can develop the same characteristics, apply the same principles and succeed in life to the same degree that David is succeeding.

Mentally, David is in as good shape as he is physically. In September of 1969, he was accepted at the St. John's Raven Court School for Boys. It is one of the most demanding private schools in Canada. While in the 7th grade, David did quite well in 9th grade mathematics. That's not bad for a little boy who the doctors said was never going to count to ten. On October 23, 1971, my wife and I had the privilege of attending the Bar Mitzvah of David Lofchick. I wish *you* could have been there to see David take that giant step into manhood. With clear eyes, a steady voice and unfaltering steps, David, amidst a large group of loving friends and relatives from the United States and Canada, became a man. His performance was understandly outstanding since he'd been preparing all his life for the occasion.

Yes, Goliath is clearly on the deck, but just as clearly he hasn't been knocked out and probably never will be. David must exercise extensively and regularly for the rest of his life. Even a few days off takes a toll. Like any active 19-year-old there are times he would much prefer to be with his friends. However, when exercise time comes, David understands what he must do and heads for the gym. Of course, it's not all work because in addition to his parents he has those two big sisters, a host of friends, and a large number of relatives who represent a lot of companionship and quite a cheering section.

One of the high points for David occurred in February, 1974, when a $100,000 whole life insurance policy was issued on David's life. The policy was issued on a standard basis which, to the best of my knowledge, marked the first time a victim of cerebral palsy has ever qualified for such a contract.

ACHIEVING IS CONTAGIOUS

Those who know the Lofchick family will quickly tell you that each member played a vital part in David's life and was privileged to grow with him. Each one is outstanding and each one contributes to the family and to the community. Bernie's growth, for example, has been equally amazing. Bernie is truly the most completely educated, uneducated man I've ever known. He officially finished the 7th grade, but he spends every day of life in "school." He learns something from everybody and his pursuit of excellence qualifies him as one of the most astute business minds I have ever encountered.

Of necessity, Bernie worked both harder and smarter in his business career and personal life. For a seven-year-period he worked seven days and seven nights every week, taking only one night off during this entire period of time. That feat alone clearly demonstrates his dedication, determination, desire and devotion. In his quest, Bernie discovered that in a successful and happy life **you can get everything in life you want if you help enough other people get what they want.** Applying this principle to his business, he built the biggest cookware company in Canada and achieved financial independence in the process.

By any yardstick David and those who helped him are quite successful. It was a team battle and a team victory with each one playing an important part in putting Goliath on the deck. Each one is playing a significant part in keeping him there.

ALL THE INGREDIENTS

With the story of David Lofchick in mind, let's turn to the "Stairway to the Top" chart. As a baby, David couldn't have his own Healthy Self-Image, the first step on the chart. Nevertheless, in the eyes of his parents he was a special little boy who deserved to have and was going to have his chance in life. They *saw* David as he is today, and they saw themselves as capable of giving him that chance. Today, David has a healthy self-image, the results of which are so completely evident.

The second "step" in your stairway to the top is Your Relationship With Others. Obviously, there were a number of people who played vital roles in the growth and development of David Lofchick. Doctors, nurses, therapists, teachers, etc., all had a part. The "blood, sweat and tears" were all made more tolerable because of the patience and love developed through the relationship between the parents, David, and the professionals involved. Without help — and lots of it — David's situation would truly have been desperate. Fortunately, he received the help he needed and became a winner. The people who helped David were winners too because **"He climbs highest, who helps another up."**

The third step we covered was the importance of Goals, how to set those goals and how to reach those goals. Every aspect of goal setting was evident in David's story. In conjunction with the goals the family had for David, Bernie also set his own personal, work, and financial goals. Initially, Bernie couldn't easily carry the heavy medical burden imposed by David's treatment, but he did what champions have always done. He rose to the occasion. Now he's getting everything in life he wants by helping David and others get what they want.

The fourth step was the right mental attitude which covers a wide area, and David Lofchick's story illustrates it perfectly. The family attitude of working one day at a time, taking one step at a time, making stepping-stones out of obstacles and reacting positively to all negative situations was conveyed to David. They fed him a steady diet of "You can do it, David." David listened to enthusiastic, positive, cassette recordings while he dressed, exercised and rode to school with his parents. Daily his trainer, the former Mr. Manitoba, Syd Pukalo, as well as his parents and close family friends, reinforced the positive factors in his life. Eventually, the proper mental diet, became a part of David's life and the habits he acquired were so good and strong that his growth and progress were assured.

The fifth step concerned Work and David's story fits it well. To give you an idea, the next time you complain about having just 24 hours in a day, let me urge you to remember David Lofchick. For years he only had a 21-hour day because he literally invested three hours a day in his physical battle to stay even with the cerebral palsy. Today his time demands are still enormous. If he doesn't work at it every day, his Goliath moves back in. Yes, he has had to work, but David and the Lofchick family *know* that you don't pay a price for good health — you enjoy the price.

David's story fits beautifully in the sixth step which is the discussion of Desire. I can honestly say that in dealing with hundreds of people, I've never met a family where desire is more evident than it is in the Lofchick family. Their burning desire for David to have his chance in life was translated into the actions they took so he could have his chance. Some of those actions were tough, real tough, because they involved a special kind of love that was so deep it demanded they overrule their natural sympathy and compassion. Many times when Bernie and Elaine forced those braces tighter according to the doctor's instruction, David would cry and plead with them to ease up or leave them off for "just one night." Bernie and Elaine would have given almost anything to comply, but their love was so deep they said no to David's tears of the moment which meant they were saying yes to his health and happiness for a lifetime.

As you view David's story, you realize that character, honesty, love, loyalty, faith and integrity are in evidence from beginning to end. In the first Segment of the book, I pointed out that any quality you are short of, you can acquire. I believe the story of David verifies this fact. To look at him, you would find it hard to believe anything has ever been wrong with him. Many times I have wondered just how fantastic David might have been if he had been a normal, healthy baby. It wasn't difficult for me to image him being bigger, stronger, faster, smarter, etc. Then one day the truth hit me like a ton of bricks. Had David started with more, he might well have ended up with less. I'm convinced he is more — maybe much more — not in spite of, but because of the cerebral palsy. That's why God tells us so clearly to thank Him for everything. [Thess. 5:18]. Yes, it's a special and wonderful miracle that the Lofchicks saw their son as a boy who was going to get his chance in the relay race of life. They got him started, passed the baton on to him and old David has been running with it ever since.

The best part of David's story hasn't been written because David is still living it. My belief is, what David does in the future will far surpass what he's done in the past. That's exciting, but even more exciting is the thought of what this story could mean to the millions of kids who have normal health. If David could start from where he was with what he had and do what he's done, think what the same principles and procedures could mean if applied to kids with good health. That thought is awesome and exciting.

David's story now has a sequel. While telling his story in Amarillo, Texas, one night, I noticed that a young couple seated on the front row was visibly moved. Later we visited privately and they sought the name of the Chicago doctor who took over Dr. Pearlstein's practice upon his death. Their fifteen month old daughter had Cerebral Palsy, and they hoped something could be done for her. They took their daughter to Chicago and after the examination, the doctor told them that their daughter had all the *symptoms* of the disease, but she definitely did not have Cerebral Palsy. She had simply been born prematurely and the doctor had incorrectly diagnosed her condition. The premature birth had caused her to be a little slower than normal. However, since they had been treating her for Cerebral Palsy she had acquired *all* the symptoms of the disease. They immediately started treating her as a normal, healthy child and in a matter of weeks the symptoms of Cerebral Palsy disappeared. Yes, we treat people the way we see them and they respond to that treatment whether it's good or bad, positive or negative. Again, that's why it's so important for us to be "good finders."

So here you are at the top of the stairway. You've climbed all the steps so you now stand squarely in front of the door leading into the banquet hall of life. At this point I call your attention to the word opportunity which is clearly written on that door. Actually, the word opportunity could be spelled AMERICA — as a matter of fact, if you will look again, it's obvious that opportunity *is* America. Only in a free enterprise country such as America could these principles bear such fruit. So let's take a look now at the land of the free and the home of the brave — America The Beautiful.

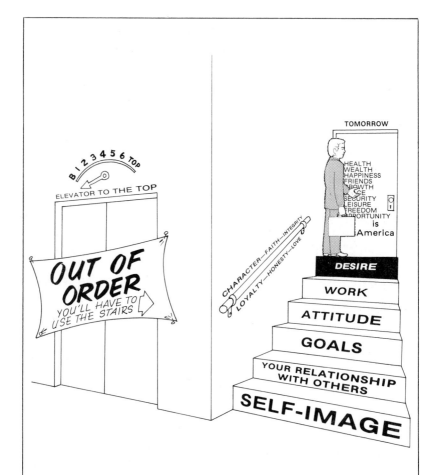

There **you** are standing in front of the glass doors of the executive suites of tomorrow. All you need now is a little push to open the door.

CHAPTER FOUR
AMERICA THE BEAUTIFUL

FREE ENTERPRISE VS. COMMUNISM

Throughout this book I've been telling you a number of stories about people like you and me. As stated earlier, I believe life is a story, so I've tried to tie these stories to life to help you be more — do more and have more. These stories involve people from every race, creed, and color and they come from every walk of life. They differ in many ways, but each shares the common bond of living in a free enterprise system which enables them to more fully use their ability.

My personal travels from Perth, Australia to Paris, France, combined with the spoken and printed word, have enabled me to compare free enterprise and America with the rest of the world — and America wins — by a landslide. Simple example: The average American newspaperboy working part time in free enterprise earns more money than 50% of the workers of the world.

I stress free enterprise at this time because some of the principles advocated throughout this book would not bear fruit behind the iron and bamboo curtains. In this final chapter, I sound the warning about some dangers we face, and what *you* can do to keep America and you, free and great.

An excellent comparison between free enterprise and Communism exists in Cuba. Before Castro and Communism took over in 1958, the average yearly income of the Cuban worker was approximately $475, everything was plentiful, nothing was rationed and you could travel as you pleased. Today, personal freedom is a thing of the past, and individual hope is just a memory. Under Communism, the average income of the Cuban worker in 1974 was about $325, which would buy less than one-third of what the $475 would have bought in 1958. Virtually everything in Cuba today is rationed and many things are unavailable. All travel is restricted and no one can leave the country. Castro stopped emigration after freedom-loving Cubans

352

by the thousands gave up everything they owned in exchange for freedom in America. In Russia, the mother country of communism, personal freedom is so limited that even their prize exhibits [athletes and artists] are closely guarded when they leave the country and their Nobel prize winners often can't leave to accept their prizes. Freedom of worship is but a foggy memory, political dissent is an invitation to disaster, and emigration to another country is a million-to-one long shot.

In material goods, the Russian works 1000 days to buy a medium size car and waits six long years for delivery. Even then travel is restricted, gasoline is expensive, and paved highways are few. By comparison, an American can buy a medium size car for 100 days work, get immediately delivery on 200 different models, and can go *anywhere* in the United States on the most elaborate highway system in the world.

A Russian works 300 hours to buy a refrigerator and waits months for delivery. In America, a better refrigerator for immediate delivery can be bought with 30 hours of work. In Russia, anything not essential involves a long line, often with disappointment at the end. It's a source of embarrassment that the free enterprise system works extremely well in Russia itself. During the highly oppressive Stalin regime, Joe Stalin agreed to let the farmers have a small patch of ground adjoining their homes to cultivate for their own personal use. This land comprises less than 4% of the total land under cultivation, but approximately one-third of the total agricultural production of Soviet Russia comes from this 4%. Specifically, this "free enterprise" land produces more than 60% of Russia's potatoes, 50% of the Russian milk supply, 75% of the eggs and nearly 50% of Russia's meat production. **Incentive is the soul of success — regardless of your nationally.**

Despite its claims, there isn't a communist country in the world that can feed itself. Communism is so inefficient that some experts believe Russia would collapse in 15 years or less if we withdrew our agricultural and technical expertise which is propping them up. Anyone who thinks in terms of embracing socialism should just *look* over the wall into Communist East Berlin or visit Cuba, China, or Russia to see the *reality* of communism instead of the *theory*. They are two different animals. Communists say they are all "equal," which *is* true. They are all *equally poor*. To paraphrase Winston Churchill, Capitalism's "problem" is the uneven division of wealth while socialism's "virtue" is the even division of misery.

THE BULLFROG THEORY

As we approach America's problems, I'm concerned about two groups of Americans. One group is like the individual who refuses to have an examination because he suspects he has cancer. He blindly says, "America has no problems" or, "don't worry, America has always come through — don't tell me about it." The second group says, "Well, what can I do, it's just me and it's too late now."

If your house were burning, you would want to know about it so you could grab a bucket of water and put it out. The purpose of this chapter is to tell you that your house [America] is burning and give you several buckets of water so you can *help* douse the flames. The fire that is burning America started much like you boil a bullfrog.

You don't boil a bullfrog by throwing him in boiling water, because he will pop out faster than you can pop him in. You put him in cold water and turn on the heat. As the water gets warm, the bullfrog relaxes and takes a nap. You know the rest of the story. He wakes up dead. He's been boiled to death.

An enemy today would not directly attack America. Germany, in World War I and Japan, in World War II used that direct assault with disastrous results. The enemy we face today is far more subtle and infinitely more powerful and dangerous than either Japan or Germany. The enemy is Communism and it started under another banner back in the 30's. At that time Americans were sold on the "free lunch" concept that they could increase their wealth by channeling it through a centralized government in Washington. So, we started electing the most "promising" politicians to political office. The "frog" was in the water and the "heat" was on. Over the years, vote-seeking politicans passed liberal legislation [liberal with the working man's money]. In all fairness, I must point out that not all "politicians" are in office. Many "politicians" are citizens who

He's gonna' wake up boiled to death.
Complacency will kill.

regularly confront the elected officials with two "demands." First, you *must* do something to reduce the ridiculously high expenditure of the Federal Government and second, you *must* figure out a way to get more federal funds for our people back home.

Federal aid has been so heavy and so extensive that today some economists are predicting that by 1990, 50% of the American people will be lending support to the other 50%. This has come about so gradually that many people are unaware it has been happening for many years. I'm concerned that the "frog" [America] is in hot water — that's getting hotter — but I'm also convinced that an aroused citizenry can solve that problem.

Many people blithely say that Americans have always come through when the chips are down — in the past this has been true, but I'm concerned. We have 100 million Americans who've never seen us weather a severe depression. We *know* how they react to success and prosperity, but realistically we don't know how they would react to adversity. These same Americans have never seen us win a war. The Korean War was a stalemate and Viet-Nam was a disaster. They don't know the sweet taste of victory or the thrill of seeing free people embrace their liberating heroes.

I'm concerned because 130 million Americans are under age 25 and the average 25-year-old has seen an average of 18,000 hours of television. During this time he will have viewed 40,000 murders, witnessed thousands of rapes and seductions, and heard "jillions" of obscene and profane words. This is hardly the "diet" that builds either character or determination.

THE BIG LIE

Throughout this book we have stressed, "as you sow, so also shall you reap." To show the effect of repeatedly seeing or hearing anything, please complete the following statements. Winston tastes good like a _____ _____. Pepsi Cola hits the _____twelve full ounces that's a _____. Drink Coca Cola the pause that _____. Duz does _____. Now check your answers on page 380. Those commercials were on television over ten years ago but chances are excellent that you got them right, because you will remember *and* believe *almost* anything *if* you hear it enough times.

Forty years ago, Adolph Hitler conclusively proved that the masses will believe the "big lie" if you tell it often enough.

Let's look at American Big Lie Number One: For the last 25 years, liberals have been telling me my generation was taught that sex was dirty — but were we? A survey of my peer group gave me a resounding *no*. When *anything* about sex was taught or discussed we were told that sex was private, that it was sacred and that it was between husband and wife. The Bible stresses the sacredness and beauty of sexual relations between a man and his wife. It identifies it as the highest expression of human endearment and that it goes beyond the procreation of the human race. But the liberal, by implication, was saying that since sex wasn't "dirty" it could be indulged in with anyone so long as it was a "meaningful" relationship.

Big Lie Number Two: In the last 25 years, we've been repeatedly told that "poverty breeds crime." However, in 1940 after an entire decade of the toughest depression in our country's history, the crime rate was lower than it was at the beginning. Significantly, there has never been a definitive study that established a correlation between crime and poverty. Crime has to do with character and integrity. What we teach our children determines whether they will be law-abiding or lawbreaking.

What are the kids being taught? By the millions they watch TV, in living color where instant coffee, instant tea and instant potatoes, along with instant happiness, instant success and instant gratification are sold. It's inevitable that the kids get an erroneous concept about true success and happiness, as well as what's involved in acquiring the big car, the big home, the swimming pool, etc.

Underprivileged youngsters inevitably compare what they don't have to what those on the TV screen do have, and they feel underprivileged. Combine this with the fact that society is telling them that poverty breeds crime and you have planted the seeds of criminal action.

Big Lie Number Three: People equal poverty and India proves it. Does it really? India is a poverty-stricken nation. England has a higher density per square mile and Holland has a 50% greater density than India, but they have a high standard of living. Africa has a low population density, but extreme poverty. America has a low density and an enormously high standard of living. Population could be *a* factor, but it is not *the* factor. However, this "big lie" has been used to support liberal abortion laws and encourage fewer babies in America with the result that in 1975 the birth rate was only 1.9 per 100 and we need 2.1 per 100 to sustain our population.

In 40 years, we will have the highest percentage of elderly people in history. They will deserve, demand and get a higher standard of living. That's proper, but these extra benefits will be supplied by the lowest percentage of workers in our history. We need more dedicated Americans raising God-fearing, law-abiding children. These kids, properly loved, taught and motivated are the solution to, and not the cause of, the problem. Actually they are our only hope for solving tomorrow's problems.

YES — WE DO HAVE PROBLEMS

I'm concerned about the enormous waste in government spending especially for programs like the one to study the effects on male students of smoking marijuana while watching pornographic movies [$121,000]. $5,000 went to Erica Jong to write *Fear Of Flying*. $2,000,000 was spent to buy Marshall Tito of Yugoslavia a yacht. These amounts are infinitesimal when compared to the seven billion dollars we have given in foreign aid to the six nations which have raised one thousand tons of opium with a street value of $22 billion. Absurd is the word I carefully and deliberately use to describe a policy that permits America to send our billions to *build* their countries. They in turn take our money — often without a simple thank-you — and ship heroin into America to *destroy* us.

A letter to *your* congressman would have an impact. We know public opinion carries considerable weight. When Americans and American businessmen started boycotting French goods in protest of the manufacture and exportation of heroin from Marseilles, France into the U.S.A., an interesting thing happened. The French managed to find and destroy more heroin producing labs in six months than in the preceding ten years.

I'm concerned about the laws that require any American to

join any organization to get a job. Theoretically, these laws were passed for the benefit of the working man. It hasn't worked this way, however, because the states which have the right-to-work laws have a lower rate of unemployment than those with "closed shop" laws.

I'm concerned about crime, forced busing, the increase in juvenile delinquency, the rising rate of crime among women, the ever-increasing use of drugs, alcohol, pornography and a hundred and one other problems, but I'm convinced there's a solution to these problems.

I'm especially concerned that American youth are not being sold on the American free enterprise system. According to the United States Chamber of Commerce and the Princeton Research Institute, 67% of our high school students do not believe a business needs a profit and nearly 50% of them cannot give you even one advantage that capitalism has over communism. 63% of the American high school students feel the Federal Government should own the banks, railroads and the steel companies. 62% do not believe a worker should produce to the best of his ability, which is another form of dishonesty. These things are frightening but don't blame the kids. It's *our* fault. We write the books, build the schools and pay the educators. It is up to us to teach our sons and daughters the advantages of the free enterprise system.

DEALING WITH COMMUNISM

I'm concerned about communism, especially as it relates to our current foreign policy, because Russia honors a treaty only if it's to her advantage. A recent study of over 1000 treaties confirms Russia as the champion treaty breaker of all time. That loud chorus of Amens you heard came from the Finns, Estonians, Latvians, Lithuanians, Czechs, Hungarians, Poles and Germans who were enslaved *after* signing treaties with Russia.

At the time President Kennedy confronted Nikita Khrushchev concerning the Russian missiles in Cuba, he was dealing from strength and was able to tell him to pull those missiles out of Cuba — or else. Russia understood the language and backed off.

However, when Secretary of State Kissinger and Leonid Brezhnev negotiated to stop the Yom Kippur War, we had a different situation. Detente' was in effect and the Russians, by agreement, were to inform us of any known crisis. Evidence is conclusive that they knew in advance of an imminent attack by the Arab countries on the Israelies, but they said nothing. During those first few fretful days when the Egyptian armies were forcing the Isralies back, Kissinger tried desperately to reach Brezhnev to urge him to stop it, but Brezhnev was unavailable.

With the tide of battle turned and the Israelies completely surrounded the Egyptian army, Brezhnev started screaming for Kissinger to stop the war. America put extreme pressure on Israel to call off their armies. I'm convinced we bowed to Russia's wishes because of their increasing military strength combined with our relative decline.

When you deal with Russia, you are dealing with an idealogy and a leadership that does not believe in God, has no regard for human life and looks upon a treaty as a piece of paper until the other side breaks it. The Communist feels what is his is his and what is yours is open for negotiaton. Brezhnev, without regard for human life and now with possible military superiority, could coldly play the high stakes game with impudence. I'm concerned about the relative decline in our military strength, but the problem has a solution.

I should pause and explain something to my Christian Brothers who might quote, "The meek shall inherit the earth" scripture. In the original Greek, the word meek meant "power — with restraint." So long as we have the power, we *won't* need to use it and hence we won't use it. If we don't have the power, history's lesson conclusively proves that we *will* need it. Like my insurance friends tell me, it's infinitely better to have it and not need it than to need it and not have it.

I'm convinced that at long last, Americans *know* the water [remember the bullfrog] has reached such an intolerable heat that they recognize their house [America] is burning. Most Americans are now asking someone to give them a bucket of water [tell me what to do] so they can personally help put out the fire. Hopefully, the rest of this chapter will provide you with several "buckets of water."

WHAT CAN YOU DO?

Fortunately, the timing has never been better because we just celebrated our 200th birthday and Americans are beginning to accentuate the positive. From coast to coast and border to border the evidence is overwhelming that concerned Americans are standing up to be counted, sounding off to be heard, studying to be informed, and working to make long-needed changes. In the past two years, I have seen more dedicated men and women enter the field to fight corruption and crookedness than in the preceding ten years. That's encouraging.

I've also seen young people by the score do an abrupt about-face. The recession and job shortage caused many to realize that demanding impossible salaries and conditions from a prospective employer who was struggling for survival afforded them little hope for a job when they were competing with a dozen other youngsters who were better qualified for that job. More importantly, many of them now realize that ultimately those who do only what they please to do are seldom pleased with what they do. That too is encouraging.

It's also encouraging to hear more and more of the liberal, big government advocates publicly acknowledging that more government spending and involvement is not the answer, that self reliance is the order of the day and the individual *is* responsible for his own conduct and personal well being.

The solution, however, is covered in the last four sentences of the speech President Kennedy was to have made in Dallas, Texas, the day he was assassinated.

"We, in this country, in this generation, are by destiny, rather than by choice, the watchmen of the walls of world freedom. We ask, therefore, that we may be worthy of the power and the responsibility, that we may exercise our strength with wisdom and restraint, that we may achieve in our time and for all times the ancient vision of peace on earth, good will toward men. That must always be our goal and the righteousness of our call must always underlie our strength for as it was written long ago, 'except the Lord, keep the city, the watchmen waketh but in vain'."

That's the foundation upon which this country was built. That is where we must return, because as William Pitt said, **"If God does not rule the affairs of man then tyrants will."** Fortunately God-fearing men and women are getting back into the political arena and President Carter openly acknowledges his faith in and dependence upon Almighty God. Equally exciting is the fact the boy scouts are now returning to their original concepts and are again teaching kids trust in God.

We need to stand straight and firm on law enforcement. We've leaned over backwards in our zeal for fairness to protect the accused. Now, in fairness to criminal and victim alike, we must look to the rights of both and make the criminal instead of the victim pay for the crime.

Another way to solve America's problems is to become politically active. Each one of us must stop saying, "those politicans." It is not *"That* Congressman," *"That* Senator" or *"That* Mayor." We must properly identify them as *"My* Congressman," *"My* Senator," *"My* Mayor," because we [that's you and I] did elect them — by our support or by our lack of support. Interested in helping America — and you? Did you vote and/or support qualified, God fearing candidates in the last election? It only takes 150 dedicated people to elect a Congressman. Even though public officials pass the laws, citizens — like you and I — elect the people who pass the laws.

One thing all of us can do, and even must do, is sell the beauty and sanctity of the family as a unit. Historically eighty-eight civilizations have risen to a dominant position in world history. Some rose quickly, some rose slowly, but without exception, they *all* fell in one generation and each one fell *after* the family unit was destroyed. In *every* case the pattern was the same, a relaxing of moral standards which led to pornography followed by promiscuity, adultery, wife swapping, and finally homosexuality. Surely America, if properly alerted, can learn from the eighty eight examples which preceded us.

A good family to look at as we "sell" the family as a unit is the James and Margaret Griffin family of Columbus, Ohio. For the last 23 years, James Griffin has been driving a truck for the sanitation department by day and working in a steel mill at night. In addition, he has two janitorial jobs before he calls it a day. On weekends he is the janitor of two schools. For the last 23 years James Griffin has worked an average of 20 hours a day supporting his seven sons and one daughter. Needless to say, Margaret has been by his side all the way. The Griffins have done this because they wanted their children to have their opportunity. The Griffin family is a closely knit unit with Joe, the older son, serving as the man of the house during James Griffin's long work hours. The Griffins are grateful that they were given a chance to use their ability and initiative to get what America has to offer. They even used their vacation on Friday nights so they could watch their sons play football. They were and are superior players. One of their sons is Archie Griffin who in 1975 became the first football player in history to win the Heisman trophy for the second time.

HAND OFF — UNCLE SAM

As voters, we need to become personally involved and elect officials who dedicate themselves to getting and keeping the government out of business and encourage more business people to get into government. One look at the Post Office, Medicare, Medicade, Social Security and the food stamp program will convince anyone that despite the efforts of tens of thousands of dedicated government employees, who have devoted a lifetime to conscientiously serving America and the general public, the government simply doesn't know how to run a business.

The need for more direction and encouragement in business principles are painfully evident when we view the rising cost of government and it's comparative inefficiencies. For example, the Exxon Corporation can ship a gallon of gasoline from Houston, Texas to New York City faster and cheaper than the Post Office can send a letter from Dallas to Ft. Worth and pay substantial taxes on the profit. Incidentally, the government can only provide as many services [like the postal service and others] as productive people and profitable businesses can support.

December, 1975, *Reader's Digest* tells a similar story. In 1915 you could make a telephone call from New York to San Francisco for $20 or you could mail 1,000 first class letters from New York to San Francisco. Today you can call after 9:00 P.M., New York to San Francisco for 65¢ or you can write *five* letters from New

York to San Francisco for 65¢. So the government is investigating the telephone company. [Like the man says, the post office is not something you'd write home about.] Of even more concern is a recent survey which shows that the rate of productivity per man hour in government is thirty-nine percent below the average productivity level of the private sector. Thirty-nine percent! No wonder our national budget runs into the red by the *billions* year after year.

PROGRESS REPORT

As concerned citizens, we need to showcase the progress instead of the problem. I don't believe in hiding problems, but I believe the best way to solve a problem is to identify it. Then we need to remember that hope and encouragement are the major ingredients in the solution to *any* problem. Example: The racial problem. Everyone knows about the problem, but most do not know about the progress we are making toward solving it. The net result is despair that no solution exists, which leads many people to quit working on solving the problem.

In 1975, Gentle Ben Williams, the all Southeastern Conference middle guard for the Ole Miss Rebels, was elected Colonel Rebel by the student body. Gentle Ben is a black man. Just 13 years earlier James Meredith, another black man, required the protection of Federal Marshalls to attend the University of Mississippi. From, "Kill the black man," to "vote for Gentle Ben for Colonel Rebel," in just 13 years is tremendous progress. We've crossed a big barrier and every day more and more Americans are recognizing that the pigment in a man's skin has nothing to do with the heart and ability that lies inside.

The black American has made more progress in the last 15 years than any people in history. We need to remind our foreign and domestic critics that *America has more black millionaires and more black people in American colleges than the rest of the world combined.* We have black senior officers in all the services, as well as black cabinet members, Senators, Congressmen, and Mayors of large cities and the numbers increase daily. In the last 10 years, the number of black attorneys, accountants, college teachers and other professionals has almost doubled. The number of black graduates has increased over 100%. Between 1968 and 1973, the number of blacks earning $15,000 each year has almost tripled. According to *U. S. News and World Report*, outside of the Deep South the average income of a young black couple is 99% as great as his white counterpart. Everything is obviously still not equal for the black man but the fastest way to make it equal is to emphasize the progress.

BE POSITIVE —
ESPECIALLY ABOUT THE PROBLEMS

In 1974 and 1975, the prophets of doom were saying that inflation, recession and unemployment spelled the end of America. Two years earlier, the same prophets were sounding the death knell because of the gasoline shortage. Five years earlier, riots on the campus were going to destroy us, but they really had a field day on Oct. 4, 1957, when the Russians put Sputnik in orbit. They told one and all, "The Russians are going to get all our secrets, reduce us to a second-rate power and beat us to the moon." History, however, has proven that Sputnik didn't spell the end of America. In fact, the Russians aroused us from a sound sleep much like the Japanese did at Pearl Harbor in 1941. Despite their advantage, we easily won the race. Today we know the only way those Russians are ever going to get to the moon is for Americans to take them there — piggy-back.

I have no fear of Russian economic and technological strength. I do fear their dedication, ideology, and goals of world conquest. Watch the next Olympics and you will note that when a Russian receives a gold medal he will, with much emotion say "I did it for the glory of Mother Russia."

One simple example of the difference an involvement like that makes in performance, is the story of Pat Matsdorf, the former world's record holder in the high jump. He set the record in a dual meet with the Russians. Interestingly enough, just six weeks earlier, he had been badly beaten in a college meet. Against the Russians, however, he jumped a full 5½" higher than he had against college competition. A curious reporter asked Pat to explain the dramatic improvement in his performance. Pat looked down and pointed at the letters — U.S.A. — on his athletic jersey and said, "I've never represented anything this big before." This kind of pride can be — must be — developed in millions of American young people and adults.

Through our problems *and* our triumphs we must keep our sense of humor, because if you think the recent problems were serious, let me urge you to open your history book to 1858 to look at a real problem. Not only was there a shortage of whale oil that year but leading "whaleologists" the world over maintained that "those dirty whales" were not turning out the same quality whale oil they had in the past. The prophets of doom assured one and all the lamps would go dim, our children would grow up in an era of darkness and education would be destroyed. Then someone discovered petroleum.

Between now and the time you read these words there could well be a dozen national emergencies and numbers of crisis in your personal life. However, as Dr. Norman Vincent Peale often says, "The only people who do not have problems are those in the cemeteries." [Then with a twinkle in his eye he says, " and some of them really have problems."] If you have problems, it simply means you are alive and the more problems you have the more alive you are. He even jokingly suggests that if you don't have man-sized problems you should get on your knees and ask God to "trust" you with a few.

We also need to remember that some good comes out of every problem. Eleven thousand lives were saved because of the fuel shortage in 1974 and America got busy toward self-sufficiency in energy. Incidentally, the character for crisis in Japanese, is a combination of the characters for "disaster and opportunity." The opportunities of America's crisis far outweigh the "disasters" caused by them and America historically takes its "lemons" and makes "lemonade."

— RESOURCES VS. RESOURCEFULNESS —

National dedication will enable us to utilize our greatest natural resource — our people — who will then develop our other resources which America has in abundance. This includes the discovered and undiscovered, the known and the unknown. I agree with Dr. Billy Ray Cox, of Harding College, who says *our major problem is not a lack of resouces but lack of resourcefulness.*

Our oil and gas reserves might be running low, but our hidden resources will more than take up the slack. Dr. Cox points out that just 300 years ago people were using coal as rocks. Just over 100 years ago, people viewed oil as the black curse and forty years ago there was no known use for uranium.

Unfortunately, we are not utilizing many of our known natural resources. One county in Wyoming has enough coal reserves to supply more energy than all the known oil and gas reserves in the entire country. Yes, it does have a high sulphur content, but American technology is on the threshold of removing and utilizing that sulphur. In short, here's a "lemon" I'm confident will end up as the principle ingredient in lemonade.

Solar heat and energy is being developed daily and some experts feel that with a concerted effort this could provide a major part of our home and office heating supply in the very near future. More progress has been made on utilizing this unlimited source of energy in the past two years than in the previous twenty. Tremendous potential also exists in the development of offshore drilling. Thus far only 4% of this land has been leased for oil exploration and drilling. The list of undeveloped resources is endless. I'm confident that American ingenuity will solve the energy problem as well as any other problem we are *positive* about solving.

As our known resources dwindle — our resourcefulness enters the picture. For example, some cities are converting garbage to energy and a process has even been developed to use chicken droppings as fuel to run automobiles. In Europe, an automobile has been tested using water as its principle fuel. Our scientists are making progress in their quest to harness the power of the ocean tides and utilize the energy of the Gulf Stream. The story goes on and on to the degree that I'm strongly convinced that the oil shortage is going to be the "lemon" which produces the best tasting lemonade this country has ever had.

WAVE THE FLAG — PROUDLY — WITHOUT APOLOGY

As Americans we must demand that our heroes and moral teaching be put back into the history books. According to the

Thomas Jefferson Research Center, when America won its independence, religion and morals accounted for more than 90% of the content of school readers. By 1926 the figure was only 6% and today it is almost immeasurable. History proves that if we give our children heroes and moral principles to live up to — they will. We need to teach our children — from early childhood — about our heroes of yesteryear. We need to tell them the stories of America — its greatness and its goodness because the spirit of America is caught — as it's taught.

We need to listen — and make certain the young people listen — to the immortal words of Patrick Henry. They come ringing down through the pages of history as he shook his fist in the face of King George III and spoke these immortal words, "Is life so dear or peace so sweet, as to be purchased at the price of chains or slavery. Forbid it, Almighty God! I know not what course others may take, but as for me, **Give Me Liberty or Give Me Death.**" A feeling of pride and patriotism and a lump in the throat is the result. Corny. Sure is. But it is also love, and love of America breeds a willingness to build an even better America.

We need to hear John Paul Jones, with his ship listing and some of his guns out of order, as he answered the pride of the English Navy's call to surrender. Outmanned, outgunned, and outmaneuvered, his indomitable spirit rose to the occasion as he answered, "**I have not yet begun to fight.**" Obviously, he hadn't because the battle immediately turned, an important victory was won, and America had a new and much needed hero.

We need to put the words of Nathan Hale, the 21-year-old America patriot who was captured as a spy, back into the history books. Offered a life of luxury with a position of power and prestige if he would capitulate — Nathan Hale, without hesitation, stool tall and helped all of us stand taller as he wrote an important page in American history with his calm response, "**I regret that I have but one life to give for my country.**"

We need to identify more closely with our national emblem, the Bald Eagle. The eagle is truly the symbol of America. Hatched on the lofty peaks amid the wind and the elements, the young eagle is taught to fend for itself at an early age. When the time comes for him to try his wings, mama eagle literally pushes him off the cliff side and he is compelled to fly.

The full-grown Bald Eagle is a majestic sight as he soars far and wide in search of food. His vision is such that at 5000 feet he can look directly at the sun and in the next instant spot a field mouse nearly a mile below. To me, this is the epitome of the America we have always been and must continue to be: powerful enough to look the strongest nations in the eye and yet compassionate enough to look down at those small nations in need and extend either the helping hand or the covering umbrella as the situation dictates. To remain *that* kind of America, we must teach our strength and heritage to our youth throughout their entire lifetime.

What *is* being taught in our schools? A recent history course taught in California produced these incredible conclusions on the part of the students. Abraham Lincoln was a "racist" and the Japanese were completely justified in their attack on Pearl Harbor. It goes without saying, when our history books teach these young people to be ashamed of their country, they [the young people] will not respect or co-operate with an "establishment" they consider "racist" [it produced Lincoln] or a warmonger [it "instigated" the Pearl Harbor attack].

We need to teach our kids to salute the flag and respect the American creed every single day. Remember when we went through the Winston, Duz, Pepsi Cola, etc. routine to show that what is planted in our minds becomes a part of us? I'm suggesting we *plant* love of, and loyalty to country through the daily Pledge of Allegiance and the American Creed. These steps will imbed Americanism in the minds of our youth and they will stand tall and be proud that they are Americans.

AMERICA SPEAKS

To show you the America I love, I'd like to invite you to take a trip with me in your imagination as we travel via the big jet, which in many ways symbolizes America. I'd like to familiarize you with this great and beautiful country and some of its outstanding people.

From Dallas we head westward across the plains rich with cattle and oil, that contribute so much to the prosperity of America. We fly over El Paso, home of Lee Trevino, the "Merry

Mex" and former golf caddy who was chased off some prestigious golf courses before his rise to prominence as one of America's premier golfers and outstanding personalities. We veer northward and take a long sweeping glance at the natural beauty of the Grand Canyon, make a fast stop at Carlsbad Caverns and look down on the uniqueness of the Mojave Desert before we come to the lush, irrigated fruit and vegetable farms of California. Here we will meet Richard Cessna, Jr., Karl Karcher and Robert Patchen.

Richard Cessna, Jr. is the president of Kidco, Inc. which has been in business slightly over a year, but they are already grossing as much as $3,000 per month. They started with a contract to sweep the six main streets of San Diego Country Estates for $150 per month. They branched out by contracting with their father, the supervisor of the estates' 110 horse stables, to remove the manure and wood shavings which they compost. They sell the compost to landscapers and local golf courses at prices lower than commercial suppliers. Incidentally, Richard Cessna, Jr. is 12 years old. His vice president is his sister, age 9. The secretary of the company is another sister, age 11, and the treasurer is a half sister who is 14. Now that is America, that is free enterprise.

Kark Karcher, a gentle giant of Midwestern stock who has an unshakeable faith in Almighty God, is in the restaurant business. His financial success started when he bet on himself and free enterprise by pledging his financial net worth to get the capital investment necessary to become an entrepreneur. [That, my friends, means he hocked his '41 Plymouth for 326 bucks to buy a hot dog stand]. From that modest start, this 8th grade dropout has expanded, until today, "Carl's Jr. Restaurants" number 127 with over 3800 employees. It's refreshing — but not surprising — to learn that Carl is an old-fashioned guy who built a successful life, [12 beautiful kids and a storybook 40 year marriage to the former Margaret Heinz] and a successful business on faith, love, character, honesty, loyal and integrity.

The next free enterprise and flag-waving American we meet is Robert Patchen who sells real estate in San Mateo, California. Bob earns approximately $1000 per month at his profession and has for nearly twenty years. This is not all the money in the world, but *Bob has never seen a house he has sold* so it's obviously quite an accomplishment. Because he lives and works in the free enterprise system that is America, Bob Patchen not only is able to pay his own way but to make a contribution as well. Question: If a 12 year old, and 8th grade drop out and a blind man can "make" it in America, don't you believe that *you* can make it even bigger? Shouldn't we make certain that stories like these reach everyone in America?

LISTEN — TO SOME BUSINESSMEN

Back aboard the jet, let's do a little sight-seeing as we fly up the coast. Look down on the forests of giant Sequoias and Redwoods before we turn right and cross the awe inspiring Rockies. Now we get a bird's eye-view of the corn and wheat fields of Kansas, Nebraska and Illinois which has helped make America the bread basket of the world. We fly over Chicago, the home of a former newspaper boy named Clement Stone, a free enterpriser who conceived a better idea to merchandise insurance and built a personal fortune, still rated at roughly a third of a billion dollars, despite the fact that he has contributed over 100 million dollars to worthwhile causes. Today Mr. Stone shares his success secrets through his books, lectures, recordings and monthly publications like "Success Unlimited."

Continuing our trip, we turn northeast across Lake Michigan and in a matter of minutes come to Ada, Michigan, the home of Rich De Vos and Jay Van Andel, two of the most successful and vocal exponents of the free enterprise system in America today. Their belief in the system is founded on personal experience. In 1957, they acquired a converted service station and started Amway, which is a contraction of the American Way. Their capital was limited and their problems were numerous, but an unlimited faith in God and country combined with an enormous capacity for work, prevailed. Today the Amway Corporation distributes its products through approximately 300,000 independent distributors worldwide who sold over $300,000,000 in 1976 in Canada, Germany, England, France, Hong Kong, Australia and the United States. As a matter of fact, just 20 years after the company started in that converted service station we can say with poetic accuracy that the sun never sets on an Amway Distributor.

LISTEN — TO THE IMMIGRANTS

Next stop — Detroit, Michigan, the home of Ilona Zimmersman, a Hungarian refugee who, living on roots and berries, escaped from her communist captors by walking across her native land at night. I met Mrs. Zimmersman about five years ago at an awards banquet where she was recognized as the outstanding real estate sales person in Detroit. As I talked with her, I had to listen very carefully because she speaks with a gutteral accent which is difficult to understand. As she talked, however, the reason for her success was apparent. She doesn't sell a house on a lot — *she sells a home on a little piece of America, the greatest land on the face of the earth.* I wish you could meet Ilona Zimmersman and some other refugees including Sam Moore of Nashville, Tennessee. They would really give you a sales talk on the way America compares to other lands. Twenty five years ago, Sam emigrated to America from Lebanon. With tears in his eyes and gratitude in his heart, he urges one and all to support the land that permitted him to move from floor scrubber in a grocery story to Board Chairman of the Thomas Nelson Publishing Company, a company which, incidentally, will do approximately $15,000,000 this year.

LISTEN — TO WHAT "ONE" DID

From Detroit, we fly south across the beautiful grasslands of Kentucky and the hills of Tennessee. We fly over the steel mills of Birmingham, Alabama on our way to Montgomery, where we land to meet a lady with sore feet. Not too many years ago Rosa Parks sat down in the wrong part of the bus. The bus driver told her to move to the back of the bus which she refused to do. Since that date — because one lady, a seamstress with sore feet refused to stand up and move back — an entire people stood up and moved forward. It was here that the haunting eloquence of Martin Luther King, who took up Rosa Park's banner, captured the imagination of the American people and set a million feet to marching for the Civil Rights of the Black man.

We leave Montgomery, Alabama and head to Alcaniz Street in Pensacola, Florida, the boyhood home of Daniel James. Daniel's mother, a high school graduate with a lot of spunk and ambition for her family, was not content with the black schools in Pensacola. She opened her own school which attracted as many as sixty students at a nickel a day — when the students could come up with the nickel. This did not qualify the James' for membership in the Country Club set but as Daniel James said, "We never had to go on charity, we were able to support ourselves, we held our heads up."

Mrs. James repeatedly told her family that if the door of opportunity ever opened for them, they were never to say, "Wait a minute, let me get my bags and then I'll go through." Mrs. James said, "You have your bags ready, you have your dedication, you have your objectives, you have your purpose. You be ready to go." There is an eleventh commandment she taught Daniel, "Thou shalt not quit" — and "make certain that your children get a better education than you do."

You might not recognize the name Daniel James but you undoubtedly will recognize the name "Chappie" James, Four Star General, U. S. Air Force, Head of the Air Defense Command for North America.

You can't do everything at once, but you can do something at once. The April, 1974 issue of *Guideposts* Magazine tells the story of Rita Warren, an Italian immigrant who finished the 5th grade. When Rita's daughter transferred from a parochial school to the public school where prayer was forbidden, she asked Rita a question. "Mom, if one woman who doesn't believe in prayer [Madeline Murray O'Hair]" can take prayer out of school, why couldn't one woman [you, Mom] who believes in prayer, put it back in school? At that point Rita went to war against the Commonwealth of Massachusetts and whipped them — hands down. It's a long but beautiful story that started in the city library and involved learning the legal procedure to follow. There were lots of trials and heartaches, including a veto by the Governor, but thanks to Rita Warren there is a one minute prayer time in Massachusetts today.

Think about what you just read. One woman changed history and benefited mankind. *You* are one person. One person [vote] kept Aaron Burr from being President of the U.S. One person [vote] kept Andrew Johnson from being impeached. General Motors, Ford, DuPont, A.T. & T., *all* started in the mind of *one* person. I repeat, *You* are *One* person. No wonder Bach was moved to write, "There are three great things in this world — an ocean, a mountain, and a dedicated man — woman." Just *one* Rita Warren in every state could move mountains and solve many of our problems. To paraphrase Rita's daughter, "if *one* woman who believes in prayer can put prayer back in the schools of Massachusetts, surely 100 *million* people who also believe in prayer can put it back in the rest of the States."

If you're still hesitant or wondering about what to do and where to start, read this:

God said to build a better world and I said How?

The world is such a cold, dark place and so complicated now.

And I'm so young and useless there is nothing I can do.

But God, in all his wisdom said, "Just build a better you."

Building a better you is the first step to building a better America. The solution starts with you and, "If everyone became a part of the solution — America would have few problems."

In St. Petersburg, Florida, the Methodist men's Bible class decided they wanted the Bible taught in the public schools. These men did not know this could not be done — so they did it. It took nearly two years of legislative and judicial procedures but today, in St. Petersburg, Florida, school children are learning what God says in His Bible.

LISTEN — TO OUR HEROES
AND THE HANDICAPPED

From Pensacola, we go West across the plantation area of the Deep South which is known as the Bible Belt. We look down on New Orleans where Andrew Jackson and his coon-skin heroes from Tennessee wrote a stirring chapter in American history. They stood behind some cotton bales and decisively defeated the British to give our fledgling nation its first respectability among European powers. From New Orleans, we go to San Antonio and stroll around the historic grounds of the Alamo. It will help all of us to stand on the very spot where Travis, Fuentes, Crockett, Bowie, Guerrero and the dedicated few made their historic stand. They set an example in their fight against tyranny that will live forever in the minds of men who want to be free.

Finally, let's stop in Waco, Texas, to look in on James Brazelton Walker. "Braz" Walker, like David Lofchick from Winnipeg, Canada, so completely epitomizes the principles we've been discussing that I wanted his story to be the final one in *SEE YOU AT THE TOP*. "Braz" has gained international recognition as an author writing about tropical fish. His photography has graced the cover of several national publications. In 1968, he received the distinguished service award of the Waco Jaycees and was recognized as one of the Outstanding Young Men of America. He enjoys his career as author, speaker and photographer — which provides him with a handsome income.

Does that sound like a typical American success story? It isn't. At age 19, "Braz" contracted Polio which affected his lungs, muscles and nerves to such a degree that he is paralyzed from the neck down and is completely dependent on a mechanical breathing device. He types his own manuscripts with the aid of an instrument designed for him by General Electric which he holds in his mouth.

Obviously, "Braz" has had a lot of help and encouragement from many people, including his loving and devoted parents. He believes life is a gift with no guarantees, and that a handicap is not a disability but an opportunity to use God-given talents and imagination to their fullest. Braz is truly grateful that he lives in the only nation in the world, at the only time in history when he could have survived. He doesn't have much to use [or does he?], but **he does not let what he does not have keep him from using what he does have.** No "Loser's Limp" for him.

WE MUST SELL EVERYBODY

I could tell you a thousand other stories about people who prove the free enterprise system is the most effective economic system ever devised by man. It's a system that works so effectively that even our relief recipients are in the upper 4% of the income brackets of the world. This means that over 3 billion people on the face of this earth aren't living as well as our relief recipients live in America.

Despite all the advantages of the free enterprise system, the most serious mistake we can make is to assume too much. We erroneously assume that we don't have to sell our youth and fellow citizens on the obvious advantages and benefits associated with America and the free enterprise system. Results have been disturbing and disappointing to say the least. This attitude has bred revolt, rebellion, discord and such acts and comments that would have our founding fathers turning in their graves.

The irony of it all is that we don't have to sell the American free enterprise system to those who come from other countries. Take the Cuban refugee as an example. Many of them waited for years to trade everything they owned for a ticket from Havana to Miami and the free enterprise system that is America. Look at the Hungarian refugees who saw their countrymen literally throw themselves in front of Russian tanks because they preferred death to slavery. They don't have to be sold on the merits of America. Nor do we have to sell America to the occupants of East Berlin who can look over the wall into West Germany and see the difference.

It has become crystal clear, however, that we do have to sell America and the free enterprise system to our children, because only one generation stands between us and all the "Ism's" in the world. It's equally clear that we need to sell the free enterprise system to those teachers and professors who often belittle the very system that sustains them. We need to sell labor leaders and union members on the concept that a laborer should be free to work as hard and as enthusiastically as he wishes for the benefit of everyone. That *is* Free Enterprise. That *is* the American way.

We need to tell more of our citizens — some of whom are theoretically responsible — that their screaming about our "problems" is drowning out the steady hum of the very system that has made us the most productive and affluent land on earth.

We also need to sell government employees and officials on the fact that government doesn't produce income or prosperity. Instead, it exists and survives because free people working in a free land support the government. We need to sell elected officials on the simple fact that the right to work and produce without undue government restraint is not only our right but our source of strength. One good look at any socialistic country will convince any clear thinker that **free enterprise is the only way to go.**

IN LOVE WITH AMERICA

If I sound like a sentimentalist who is in love with America, I plead guilty — but with cause. I've been in many other countries, but I've never seen one that even comes close to America. We're the only country that has a long line of immigrants waiting to get in and no barriers to keep anyone in who wants to leave. The America and the Americans I love, voluntarily gave over $27,000,000,000 to charity in 1976 alone. The America I love is so compassionate, it responds generously when there's a famine in Africa, an earthquake in Chile or a typhoon in Korea. The America I love is so understanding that our conquered enemies, like Japan, Germany and Italy, received billions of American dollars for the rebuilding of their devastated countries.

The America I love spends untold millions of dollars on the development of drugs and treatment that will benefit mankind throughout the globe. The America I love developed the cure for polio, found a way to send men to the moon and is working every day on cures for cancer and other terminal diseases. The America I love is an understanding, compassionate one. It's so structured that even when we have our Watergates, any fair-minded citizen recognizes that individuals are responsible and not the government or the free enterprise system.

As a matter of fact, Watergate, more than any single incident, completely vindicates our system of government and free enterprise. For the first time in our history the President and Vice President of our country [who had been overwhelmingly elected] resigned from office in unrelated scandals. Despite this fact, the transition to our new leadership never missed a step. There were no riots, strikes, demonstrations or loss of momentum.

In my mind, there is absolutely no doubt that America is still the land of the free. Still the home of the brave. Still the land where anyone can get anything he really wants — provided he is willing to take the necessary steps. Yes — I'm completely convinced that though our land is not perfect, it is far ahead of any other land on the face of the earth. It is truly America the Beautiful, and it is time that every loyal American started standing up and speaking up for the land which is truly the last hope for freedom in the world today.

AMERICA IS IN YOUR HANDS

As we complete our trip we are forced to conclude that as Americans we have a tremendous country with absolutely unlimited opportunities accompanied by equally awesome responsibilities. We're the last, the one and the only hope that a dwindling free world has. **Freedom, like health, is often appreciated only after we no longer have it.** Historically, freedom, once lost, is difficult to regain. According to Freedom House, a nonpartisan organization devoted to the strengthening of free societies, as of Jan. 1976, only 19.8% of the world's population was free. This figure is down from 35% in January of 1975. America is *all* that stands between that 19.8% and slavery.

The United Nations either can't or won't do anything to protect the free people of the world. Since its inception, over one and one half *billion* people have lost their freedom. In short, the U.N. has failed to function as a positive factor for peace and is little more than a pawn of the Communists and Third World Nations. Its 1975 resolution on Zionism, its ineptness in enforcing the Viet-Nam peace and a thousand other incidents, including its refusal to act in the face of undeniable proof that the North Koreans deliberately machine-gunned more than 5,000 American prisoners and buried them in mass graves, should clearly prove that the U.N. either cannot or will not function.

The voting structure of the U.N., combined with the fact that since 1945 a Communist has held the post of Undersecretary General of Political and Security Council Affairs, renders the U.N. ineffective as an unbiased body for world peace.

With Communists in control of that office, as Rus Walton points out in "One Nation Under God," "it's like asking the fox to guard the henhouse — and we are the chickens."

One reason I wrote this book, and created the "I CAN" course for schools, is to help alert America to the greatest crisis in our 200 year history, *and* to help build our strength by building our people. I wanted to be able to — at *any* time — look my children and your children in the eye and say, I did my part — and then some — in fighting the battle to insure each of you the same opportunity for the good life which America has so generously bestowed on me. It *is* true — only one generation separates us from all the "isms" in the world. Dorothy Thompson says, "*no one* can have life, liberty or the *possibility* of happiness unless his *country* is alive, free and happy."

What about you? Are you accepting your responsibility? If everyone in America was doing exactly the same thing you're doing, would our country be getting better, or worse? That's a question for you and your conscience. If you really love America, you will enthusiastically join the ever-increasing throng working to make a great America even greater.

THIS EXCITES ME

This I believe — if being on the winning team, if being on the side of right and decency means anything to you as an individual, then you will join the fastest-growing team in the world. The "Do Something for America" team, the "Sell America" team that actually started nearly twenty-five years ago. At that time, the voices for America were few and far between. The scoffers were gaining momentum and growing stronger by the day, until they peaked in 1973. At that point, the concerned, dedicated, thinking Americans started to awaken and realize we were losing our country by default. The hue and cry has arisen all over our land to "do something," but the downward slide has been underway for so long that it has taken us two years to halt the trend. In my judgment we "bottomed out" and leveled off in mid 1975.

As I write these words aboard another aircraft on my way to Winnipeg, Canada, I write as an American who is convinced we are doing something to regain the moral strength and integrity that is the foundation stone for all great nations. The editorial pages of newspaper and magazines from coast to coast, border to border and from small hamlets to big cities are all espousing the causes of common sense, moral responsibility and an honest day's work for an honest day's pay. As I fly into *all* parts of our great country, I note with enthusiasm and considerable optimism, that even the most liberal newspapers and politicians are calling for *less* governmental interference and more individual initiative and responsibility. The free-wheeling, pleasure-seeking citizen of yesterday is growing into a more sober-minded mature individual who recognizes that *all* of us have *everything* to lose unless we *individually* play a part in leading America back to a land of laws and principles.

Fortunately, responsible people have awakened and are organizing voter education groups to inform the citizenry on issues and candidates. Parents by the thousands are discovering the *necessity* of learning what their children are being taught in school as the first step in making certain the right material is taught. I have personally seen and talked with more God-fearing people who are speaking up for both God and country in the past two years than I had in the preceding ten years. I make no claims to crystal ball ownership, but based on what I see and on what concerned citizens are *doing*. I fervently believe that America's tomorrows are going to be better than its yesterdays. I *know* they will be if *you* do *your* part — and sell someone else on doing the same thing.

WHAT WILL YOU SAY

Chances are you and I will someday cross paths, because I speak to a large number of people as I crisscross our land many times each year. If we do, I hope you'll say, "Hello," and tell me that you've read this book. What you then say will tell me a great deal about its effectiveness. If you tell me you enjoyed the book, I'll smile. But truthfully, I'll be hoping that you'll say more. If you tell me you got a lot out of the book, I'll smile even more broadly, but I'll still be hoping you'll say more. If you tell me what you've done and are doing to build a richer and more rewarding life since you started the book, then I'll truly be thrilled.

I say this because this book was not written to entertain you, although I've tried to make it enjoyable so you will read and re-read it. It isn't written to inform you, though I believe the message includes a considerable amount of information. *It was written to motivate you into action.* Anything less than that is unacceptable to me — and should be for you, because **you are the only person in existence who can use your potential.** It is an awesome responsibility.

Since Webster defines "opportunity" as a "fit time," you are fortunate because now is truly a "fit time" — for you. The information in this book, properly used, will enable you to use that potential and go where you want to go, do what you want to do, have what you want to have and be what you want to be.

I can say this without boasting, because I serve as a reporter bringing you the wisdom of some of the greatest minds this country has ever produced, as well as some of the infinite wisdom of Almighty God. I also bring the practical experience acquired in 30 years of being in the people-building business. With these thoughts in mind, I can say with humility and yet with confidence that **you now hold in your hands information and inspiration that will unlock the treasures you seek in the tomorrows of your life.**

I would also like to assure you that had I been on trial for my life — charged with telling you how to live a richer, fuller, more rewarding life and you were my judge and jury, I would have written the book exactly as I did. If I were looking into your face as you read these final words I hope I would see a broad smile, as well as a twinkle in your eye. That's what I should see because the symbolic you, on a following page, is standing in the banquet hall of life with all the good things this world has to offer spread in front of you. They are all available, and yours, if you really want them — and if you build your life on the foundation stones of honesty, character, faith, love, integrity and loyalty.

Now that I have shared these thoughts on how to reap richer rewards from this life, let me urge you to follow the admonition expressed in Matthew 6:33, **"But seek ye first the Kingdom of God and His righteousness and all these things shall be added unto you."** Ten chapters later, St. Matthew tells us why this is good advice in Matthew 16:26, **"For what is a man profited if he shall gain the whole world and lose his own soul?"**

Sentence completions from page 355
Winston tastes good like a [cigarette should]
Pepsi Cola hits the [spot]
Twelve full ounces that's a [lot]
Drink Coca Cola the pause that [refreshes]
Duz does [everything]

THE BEGINNING

Confusing? It shouldn't be. Oh, I know you just made your first trip through *SEE YOU AT THE TOP*, and I know most people would be thinking in terms of "the end." But you're not most people. You are you and you now know there never has been and there never will be another *you*. You know that you're created in God's own image only "slightly less than the angels." Knowing this about you, and others too, you never look down — nor up — to any man. **You understand that no one can make you feel inferior without your permission**, which you now refuse to give to anyone. You obviously know that **you can get everything in life you want if you help enough other people get what they want**. You also understand that **ability can take you to the top, but it takes character to keep you there.** That while there is plenty of room at the top, there is not enough to sit down.

So you see, this is the beginning of that new way of life which clearly demonstrates that happiness isn't pleasure — it's victory. Perhaps the most important thing is that you know and accept the fact that the beginning must always remain the beginning, because **success and happiness are not destinations, they're exciting, never-ending journeys.** Your beginning puts you in the enviable position of being both a "go-getter," which you are, and a "go-giver," which you're beginning to be.

So, as I say "Welcome" to the beginning and "Good-bye" to the old you and the old way of life, I shall close the book "differently," which shouldn't surprise you, since I opened it "differently". In today's world we have many people who end a visit or a phone call by saying, "Have a good day." That's nice and pleasant but I believe life has considerably more to offer than just a "good day." I believe that if "you believe" in yourself, your fellow man, your country, in what you are doing and in Almighty God, that your "good days" will extend into a good forever and I truly will *SEE YOU AT THE TOP.*

YOU CAN HELP

Massive research by Harvard psychologist, David McClelland, which included the study of children's literature of forty contemporary nations, as well as Greece and India, revealed a significant correlation between achievement orientation of children's books and the rate of economic growth of their nation for the next *twenty* years. His research provides convincing evidence that ambition and achievement which result from it, is far more the result of education and culture than it is genetic inheritance.

If you agree with the basic philosophy in *See You At The Top* and feel it would benefit the youth of your country, would you help us introduce the "I CAN" program to your local schools? To comply with state and federal regulations, an edition of *See You at the Top* minus all scriptural and religious references is available for use in public schools. If you are willing to help, please drop me a note in the mail and include the name and address of the school administrator. I will send you specific information about the course and ask you to personally place it in the hands of the administrator. We will take it from there.

This course is quite comprehensive and includes a Teacher's Guide, a Creative Ideas Manual and two series of recordings. One series follows the format of the book and is used in the classroom to re-inforce and add another dimension to the learning process. The other series includes 80 short motivational messages [three minutes] to be played over the public address system at the beginning of each day. This series is entitled, Zig Ziglar's Lift For The Day and since every student and teacher hears these messages, the entire school benefits.

Many schools, churches, businesses and even correctional institutions around the country are implementing this program. Results have been exciting, but time is of the essence.

Naturally, I'm biased, but I firmly believe that if this course is taught in your schools, it will make a difference in the lives of your youth – and you will have played a significant part.

Thank you, God bless you, and I will See You At The Top.

Zig Ziglar
The Zig Ziglar Corporation
12011 Coit Road ● Suite 114 ● Dallas, Texas 75251
(214) 233-9191

Zig Ziglar's
CONFESSIONS OF
A HAPPY CHRISTIAN

192 pages $ 6.95

In this exciting new book Zig Ziglar puts to rest the absurd notion that Christians should have long faces and short pocketbooks. He shares the excitement and benefits of serving Jesus Christ **NOW**, including what has happened to him in **all** areas of his life since July 4, 1972, when he was born again and declared his complete **dependence** on Jesus Christ.

Some of the exciting subjects:

- A Declaration of Dependence
- On The Fence
- Come Into My Heart
- You Are Not Good Enough
- The Jesus I Love
- But Lord, I've Got a Car Payment—And It's Due Next Thursday
- Shhh—Don't Tell 'Em About Jesus
- We All Make Mistakes
- How Will You Bet?
- Goodies From God's People
- Just A Coincidence
- An Open Mind and an Open Bible Will Make You a Christian
- Are Christians **Really** Different?
- Satan's Sales Meeting
- The Good Things God Gives Us—or A Heavenly Smorgasbord on Planet Earth

THREE WAYS TO ORDER

- From your local bookstore.
- From The Zig Ziglar Corporation, 12011 Coit Road, Suite 114, Dallas, Texas 75251; (214) 233-9191.
- From the publisher: Pelican Publishing Company, 630 Burmaster Street, Gretna, Louisiana 70053; (504) 368-1175.

IN RESPONSE TO YOUR INQUIRIES

A series of audio and video cassette recordings based on *See You At The Top* is now available.

A customization of *See You At The Top* for your company including jacket, foreword and introduction can be printed. This would give added impact and prestige to your training and motivation program.

For information concerning quantity prices on this edition, a personal appearance by **Zig Ziglar**, the cassette series, or complete details on the customization process write:

Zig Ziglar
The Zig Ziglar Corporation
12011 Coit Road
Suite 114
Dallas, Texas 75251
(214) 233-9191

KEEP IT UP

In each segment I have suggested certain books or publications which I feel reinforce and supplement the information covered in that segment. The major purpose is to urge you to utilize the proven educational and motivational material that can help you reap the full rewards which are available.

I conclude with these recommendations:

For your spiritual well-being,
New American Standard Version
King James
The Living Bible
Guideposts Magazine
Carmel, N. Y.
For your physical well-being,
Dr. Kenneth Cooper, *Aerobics.*

For your continuing financial and motivational well-being,
W. Clement Stone, *Success Unlimited*
Chicago, Ill.

For your general well-being,
Readers Digest
Pleasantville, N.Y.

Bits and Pieces
The Economics Press, Inc.
12 Daniel Rd.
Fairfield, N.Y. 07006

For your "I'm Sold on America" well-being,
Richard DeVos and Charles Paul Conn, *Believe*
Daniel Marsh, *Unto the Generations*
John Nobel, *I Was A Slave in Communist Russia*